Echoes from the Bluffs

To Chris and Edie
Rohrer

[signature] 10-23-23

Echoes from the Bluffs

Michael H. Logue

Scan this code to
order Echoes!

Cover design by the author.
Cover photo: *Vicksburg from the River* by Layne Logue. © All rights reserved.

ISBN 978-0-578-27928-2

To my wife, Becki,
for always believing in me and
for being the best half of all I do.

&

To my amazing children, Adam and Amanda,
for sharing and passing along PopPop's passions,
history, and tales with my grandchildren.

To God always be the glory.

CONTENTS

CONTENTS
(Continued)

Families with new soil could turn to growing cotton. Zeph's 200 acres purchased from Chief Vann in 1803 was too exhausted to try that risky crop.

No family bonds held him to Turkey Creek. It was time to start fresh. Turkey Creek carried the collected Coody and Pace families down the Savannah River to passage to New Orleans.

The Mississippi Territory, barely a decade old, held lands to the north that were only accessible over rugged game migration trails and indigenous paths that had been hammered into treacherous *military roads*. Zeph's loaded cart faded from the glow of New Orleans into the deep, dark Louisiana swamps and protruding ridges to Fort Adams on the Mississippi-Louisiana boundary.

He heard enroute about the country *north of civilization* that had teased the adventurous and spit them out in so many pieces. A new comet in the sky was disturbing even the brave. What did it foretell?

Along the way, Zeph dodged and warded off highwaymen and the wandering remnants of the Natchez people and other survivors of the indigenous collapse. Recent slave revolts had produced marauding escaped slaves. White refugees were to be avoided or appeased when confronted.

At wayside hamlets, villagers were suspicious of strangers who might bring a plethora of disease, the real demons lurking in the night mist and vapors.

Campfire stories brought tales of massacred forts and a *"River of Death."*

At Fort Adams, flatboats were carrying burned-out pioneers south. The nearby Territorial Capital, Natchez, was struggling to construct a successful economic model. Zeph's concerns were heightened by reports that the very familiar *Hopewell* treaties were being replaced by mass sales of tribal lands. One of the major treaties had been signed at Fort Adams.

In the days spent at Fort Adams, where they resupplied their modest caravan, merchants mentioned the hundreds of pioneers and large grant patentees who failed to make a go of it on the Loosa Chitto and Bayou Pierre just south of *Walnut Hills*. The *pioneer* concept was giving way to a *commercial farmer* system that was producing rivalries among former friends.

Stalwart pioneers. like those back in South Carolina, had evolved into livestock farmers and some were experimenting with poor strains of cotton.

Fortunately for pilgrims, recent treaties had opened lands in the Territory. A new Warren County was comprised of a few clusters of homes divided by great expanses, living in relatively secure, cooperative independence.

After registering at Fort Adams, the wide-eyed migrants departed for Natchez only to feel the very ground rumbling under their feet. Word floated downriver that the Mississippi River had changed course and much of the country to the north was in shambles.

, At Natchez, they joined a crowd on the Mississippi to watch a new smoke-belching boat land at the docks. The protocols of a pioneer way-of-life on the lower Mississippi river seemed to be changing with every milepost.

Reaching Bayou Pierre and Port Gibson, hopes were lightened by modest successes of fledgling businessmen and yeoman farmers who were struggling but enduring the flood of agricultural crops originating in the Ohio Valley.

The Grand Gulf trading post verified their homesteader list: a gun, an axe, some spades, and a plough. They purchased an optional cow.

As they approached Warren County, chatty veteran neighbors seemed to be optimistic and fellow pilgrims at the Grand Gulf trading post were downright enthusiastic. *"We can do this,"* Zeph must have mused.

His experienced group could easily build and manage eight to ten acres of corn and peas, a large vegetable garden, orchards, a drove of hogs, and a herd of thirty cattle. The only thing lacking in South Carolina was good soil.

Their primary cash crops would be indigo and tobacco but markets for commercial meats and agricultural products were a stable option.

Zeph alone could cultivate to six acres of cotton. His family, with several hands, could service more acres of corn, or fifteen to eighteen acres of cotton. Growing cotton would require slave help, a system he understood from his days as overseer for Chief James Vann.

Given their experience and determination, he trusted that their journey would pay the desired dividends for this "*redbone*" family in Walnut Hills.

After a lengthy pilgrimage of *"here and there,"* Zephaniah Coody and Mary Pace Coody finally appeared in the tax rolls of Warren County in 1814. The family eventually took root on the SW 1/4 of Section 41, Township 15, Range 5 East *(see map below)* on November 1, 1816, north of today's Redbone Road.

The next year, Mississippi was admitted into the Union and included the community of *Vicksburgh*; the *"flush times"* were soon to come to the county.

The Coody family would fully experience the glad and sad times of the *Cotton Rush*. Zeph owned about nine slaves. His granddaughter Eliza, though, would marry an *abolitionist preacher* wounded twice in his local pulpit.

Zeph and Mary, as well as most of his siblings and children, would not survive to witness the Civil War. He and Mary would be spared the pain of losing children in that great upheaval.

Such are but a few of the *Echoes from the Bluffs* of western Mississippi.

Zephaniah and Mary Pace Coody are the author's third great-grandparents, among the first families of Warren County, Mississippi. Their son Archibald, also the author's ancestor who made the journey from Turkey Creek, South Carolina, is on his right.

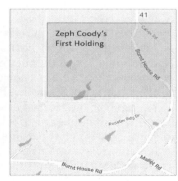

Part I
The Ancient Echoes of This Unique and Epic Landscape

The geological platform of transitions, tragedies, and triumphs

The Mississippi River from the Yellow Bluffs at Vicksburg, Mississippi.
Photo by the author (MHL).

A
The Mississippi River
The Grand Theater

The Mississippi River was born in a geological cataclysm and the explosive confrontation of three continents. Fire, ice, destruction, and natural conflict were its ancestors. Nature's forge hammered from an evolving landscape the nation's most important river system, the center of north American civilizations, and the center stage for the continent's greatest conflict.

About 300 million years ago, the tectonic plates carrying today's North America, South America, and Africa collided and fused, creating the super-continent *Pangea*. The grinding, upward thrust produced a single, continuous mountain range that would eventually form today's Appalachian and Ouachita-Ozark ranges.

In the process of Pangea fracturing into today's continents, the future North America moved over an intense *volcanic hotspot*. The upwelling of magma lifted a section of that mountain range about two miles, forming an arch. Forces of nature gradually eroded the uplifted land away.

As North America moved away from the magma fountain, the crust beneath the arch cooled, contracted, and subsided about two miles, forming a trough, the ***Mississippi Embayment***. As sea levels fell, the Gulf of Mexico remained, filling the Embayment.

The Embayment stretches from the Gulf of Mexico to present-day Cairo, Illinois, and beyond. It is a product of the Cretaceous and Early Cenozoic periods, 50 to 100 million years ago, when dinosaurs roamed and vanished. The evolving Mississippi River stands equal to any dramatic planetary change of its era.

Today's Mississippi River basin is a geological infant. Just 20,000 years ago, the earth was beginning to warm from the last Ice Age. The great Laurentide Ice Sheet began to melt and shrink. The waters of the melting glaciers carved channels into the landscape. A complex veinous system of streams fed several main arteries which combined to form the Mississippi River.

Over time, this maze of rivers delivered enormous loads of sediment into the Embayment, creating its foundation as *Big Muddy*.

The Mississippi carries enormous power in its velocity, ferocity, and volume. In ancient eras, the river dumped 1,280 *cubic miles* of sediment into its Embayment, the equivalent of 1,280 square soil blocks a mile high and a mile square.

In 1951, scientists recorded the Mississippi River depositing 1.5 million tons (300,000 five-yard dump trucks) of sediment into the Gulf of Mexico *every day*. Imagine a never-ending line of dump trucks from *New Orleans, Louisiana, to Pittsburgh, Pennsylvania*, every day dumping into the Gulf.

Charles Kuralt, the ever-insightful traveling CBS correspondent, surmised that the Mississippi River would not satisfy its need to move land until it had moved the entire state of Illinois to the Gulf of Mexico.

Engineers agree that, given time and an opportunity, Old Man River would wash away the Rocky Mountains. It made quick geological work of the original mountain in the center of the Continent just to get to the Gulf.

The Restless, Wandering Giant

By the time of man's appearance on the continent, the Mississippi River fabric of streams covered 42 percent of our future contiguous country. Economies of many prehistoric, historic, and modern cultures have depended on this river system to travel and exchange goods and culture. It was the *seedbed* of the world's largest economy in 1860, the antebellum South.

From today's Yellowstone River to the confluence of Pittsburgh's Monongahela and Allegheny rivers that form the Ohio, to the Gulf of Mexico, the Mississippi is the *world's longest river*.

Stretching 2,350 miles, it provides an outlet for ten states and two Canadian provinces, carrying goods to world markets by way of Baton Rouge-New Orleans, the *world's largest port complex*.

The Mississippi River is much larger than China's Yellow River, double that of Africa's Nile and India's Ganges, and fifteen times that of Europe's Rhine. Only the Congo and the Amazon can best it in certain categories.

The Mississippi River is a classic *meandering*, alluvial stream. Deceptively silent but violent, unconfined by rock formations, its currents hold its soil banks in a constant state of stress, anticipating *Old Man River's* appetite and his next *movement*.

Beneath its churning waters, the river is constantly rearranging itself by

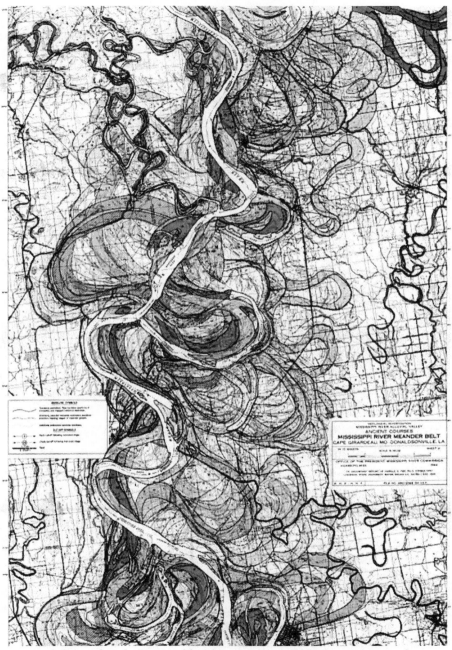

Cartographer and geologist Harold Fisk's amazing graphic above captures the wandering Mississippi River over time, each curve a former river trace.
U.S. Army Corps of Engineers image.

depositing sand near slow-moving points and attacking the banks on the channel's opposite side. Underwater sand waves can reach a height of fifty feet. The river constantly seeks to reach an unreachable equilibrium. Change is its only constant.

Contorting itself into a series of tight, long bends, the river eventually abandons them for a shorter downhill route, forming oxbow lakes, new channels, sloughs and bayous, and countless scars scattered over miles of its border states.

Satellite views can easily track the Mississippi's ancient wanderings. The Ohio River, in fact, once entered the Mississippi near present-day Vicksburg eons ago.

The river's scars became historic landmarks and settlements such as Louisiana's Lake St. Joseph and Lake Providence.

Modern flood control and navigation works have restricted the river's movements to a large degree. Winking at man's modern engineering successes, the river reminds man daily, *"I can lick any Engineer in the house."*

Appearing calm and confined, the Mississippi exerts a constant, powerful draw on its tedious chains, feeling all points in the system for the weakest link minute by minute.

The Mississippi River possesses a benign willingness to pull the yolk of civilization and sustain its delicate ecosystem. Conversely, its destructive side can be unfathomable to those who have never seen or experienced such a beast.

The Amenable Adversary

As the lifeblood of economies, the Mississippi has no equal. Many countries can produce goods more cheaply than the United States, but the Mississippi allows America to win marketplace competitions by providing a much cheaper, more reliable means of moving bulk loads and quantities of goods to domestic and foreign markets.

Any malady that interrupts this dizzying supply chain, natural or manmade, sends shudders through national and international markets.

A severe drought in 1988 caused a major shutdown of the Mississippi River. Worldwide interests were checking frequently on the status of their commodities stranded from Natchez to Greenville, Mississippi. The traffic jam was costing each of the 110 towboat operators about $10,000 per day.

Such system slowdowns cut deeply into U.S. and world markets. A navigation expert once said that the 1988 drought stoppages cost the U.S. the European wastepaper market at that time.

For *Ole Man River's* bounty, he demands a healthy respect of and conformance to his hydraulic rules and nuances. He has sternly disciplined indigenous cultures, pioneers, town builders, and engineers who *grew too comfortable* and *drew too close*, teased by decades-long drier weather patterns devoid of disastrous floods.

The prehistoric city of *Cahokia* near present day St. Louis, Missouri, was the victim of such a rebuke.

The 600-year-old population center with tens of thousands of residents rose during a millennial *dry cycle*. About 1200, the Mississippi was loosed by the end of the Medieval Warm Period. An epic flood brought the beginning of the end of the great city and culture of Cahokia.

Humans dwelling along its banks learned over following centuries to tread lightly around the river's fragile temperament. Thereafter, they tended to build the river's requirements much more closely into their patterns of life.

Settlers who grew too *familiar* with the *Old Man* would also inevitably face his plagues, as vicious as those of ancient Egypt. No family was spared the tragedy of epidemic loss at the hands of malaria, dysentery, cholera, yellow fever, and other ravagers that fermented in the river's miles of buffer swamps.

The loss of entire families and communities are recorded on tombstones with common or consecutive death dates. Vicksburg would lose its founders to yellow fever and, in 1878, a tragic portion of its citizens. In 1843, Grand Gulf, Mississippi's 1,000 citizens were sifted by a yellow fever epidemic.

In 1855, the insatiable Mississippi River decided to claim what was left of that hard-luck hamlet below Vicksburg at its juncture with the Big Black River. In just five years, it claimed 55 Grand Gulf city blocks.

In 1862, the river brought war which burned most of the town's skeletal remains, leaving a few buildings and the tombstones on the bluff above as the only *Echoes* of those who had held out so much hope for their town.

Before 20th-century flood-control and channel-stabilization works reeled in the river's mayhem, it devoured numerous other prosperous communities and their hopes over the years, Napoleon, Arkansas, and Rodney, Mississippi, among them.

Early settlers and entrepreneurs of the Walnut Hills community and the surrounding area would flourish or fail as they carved out a tedious life and economy on and within the grasp of *Old Man River*.

The 1844 Flood typifies the harsh realities of the day. Flooded area counties did not produce a single pound of cotton for struggling investors that season. Their lives were on edge every year. One planter, in dire straits with the others, warned, *"Anyone calling in loans will be just cause for pistols!"*

Napoleon, Arkansas, a community eventually consumed by the Mississippi River. *From "Our Whole Country" by John Barber, 1861. (Wikipedia, WKP).*

At War On and With the Mississippi

By 1863, Ulysses Grant was operating at the *genius level*, recrafting the art of warfare. His overland campaign for Vicksburg is today considered the most brilliant in American history and a modern model of war.

Like his name sake, the mythological Odysseus, Grant's military prowess in late 1862 had been forged by painful learning experiences, extreme political pressures, confrontations with the military *giants* both friend and foe, and his undeniable adaptability, courage, and relentless determination.

Yet, his years at West Point and experience to date had not prepared him for war on one of the world's wonders. And the importance of his mission was obvious to even the lowest ranks of his soldiers in the Western theater of operations.

"Vicksburg is the key!," Abraham Lincoln said. *"The war can never be brought to a close until that key is in our pocket."* In Grant and his Army of the Tennessee, Lincoln had mobilized an *irresistible force*.

The capture of the commercial center of the richest state in the nation would, in essence, take the rebellious states of Texas, Louisiana, Arkansas, and Missouri out of the war, along with the critical Confederate port at Matamoros, Mexico.

The South would be starved of its vast stores of rice, sugar, salt, hogs, molasses, beef, horses, soldiers, corn, and lead. The Mississippi River was the Confederacy's jugular and Vicksburg was also Jefferson Davis' beloved home – *to be held at all costs*.

Davis had possession of the prize, Vicksburg – the *immovable object*, the impregnable *Gibraltar of the Confederacy*. Vicksburg, he stressed, was *"the nail head that holds the South's two halves together."*

Adding to Lincoln's dilemma, the Mississippi River had been closed to traffic by the Union since the start of the war.

Northern shippers and business concerns were being deprived of the all-important artery of commerce to New Orleans and, from there, the world. Great Britain depended as much on American corn and wheat as it did on American cotton. Businesses interests from the Rockies to the Appalachians were feeling the calamitous effect of the traffic stoppage.

Indiana's war governor, Oliver Perry Throck Morton, threatened his friend Lincoln with secession of the Northwest states from Iowa to Ohio if he did not quickly reopen navigation on the Mississippi.

The resulting *Northwest Confederacy* would form an alliance with the already seceded states to reopen the river and Southern trade. A *Union* without the Mississippi River did not appeal to the Northwesterners.

Lincoln would lose much of his remaining Union and certainly any chance of restoring it without the Mississippi River.

Morton's message was reinforced by Lincoln's leading war strategist, Maj. Gen. Henry Halleck, ***"Vicksburg is worth forty Richmonds."***

A Subtropical Proving Ground

Grant's army of Northwesterners were frontiersmen equally as rugged as their foes. Yet they were forced into an extremely different climate, one where Southern boys thrived. The environment of the subtropical Mississippi River near Vicksburg was as tortuous, in every season, as the untamed Amazon.

It was equally bitter for reinforcements who followed from the upper New England states such as New Hampshire, Rhode Island, and Massachusetts.

When Maj. Gen. Winfield Scott was calculating the troops needed to put down the Southern rebellion, his estimate of 300,000 knocked war planners back. He reminded them that he had to consider losses to *"southern fever."*

Even the vaulted Robert E. Lee did not believe a Northern army could maneuver in Mississippi past spring. *"Grant would be forced to retire,"* he said.

Arriving at Young's Point, Louisiana, in February 1863, a soldier noted the weather to be *"like June at home. The peach trees are already blooming."* Winter days with highs near 85° suggested that the Vicksburg operation must be concluded before the exhaustive June heat which would reach *104° in the shade.*

The rugged *man's man* Maj. Gen. William T. Sherman exclaimed, *"It is cruel to march men in such heat."* Soldiers resented leaders who did.

Soon after his 1863 New Year's arrival at Vicksburg, Maj. Gen. John McClernand expressed deep concern for the poor health of his XIII Corps in the poisonous environment.

Camped in the blackwater Mississippi swamps facing Vicksburg, soldiers of the Chicago Mercantile Battery complained about their drummers beating day and night. They lamented that *"one funeral procession after another"* was burying their comrades in horrid graves in the river levee. Many Union remains were washed up and away by the disrespectful Mississippi River.

Northern missionary and relief organizations rushed with limited resources to provide what they could to stem the suffering of their soldiers in the Louisiana jungles.

Grant's treacherous, disease-ridden 1863 canal operation at DeSoto Point, La.
Image by Henri Lovie, Frank Leslie's Illustrated Newspaper, March 28, 1863.

Before they ever faced Pemberton's forces, Grant's men would face an army of natural enemies: ticks, lice, mosquitoes, and a varmint new to the Northern soldier, chiggers with their maddening itch.

Swamps filled with dislodged and agitated man-eating alligators, disgusting leeches, and monster water moccasins kept soldiers on almost debilitating alert.

The Mississippi swamps offered zero in the way of the gallon of fresh drinking water every soldier needed daily. The water was so sediment-laden that locals joked that it was *"too thick to drink and too thin to plow."*

A barrel of Mississippi River water intended for drinking would be left standing for many hours to allow the muddy sediment to settle to the bottom. The water could then be *racked* like wine, the cleaner top water drained away. Left in the sun, barrels of Mississippi River water would get warm to the taste and various *wigglies* would need to be strained.

Dysentery, the leading killer of the war, was on parade in Louisiana.

A Treacherous Lifeline

Union quartermasters would be dependent on tender, vulnerable vessels moving a million pounds of war material and supplies daily to keep Grant's army postured for victory at Vicksburg. The 500-mile transport route from Cairo, Illinois, was one long, treacherous enemy and environmental gauntlet.

In 1863, the Mississippi could be a *new river every day*, its shifting sands and freely fluctuating depths producing shoals capable of grounding unsuspecting pilots. An immobilized steamer was a *sitting duck* for enemy marauders. The Mississippi River loved to *pile on*, using its current to rip a stuck vessel apart.

As dangerous as icebergs in the Atlantic Ocean, trees, living and dead, are pulled into the channel of a falling, receding river where they become ragged floating and submerged *snags*. These timber *traps* could hold a steamer hostage for hours or rip its belly open entirely. The Mississippi River's snags were more effective than the enemy at sinking vessels.

River pilots with deep-draft war vessels might expect a river adequate for naval operations in winter and spring. Adm. David Glasgow Farragut, however, found his deep-draft vessels vulnerable in front of Vicksburg as summer began dropping river stages in late July.

In the river's smaller tributaries like Steele Bayou north of Vicksburg, a war vessel drawing more than six feet of water would quickly become a liability. Maritime designers on both sides prioritized creating solutions for *brown-water* warboats.

Since the earliest days of steamboating, prosperous river shippers had engaged in a game of *Russian Roulette*, betting lives and property on operational costs, schedules, capacity, and fire-stoked wooden vessels powered by high-pressure steam boilers that were ticking time-bombs. Vessels rarely survived five years under this business model.

The added pressures of combat, wartime profits, personal or political urgency, and inexperienced crews meant tragedy was just around the bend.

Boiler explosions were commonplace on the Western rivers and always catastrophic. Even an exploding 30-gallon home hot-water tank has the capacity, the experts say, to blow an automobile fourteen stories high with a launch speed of 85 miles per hour.

Western steamboat engine boilers came in multiples and featured fire-tube boilers exponentially larger than a home system. Crews feared these over-sized bombs.

On April 27, 1863, the steamer *Sultana* fell victim to the convergence of these hazards faced by the vessels of her day. The *Sultana*, designed to carry 376 passengers, was gravely overloaded with more than 2,200 Union prisoners of war headed home from a Vicksburg collection center.

An illicit deal had been made to capitalize on the $10-per-soldier passenger fee, netting the crooks about $3/4 million in 2023 dollars. About 1,800 survivors of the horrible prisoner of war camps at Cahaba, Alabama, and Andersonville, Georgia, were on the boat's manifest.

Echoes of jubilant *Sultana* soldiers still ring today from Vicksburg's waterfront. *From a Civil War tintype, April 26, 1865, Helena, Ark. (WKP)*

Near Marion, Arkansas, across the river from Memphis, Tennessee, the *Sultana's hastily repaired* boilers exploded at 2:00 a.m. Over 1,700 died horrible death is many forms as a result. The Mississippi River holds the *dark record* for the **worst maritime disaster in American history**, worse than the sinking of the *R.M.S. Titanic*.

Ventures into the Mississippi's tributaries, the Yazoo, the Red, and the Arkansas led to *steamboat graveyards*. RAdm. David Dixon Porter's trapped flotilla had to be saved by Sherman during his Steele Bayou Campaign.

On the Red River, Porter came within a whisker of abandoning his entire surviving fleet trapped by falling stages. Many had already been sunk or destroyed on the expedition.

An extreme hairpin river bend in front of Vicksburg *(see photo next page)* required vessels to slow down to navigate the turn. The river created a perfect *killing field* for Confederate gunners. Even the Union ironclad *U.S.S. Cincinnati* was sunk in Vicksburg's artillery crossfire in the bend.

When Grant had no recourse but to run his Army transports by Vicksburg's line of 75 guns on April 16, 1863, contract pilots refused the *suicide mission*. Soldiers volunteered or *were volunteered* to man and pilot the vessels.

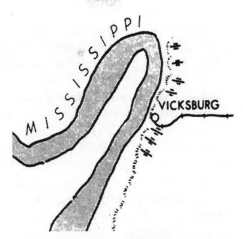

On one run, Maj. Gen. John Logan warned his soldiers that any man abandoning his post on a transport would be shot. Several received the Medal of Honor during those hazardous operations.

Conversely, the west channel of Vicksburg's treacherous Tuscumbia Bend (*above*) proved to be a relatively safe harbor for Union vessels and for the mortar boats that fired over 7,000 of their 200-lb. mortar shells into Vicksburg for 47 days and nights.

Evolve or Perish

The Mississippi River would become a primordial, intensely interactive war gameboard, willing to test the old rules of warfare and to change the daily landscape at a whim.

The challenges of the Mississippi River would certainly demand the greatest minds of the era. Strategies, weaponry, and innovative measures and countermeasures all demanded an evolution or revolution in the art of war for success in the *brown waters* of the Western theater.

Brown-Water Navies

For the first time in history, a successful military outcome depended on hundreds of fragile steam-powered transports and steely-eyed pilots instinctive to the river's tricks and turns and adaptative to frequent on-the-fly changes in riverine tactics and technology. Strange new vessels on both sides would go into urgent construction with the ink not yet dried on the draftsman's plans.

Floating Union Army monsters appeared near Cairo, Illinois, in January 1862, 800-ton ironclad gunboats conceived by the preeminent engineer of his Age, self-taught James Buchanan Eads, who designed the first bridge across the Mississippi River at St. Louis, Missouri. It was Eads who came up with the strategy of converting Western steamboats into ironclad gunships.

Designed by the U.S. Navy's Samuel Pook, these forerunners of battleships and tanks were also built by Eads, seven 175-foot behemoths completed in a miraculous few months and named for cities along the Ohio and Mississippi rivers.

These Western vessels were battle-tested weeks prior to their more famous sisters, the *U.S.S. Monitor* and the *C.S.S. Virginia*.

To overcome the low river stages that hindered Farragut's war vessels in the summers at Vicksburg, Eads' ironclads were designed to navigate on just six feet of water, or *"on a heavy dew."*

For lesser depths, vessels such as Lincoln's 176-ton *U.S.S. Cricket* required only eighteen inches to float. *"Our web-footed Navy can go wherever the ground is a little damp,"* President Lincoln quipped.

The *U.S.S. Cairo* and her 175-man
U.S. Navy History and Heritage Center (USNHHC).

There was a corresponding Confederate rush to field a large fleet of gunboats converted from steamboats. The Confederate mantra of the day was, *"If it floats, put a cannon on it."*

When Louisianians ran short of packets to convert, they modified a drydock into a floating battery, the *C.S.S. New Orleans*. The strange but powerful battery was unnerving to approaching Union crews.

These opposing navies would see the **first major action involving ironclad vessels and rams** on May 10, 1862, at Plum Point, Tenn. **It was also the first true naval battle in the Western theater.**

Two of Eads' *unsinkable* ironclads, the *U.S.S. Cincinnati* and *Mound City*, were sunk at Plum Point in previously unimagined warfare. Both of these durable, resilient vessels were *raised, repaired, and returned to service*.

The Battle of Memphis would be a major test for the **U.S. Ram Fleet**.

Afraid of the Beasts

As 400 shipbuilders worked around the clock on Ead's *"smoke pots"* using lumber from mills in four states, they lacked one a key resource – crews. Experienced seamen, for the most part, had already joined the *blue-water* Navy. And, obviously, there were no experienced ironclad crewmen.

The sight of a belching, hot, overcrowded ironclad bristling with thirteen heavy guns would have concerned the average Northwestern soldier or sailor facing an ironclad assignment. But it was those tubular steam boilers that Eads had installed that gave the recruits the greatest pause.

The unpredictable pressure cookers were the same that were infamous for destroying boats and claiming passengers and crews. The *U.S.S. Mound City* suffered a perforated boiler in battle on Arkansas' White River. Eighty-two sailors were buried on site, most dying a horrific steam-related death. Only 25 sailors were unhurt of a crew of 175.

The *U.S.S. Cairo's* fearsome tubular boiler system, floating bombs.
Image from the Gary J Millett Collection. (GJMC)

Filling the ironclad crew rosters required an inventive personnel system. Immigrants were offered American citizenship for serving. About one-third of crews on Eads' boats were immigrants from a variety of countries.

The ironclads were too small to sleep 175 sailors inside, so they slept at night in hammocks up on the upper *hurricane deck*, exposed to the worst enemy of both sides, the mosquitoes. Crews were exposed every night to the river's plague and auge.

During the day, the summer temperature inside ironclads were known to exceed 130°. *Coal heavers* feeding a ton of coal per hour into the blazing fireboxes suffered mightily in the cramped lower dungeon of the keel.

Yet Ead's vessels had modern amenities such as the paddlewheel distribution system that provided running water aboard the vessel.

A New Quick-Response Fleet

Confederate guerillas found that a high bank on the top of a meander loop, where the river was closest to the bank, was the perfect spot to catch slow-turning Union vessels. A single cannon and a few marksmen, firing head on for 30 minutes, could easily dispatch an unsuspecting steamer carrying large quantities of soldiers or badly needed supplies and artillery.

Bushwhackers also kept watch over Union recoaling stations where vessels came to shore at overgrown locations to load coal, often *one bushel basket at a time*. Steamer crews were required to stop periodically and chop large loads of firewood to feed their boilers, making them extremely vulnerable to guerilla activities.

RAdm. David Dixon Porter countered this threat quickly by building lightly armored steamers (*tinclads*) with soldiers and artillery to patrol convoys of packets. A tinclad might accompany a group of ships or protect vessels entering its assigned *river zone*. The Confederate threat was so widespread that Porter had difficulty meeting demand, even with 34 tinclads.

Col. Charles Ellet created a special strike force for such occasions, the *Mississippi Marine Brigade*. Not attached to the Marines, nor answerable to Grant or Porter, this unit was meant to provide quick response to Confederate shore raiders.

Despite the daily, unprecedented challenges, Grant and Porter never wanted for supplies, unless Grant deliberately deprived his Army by cutting his own supply line. Porter's open river lanes facilitated enormous river-based supply depots at Milliken's Bend, Louisiana, and Grand Gulf and Haynes Bluff, Mississippi.

In late March 1863, Maj. Gen. John McClernand assessed that the Union Navy had complete *superiority* on the Mississippi and that the Trans-Mississippi Department in Louisiana and Texas was completely separated from the rest of the Confederacy. The Confederacy's jugular had been cut.

One Union soldier, settled into his Siege trench, bragged of the efficiency of his Army's supply system. *"We're getting fat sitting here at Vicksburg."* He and his mess mates were receiving three pounds of food per day. The system was so safe by June 1863 that relatives visited their Union soldiers and brought homemade treats and store-bought clothing with them.

Mines and Rams

Col. Charles Ellet was also the *brainchild of ram technology* in the Civil War. Vessels with reinforced prows could easily rupture the hull of even the strongest of ironclads. The Confederates also adopted this technology, inflicting heavy damage on both Union wooden and ironclad vessels.

Innovative ironclad and ram technology doomed the greater part of the Confederate navy at the Battle of Memphis, June 6, 1862.

An effective Confederate device the Union sailors called *"those infernal machines"* was the underwater mine, then called a *torpedo*. Using a few dollars worth of readily available supplies, Rebel *submarine batteries* could sink a $100,000 ironclad. During the Vicksburg engagements, the *U.S.S. Cairo* and her sister, the *U.S.S. Baron DeKalb*, fell victims to mines in the Yazoo River near Redwood and Yazoo City. **The *U.S.S. Cairo* was the first vessel ever sunk by a mine in warfare.**

No Navy! On Second Thought!

When Grant was planning his Vicksburg Campaign at the end of 1862, he was greatly miffed when his boss, Maj. Gen. Henry Halleck, set up *"joint operations"* in Grant's theater at Memphis, without consulting Grant. Grant had **no intention of employing the U.S. Navy** in his operation.

Grant, however, eventually moved into Mississippi on April 30, 1863, with **the largest amphibious operation in modern history**. The Grant-Porter record would stand until 1942's *Operation Torch* in Africa during World War II. The previous record holder was Persian King Xerxes when he invaded Greece in 480 B.C.

Later, Grant would declare that he **would not have contemplated** going against Vicksburg without Porter's close partnership and his fleet. He freely credited Porter and the Navy with half of the success at Vicksburg.

Underpowered Giants

As powerful as Eads' ironclads were, they were built using standard steamboat propulsion systems. Going downstream, they could achieve about six knots. However, their extreme weight and undersized engines made creeping upstream against the Mississippi's powerful current and Vicksburg's long gauntlet of heavy guns *suicidal*. If the vessels were forced to burn wood due to a lack of coal, a tug would probably need to help pull them back upstream.

For this reason, when Grant needed Porter to run Vicksburg's batteries south to Grand Gulf on April 16, 1863, Porter reminded him that his ironclads could not return upstream until Vicksburg had fallen.

Treasure-Lined Shores

Northwesterners familiar with the river knew that the massive area plantations and their elaborate mansions were near the river landings, vulnerable to fire from Union vessels and raids by their soldiers and sailors.

Aside from the normal booty from looting plantations, raiders were likely to find large stores of bales of cotton, many thousands in some places. Due to wartime cotton-price inflation, a single 450-lb. bale of cotton might bring a looter, in 2023 dollars, $30,000. By comparison, a 500-lb. bale of cotton in the 2023 Mississippi cotton market was roughly $375.

Lincoln wanted cotton sent north to pay for the prosecution of the war. Captured Confederate cotton stamped "C.S.A" was restamped "U.S.N." Confederates said that stood for *"Cotton Stealing Association of the U.S. Navy."*

Many Southern planters burned thousands of bales in advance of the Union arrival, untold millions of dollars going up in smoke.

Grappling with the *Old Man* Himself

Union efforts to change the course of history by changing the course of the Mississippi, though unsuccessful, are legendary. When newly promoted RAdm. David Farragut attempted to capture Vicksburg in the summer of 1862, Brig. Gen. Thomas Williams brought thousands of soldiers assigned by Maj. Gen. Benjamin Butler to dig a 1.5-mile canal through heavy clay at the base of the meander loop below Vicksburg. If the river could be coached into leaving Vicksburg for the new route, Vicksburg might well be rendered irrelevant.

Williams' soldiers from cooler upper New England were fighting hand-to-hand an Amazonian swamp in sweltering, disease-ridden, mosquito-infested, 110° heat indices.

The Mississippi River plays for keeps. Williams failed, leaving several hundred soldier and slave graves clutched by the blackwater backwaters. Hundreds of slaves promised their freedom in return for labor were found wandering emaciated in the sweltering swamps.

When Grant arrived in January 1863, Lincoln wanted the Williams canal

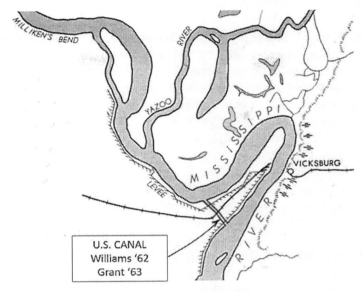

Adapted from a 1954 NPS handbook by William Everhart.

project revived. Grant started two more canal projects at Duckport, Louisiana, a little farther north, and at Lake Providence, Louisiana, nearer the Arkansas state line.

The canal projects essentially failed in their intent, leaving hundreds more Northwesterners buried in the river levee and fields. In a show of defiance, the Mississippi River unearthed and washed away many of the Union soldiers and workers buried in the levee over the next few years.

Thank God for unanswered Union prayers. Had the Union Army engineers succeeded, Grant's canal at Lake Providence in all probability would not only have bypassed Vicksburg, but also Natchez, Baton Rouge, and New Orleans, sending the Mississippi down through central Louisiana into the Atchafalaya River system.

The lazy Mississippi River has fought tooth and nail for the last century and a half to take its *preferred, shorter course* to Morgan City, Louisiana, thwarted only by our modern U.S. Army Corps of Engineers.

Mark Twain, in his epic *Life on the Mississippi*, mentored, *"Ten thousand River Commissions, with the minds of the world at their back, cannot tame that lawless stream, cannot curb it or confine it, cannot say to it, 'Go here' or 'Go there,' and make it obey."*

In a show of complete disdain for Grant, the Mississippi River, which would not "Go here!" in 1863, changed course on its own, cutting through

DeSoto Point on April 26, 1876, *the day before Grant's birthday.*

After a yearslong futile attempt to force the river away from its 1876 cutoff attempt, the Army Engineers were left with no recourse but to tell the docile Yazoo River to "Go there!" into the Mississippi's old bed in front of Vicksburg.

In 1903, the *Old Man* chuckled as Vicksburgers jubilantly celebrated *Canal Day*. The ingenious Army Engineer response to the Mississippi's mischief was realized when a dike was blown to direct the Yazoo River Diversion Canal into the city's waterfront.

Old Man River, in the meantime, enjoyed his long-planned shorter route to the Gulf of Mexico.

Veteran boaters, pilots, sportsmen, and even engineers consistently warn, *"Never give the river an edge. He will beat you every time."* The image below can be spotted even today hanging on the walls of river experts' offices as a constant reminder of the Mississippi's contentious ways.

B
The Yazoo-Mississippi Delta
Land of Dreams and Nightmares

The Mississippi River refuses to confine itself to anything resembling a consistent three-dimensional form, as some rivers might.

The Mississippi on any given day might be fifty feet higher or lower than it was just a season ago. A record low water so shallow that you can see the river's bottom from the air may be followed in the near future by a monumental high water that presses the tops of earthen levees so massive that they can be seen from space.

For questions about the river's width, a reasonable answer might be, *"Three quarters of a mile at Vicksburg"* — as long as the *Old Man* is behaving himself.

In his more vexatious seasons, accurate measurements of the Mississippi River might require a degree in river hydraulics, many years of river-watching experience, and an expansive system of river gages.

The river is monitored not in *miles wide* but in inches or feet and *cubic feet per second (cfs)*. The peak flow on the Mississippi was 2.3 million cfs in 2011. That 2011 record flow equated to 17.3 million gallons **per second**.

During the 1927 flood, the river broke free of its pitiful flood control chains. Some find it hard to believe that it was possible to ride a packet steamer from Greenwood, Mississippi, across the river's watery expanse to Monroe, Louisiana, a distance of 132 miles, without ever touching bottom.

If modern north Louisiana flood control levees were to fail today during the worst flood anticipated, termed the *Project Flood*, the Mississippi River would put eight feet of water in the Monroe, Louisiana, airport, 75 miles from the main channel.

The river has never relinquished its claim to its overflow lands. It is in these transitional areas, where the river chooses to periodically stretch like

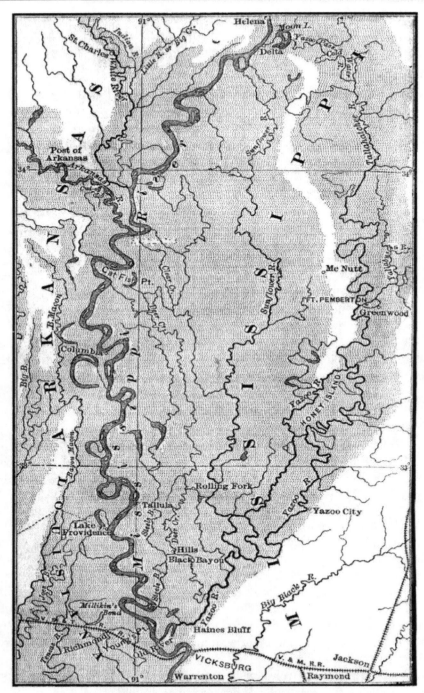

The Yazoo-Mississippi Delta of the 1860s.

an awakening, chained giant, that life can prove to be extremely tedious, yet still vastly rewarding for those willing to brave sharing the Mississippi River's bed with him.

The sirens of the *Mississippi Delta* have enticed even the earliest of man into this natural *Eden* by leaving a dark richness in its alluvial soil, its overflow nourishing an abundance of beauty, flora, fauna, and people.

> *"The Mississippi Delta is not always dark with rain.*
> *Some autumn mornings, the sun rises over Moon Lake,*
> *or Eagle, or Choctaw, or Blue, or Roebuck, all the wide,*
> *deep waters of the state, and when it does, its dawn is*
> *as rosy with promise and hope as any other."*
> *Mississippi Author Lewis Nordan*

The Mississippi's overflow lands wrap around Vicksburg on three sides, natural barriers to modern migration and development. Throughout history, these marshy, ancient forests, scattered with deceptively *high ground*, have both discouraged and encouraged many. Only the bravest take the bait of the Delta's natural bounty.

The spirit of early Mississippi pioneers still lives in the Delta. Many have thrived in her *school of hard knocks,* but they have learned that the Delta grades on a *hard curve.*

Defining "the Delta"

Author David Cohen wrote that the Mississippi Delta begins in the lobby of the Peabody Hotel in Memphis, Tennessee, and ends at *Catfish Row* in Vicksburg, Mississippi. Cohen and Norden's *Mississippi Delta* is actually the *Yazoo-Mississippi Delta,* the historic shared floodplain of the Mississippi and Yazoo rivers.

The far northwestern sliver of Mississippi, the Yazoo Delta is 6,250 square miles of rich, black alluvial deposits many feet deep.

It is 60 miles at its widest point from the Yazoo River to the Mississippi River, its western border. Its eastern limits are the hill lines and bluffs from Vicksburg to Memphis. In the state of Mississippi, 19 counties claim kinship with the Yazoo Delta, ranging from DeSoto County to Warren County.

Man Enters the Delta

The earliest people moved into the Delta about 1,000 B.C., the *Yazoo, Tunica, Koroa, Tioux,* and *Ofogoula,* followed by the *Mississippians* about 1,000 A.D.

The *Mississippians* were small-scale yet advanced farmers with impressive *towns*. They applied advanced crop-rotation principles. Their *mounds* still stand in the Delta and along other reaches of the Mississippi River where the *Mississippi Mound Trail* honors their amazing culture.

A mound built by a Delta civilization that thrived from about 1000 to 1450. *Located at the Winterville Mounds State Park, Washington County, Mississippi.*

The early Delta inhabitants enjoyed a rich ecology of migratory birds, ducks, geese, eagles, and panthers, with virgin forests of cypress, tupelo, sweetgum, hackberry, and cottonwood. Higher elevations abounded in forests of other hardwoods. Dense river cane choked streams, sloughs, creeks, and rivers teeming with fish, mammals, and mussels.

Paradise Lost

In 1542, Hernando de Soto's entourage avoided the heart of the Yazoo Delta, choosing a route that took them away from its swollen tributaries and swamps. Tribal *runners*, however, from the powerful Delta *Quigualtam* chiefdom and others made contact with the Spaniards along their route.

De Soto's intent to enslave and loot the Chickasaw had every chiefdom in his path anxiously awaiting the chance to demonstrate their strength, superiority, and resolve to the newcomers. When de Soto, claiming to be the god *Son of the Sun*, requested that leader Quigualtam report to the Spanish camp, the powerful chief rebuked de Soto.

"As to what you say of your being the Son of the Sun, if you will cause him to dry up the great river, I will believe you. As to the rest, it is not my custom to visit anyone. Neither for you or any man will I set back one foot."

De Soto's actions and insolence forced his caravan to skirmish and battle with each indigenous town along the way, all notified in advance and primed for war prior to his arrival.

To De Soto, the Mississippi River and the Yazoo Delta were obstacles to overcome and survive which, of course, he did not. He was laid to rest in the Mississippi River months later near present day Vidalia, Louisiana, claimed by the river's plagues. De Soto's burial in the Mississippi River is featured in Constantino Brumidi's sculpture, *below*, in the U.S. Capitol Rotunda.

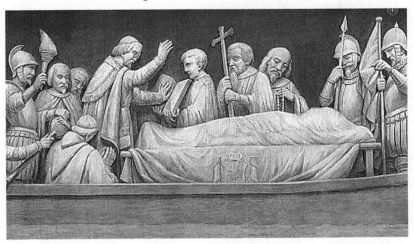

After de Soto's death to the river's disease, his remaining few survivors were chased downriver by arrows flying from an armada of giant, elaborate battle canoes. When one pursuing native group reached the limits of its territory, another was waiting to continue the chase. A few of de Soto's explorers survived to tell the story.

While the native towns celebrated their victories over the haughty Spanish explorers, *De Soto's Revenge,* the diseases left behind by the Europeans, began to slowly diminish the native population.

De Soto's meddling in native affairs left behind political unrest among the native towns. Decades of drought would also contribute to the eventual collapse of these societies.

Though de Soto claimed the area for His Majesty Carlos V, the Spanish king showed little interest in the wilds and agrarian towns the Conquistadors' wake left in ruin and collapse.

Europeans would not seriously try the region again until the French established Fort St. Pierre near the mouth of the Yazoo River in 1719. They quickly learned why *Yazoo* was translated *"River of Death."*

The French would dally for decades until the 1763 Treaty of Paris gave the

Los Nogales area *(present day Vicksburg)* to Spain.

In 1790, the more-friendly Choctaw would cede land to Louisiana governor Manuel Gayoso De Lemos for *Fort Nogales* to be built overlooking the bend of the Mississippi River. The lower miles of the Yazoo Delta and a native mound could be admired at *a safe distance* from the fort.

A Very Tentative Foothold

As the 19th century arrived, there was still little interest in settling lands from Fort Nogales north. Economic activity, save a few pioneer families and scattered trading posts, was sparce, struggling but surviving.

The Spanish opened the Mississippi to American commerce in 1795. At the time, less than one flatboat per day passed the Delta's shores.

Grand Gulf, at the mouth of the *Loosa Chitto* (today's *Big Black River*) had 200 settlers. Fort Nogales, on the tip of the Yazoo Delta, had 16 or 17.

Civilization, as defined by the Europeans, ended at Mint Springs Bayou at the northern base of Fort Nogales where the indigenous nations extended into the Delta to the north and east.

Developing the area was an extreme task. The first road to the hamlet of Los Nogales and Fort Nogales was a military communications trace from Grand Gulf not opened until 1791.

Rare flatboats pushed upriver by poles were inadequate to move heavy farming and industrial implements north. A typical homesteader in Los Nogales did well to obtain a few spades and a plough.

By 1794, the area's Choctaw had realized their drastic mistake of trading local furs to Europeans. Hundreds of thousands of hides and furs had been sent to market from the fur-rich Delta.

As the century turned, the Choctaw, without sufficient game, hides, or fur would turn to raiding farms to survive. Their area society was in shambles.

The Spanish Fort Nogales complex north of present-day Vicksburg.
From a 1796 map by the French spy Georges Henri Victor Collot.

The Louisiana Purchase of 1803 was a huge drawing card of fresh land for the bravest of Deep South pilgrims. It was, though, the stability that followed the War of 1812 that opened the flood gates to a westward move into the Mississippi Territory.

The Yazoo-Mississippi Delta would quickly garner the attention of wealthy, land-hungry speculators chasing unimaginable fortunes.

The Birth of an Empire

In 1820 and 1830, the Federal government signed the Treaties of Doak's Stand and Dancing Rabbit with the Choctaw and Chickasaw nations, respectively, giving the United States title to the entire Yazoo-Mississippi Delta.

Thomas Jefferson's dream of a western United States occupied by small yeoman farming households was about to disintegrate. Moneyed interests in the east were paying individuals to secure and work expansive land grants for them to create incredible agricultural holdings.

At about the same time, agricultural and mechanical genius Dr. Rushworth Nutt of Rodney, Mississippi, perfected his hybrid *Petit Gulf* cotton on his Laurel Hill plantation. Until Dr. Nutt's discovery, a cotton hybrid had not been developed that was easy to pick and thrived in the South's interior.

At Laurel Hill, Nutt was also the first to connect a steam engine to a cotton gin. Eli Whitney's 1794 cotton gin when powered a mule had already increased the production of clean, deseeded cotton *500 times*. Nutt's steam-powered gin increased the rate another *tenfold*. The pair had reduced ginning labor and increased ginning output 5,000 times over previous methods.

Laurel Hill Plantation, Rush Nutt's homeplace, cradle of the Cotton Empire.
Image from the Historic American Buildings Survey, Library of Congress.

New modes of transportation were also stoking the burgeoning cotton industry. When the area's first locomotive, the *Mississippi*, went into operation in Natchez, Mississippi, in 1837, the cost of hauling cotton began its decline from $4 a bale to $1 a bale, about $140 to $35 per bale in 2023 dollars.

Fleets of steamboats stopping at scores of river landings were carrying a hundred times more cotton, passengers, and building blocks of farms, towns, and cities than the old downstream, one-way-only flatboats ever could.

These innovations, combined with Andrew Jackson's removal of most of the area's indigenous people, created *the perfect economic storm*, the largest financial explosion on the planet, an ***international economic phenomenon*–the "*Cotton Rush*."**

Mississippi was preparing for launch as **the richest state in the nation**. Natchez was set to become the ***City of Millionaires***.

Vicksburg would take its place as the commercial center of Mississippi— and its second largest city—just 60 years after boasting an area population of a *few dozen*.

Ships of Dreams and Nightmares

The embers of Mississippi's blazing fires of agricultural ardor were uncontainable. The fires of prosperity spread rapidly northward, ushering in the Delta's age of opulence.

The architecturally stunning steamers brought dreamers of every kind — planters, businessmen, attorneys, merchants, speculators, and families—into this young state desperate for them.

These *floating palaces* also transported the engines required to power their new economy, the enslaved – and their *living nightmares*. By 1840, the enslaved represented 195,111 of Mississippi's population, exceeding the white population of 189,540.

By 1860, Mississippi would require the labor of half a million slaves. To feed lavish lifestyles, planters fell into a vicious cycle: *to pay my debts, I must buy more slaves and grow more cotton to buy more slaves to grow more cotton to pay my debt*, and on and on.

The cycle fanned fierce national debates when cotton began exhausting Southern soil, stiff U.S. tariffs started shearing profits, and slaves idled by depressions began sapping planter finances. Planters believed that their cash-flow woes could be solved simply by opening new lands to cotton production and, of course, slavery.

It was against this backdrop that the starkest of contrasts unfolded on the wharves in west central Mississippi: the *endowed* hopefuls arriving with the *enchained* hopeless. In a sad twist of timing and fate, many of the enslaved had been *"sold down the river"* to the benefit of throngs of failing Virginia tobacco farmers who were desperate to reduce their *chattel* holdings.

At the same wharves, Army packets were loading another desperate cargo, the remnants of the displaced Choctaw and Chickasaw nations on the wretched *Trail of Tears* to assigned homelands west of the Mississippi River.

Such was the backdrop of civilization in the early Yazoo-Mississippi as black hands, white cotton, and red displacement prepared the seedbed for the *Cotton Rush*.

Opening the Yazoo Delta

With land and technology in hand, vast cotton fields began to replace ancient forests. The visual, social, ecological, and economic shape of the Delta was beginning an irreversible transformation.

By 1834, speculators from Clinton, Mississippi, had sold carefully placed lots 40 miles north of Vicksburg on the Yazoo River. Construction was underway for the new town of *Manchester*, named for England's *cotton metropolis* with its scores of cotton mills. The named streets featured a bank, two hotels, businesses, and homes. Steamboats called regularly.

By 1840, Manchester, soon to be renamed *Yazoo City*, had over 1,000 white and black residents and was shipping 25,000 bales of cotton per year worth $40 million in 2023 dollars.

A few years later, Wade Hampton III of the very successful South Carolina Hamptons bought land in the Yazoo Delta. By 1860, Hampton had acquired

900 slaves working properties in two counties.

Choctaw leader Greenwood LeFlore, who sold the land on which the town of Manchester was built,. owned 400 slaves. His home was decorated in the finest French furnishings.

As the interior of the Delta was being transformed, so also was its Mississippi River shoreline. Earlier, steamboats had connected New Orleans and Natchez. Now, Delta river communities such as Commerce, Bolivar, Prentiss, Greenville, and Vicksburg blossomed when steamboats began landing at *their* landings.

In 1844, the town of Greenville, founded in 1824 – a year prior to Vicksburg's charter – had become the trading, business, and cultural center for the Delta region's large cotton plantations and its county seat.

The two previous county seats, New Mexico and Princeton, had joined the list of those towns gobbled up by the meandering Mississippi River. Greenville claimed the title *"Queen City of the Delta."*

War Creeps into the Delta

The Yazoo-Mississippi Delta would play a major and continuous role in Vicksburg war operations. Its miserable terrain would confound the Union's best minds by protecting Vicksburg's northern flank and providing ambush points for smaller Confederate forces.

On his first attempt to capture Vicksburg in December 1862, Maj. Gen. U.S. Grant avoided the troublesome terrain of the Delta entirely. He moved down the Mississippi Central Railroad toward Jackson. Maj. Gen. William Sherman steamed down from Memphis and landed on the Yazoo River north of Vicksburg at Chickasaw Bayou on the Delta's southernmost tip.

Hardly a Union boot had touched the Yazoo Delta proper in 1862. Vicksburg was protected on the north by this prehistoric, soggy, dark buffer.

Desperate to find any means of getting around Vicksburg in February 1863, Grant and Porter undertook the risky *Yazoo Pass Expedition* to gouge a long, treacherous canal through the upper Delta's Moon Lake opposite Helena, Arkansas. Their mission was to gain access into the Yazoo River system nearer Memphis, Tennessee, bypassing fortress Haynes Bluff above Vicksburg.

Union *pioneers*, 400 of them, dug two holes in the Mississippi River levee to allow the landside to reach stages suitable to float their vessels. It would be several days before the flow rushing through the breach could safely pass a vessel.

After fighting through many miles of some of the Delta's worst swamps and entanglements that tore chimneys and superstructures from vessels, Union forces reached the distant Yalobusha-Tallahatchie river juncture that formed the Yazoo River at Greenwood *(see map below)*.

Because speedy Union maneuvers in the Delta were not possible, the enemy had time to respond at decisive points. A hastily constructed Confederate cotton-bale *Fort Pemberton* at the river juncture blocked Union Navy and Army hopes of success.

The demoralized convoy backed out into the Mississippi two months after the start of the disastrous campaign, fighting mosquitoes, poisonous reptiles, and alligators that amassed in the Delta spring. Buffalo gnats were in such great swarms that they were killing convoy mules.

Later in life, Porter would lament, *"I never wanted to hear of the Yazoo Pass again."*

While Union forces were slogging through the marshy jungles just south and across the river from Helena, Arkansas, Porter had also launched an expedition with five City Class ironclads up narrow Steele Bayou, several miles into the Delta from bastion Haynes Bluff.

Porter hoped again to find a route to bypass Haynes Bluff *(see map next page)*. Confederate raiders harassed Porter unmercifully, trapping his boats by felling trees ahead of and behind his flotilla.

When it looked as though all was lost, Sherman's troops arrived in the nick of time to save Porter's flotilla.

Porter returned to the safety of the Mississippi River after what he termed *"an eleven-day excursion into futility."* Porter considered the Delta's streams and bayous *"a green hell."*

Even the largest amphibious operation since Xerxes invaded Greece 2,500 years ago could not conquer the Yazoo Delta.

In May 1863, when Grant successfully acquired a beachhead at Port Gibson, Mississippi, he thought that he should immediately turn north and take

Porter's Steele Bayou Expedition Theater

Vicksburg from the south using the Warrenton Road.

When a Union expedition under Maj. Gen. James McPherson found more miles of slushy swamps between Vicksburg and the Big Black River, as well as a Confederate defensive line on Redbone Road, Grant chose to go the long, dry way around. The result would become the **most brilliant military Campaign in American history**.

Porter never went back to the Yazoo Delta.

There were numerous short-term, mostly unsuccessful Union incursions and distractions into the Delta in 1862 and 1863. Frederick Steele even made a mess of Greenville in 1863.

After the fall of Vicksburg, the Delta harbored Wirt Adam's Confederate cavalry and other Confederate guerillas. Mississippi's *Gray Ghost* and others proved to be a headache for Union occupation forces.

Confederate Mississippi River raiders in the lower Delta remained a threat to shipping and a distraction for Union leaders and troops for the remainder of the war.

In the long run, knowing the infeasibility of major military operations in the Delta, Union commanders and scattered Confederate forces settled into a Delta *coexistence*. The war in the Delta concluded in a draw, the only victor— the Yazoo Delta itself.

C
The Yellow Bluffs
The Rich, Impregnable Crucible

An hour west of Amarillo, Texas, the bottom suddenly drops out of the flat north Texas landscape. The gently rolling plain immediately, with no transition, gives way to far-below canyons and eye-level plateaus and buttes.

Travelers might exclaim, *"We are in the West!"*

Travelers entering Warren County by way of the Big Black, Yazoo, or Mississippi floodplains leave behind flat or gently rolling countryside and are confronted with a similar transition, steep rises and falls on a natural roller coaster of drastic bluffs and ravines.

The rugged geologic origins of the City of Vicksburg are somewhat muted now thanks to centuries of work of mules with earth-moving *slips* and their descendants, earth-moving machines.

Entrepreneurs have long understood that the best investment in Warren County is earth-moving equipment. *Pushing the top off of a worthless bluff into an equally worthless ravine creates valuable flat land for construction.*

Our prehistoric foundation is visible everywhere: malls situated under tall, yellow banks; buildings on the edge of seemingly hard, yellow cliffs; and major roads or streets splitting yellow cuts in the earth that create a perfect venue for graffiti artists with trowels.

To one wartime observer, Vicksburg resembled, *"Great leftover scraps of creation that God dropped into piles and then sprinkled with houses."*

Indeed. Period drawings of antebellum Vicksburg reveal homes perched on sporadic knolls surrounded by jagged lots. Older homes and businesses today stand at street level, the rear of the structure often supported by brick walls or columns or wooden *stilts,* some thirty feet high, to level the floors.

The undulating landscape hides landmarks and makes driving very tedious. Many a young driver has burned out a clutch trying to perfect a standing start on a Vicksburg hill. Just a little wintry mix shuts the city streets down.

Land and River Intertwined

The Mississippi River is the source of *everything Vicksburg*, including its geological building blocks. An Illinois soldier spoke of Vicksburg's terrain: *"There are but two forces in the Universe that could have piled up, cut down, and fashioned Vicksburg – viz God and the Mississippi River."*

The very ground on which the South's Gibraltar stands began to rise 70 million years ago during the Cretaceous period.

The Mississippi Embayment, discussed earlier in Part I, Section A, became filled with eroding sediments. These sediments were compacted and cemented, forming the levels of limestone rock visible along Vicksburg's riverfront today.

By the Oligocene period, 35 million years ago, an inland sea that had formed in the Embayment was filled with sediment, its shore very close to present-day Vicksburg as it retreated south. Rock layers, the *Vicksburg Group*, were exposed. *(The **Vicksburg Group** is important geologically as a record of the last significant worldwide rise and fall of sea levels).*

As northern glaciers moved, they ground bedrock and other rock debris into a fine flour-like soil that was washed down the Mississippi trough. Reaching the river's floodplain, the powdery soil comprised of granite dust and calcium carbonate (*chalk*) dried during low water levels and was picked up by winds and deposited on the Mississippi's eastern rock shore.

This yellow compacted soil, called *loess* after the German word for its *loose* nature, colors the Yellow River (*Huang He*) in China.

Loess deposits are visible locally from Natchez to Vicksburg, from the Mississippi River to near Bovina 10 miles to the east.

An extensive loess formation near Council Bluffs, Iowa, creates the Loess Hills State Park.

A Wonder of Men

In the early 19th century, geologists and naturalists came to western Mississippi to study the thick soils and underlying bedrock.

French naturalist Charles Alexandre Lesueur visited Vicksburg in 1828 to collect some of its abundant, easily accessible fossils. English geologist Charles Lyell visited the area in 1846 and published his findings in *A Second Visit to the United States of North America*.

Eugene Hilgard, the *Father of Soil Science*, studied western Mississippi soils extensively in the mid-1800s.

During the Siege of Vicksburg, Capt. John Wesley Powell, the one-armed geologist who later led the first expedition down the Colorado River through the Grand Canyon, collected fossils near Vicksburg while serving as an officer in the 2[d] Illinois Light Artillery.

Early settlers were attracted west to the area between Vicksburg and Natchez due to the rich loess bluffs. This soil is rich in bases and nutrients. Its silt-sized particles allow plants easy access to water. It drains well, making it readily available for spring plowing and planting. Its lack of clay makes it easy to excavate and transport.

These soil qualities produced land prime for growing cotton. In fact, the cotton fields of the loess hills rivaled those of the Delta during much of this period, typically out-producing them.

A loess sunken road in Claiborne County near Port Gibson, Mississippi.
Photograph by Amanda Logue Boone. (ALB)

Loess soil prefers a vertical orientation and erodes heavily when it is not cut at 90-degree angles. Historic erosion is responsible for the horrendous 200- to 300-foot bluffs and ravines that define Warren County. Wherever water can gain a foothold in loess soil, homes, businesses, and infrastructure are at risk.

Erosion is the primary enemy faced in the battlelines of the Vicksburg National Military Park. Shifting loess has devoured roadbeds and uncovered remains in the National Cemetery. Shifting loess has threatened monuments, collapsed or *slumped* multiple park tour roads, and created other engineering and historical protection issues.

Because loess does not hold water, there were no natural lakes or ponds in early Vicksburg. Citizens found it necessary to create underground *cisterns*, fed by roof runoff down a drain spout. This system was extremely vulnerable to drought.

During Grant's Mississippi Campaign, the area was experiencing a severe drought, adding suffering to soldiers and citizens alike. Confederate soldiers complained that Vicksburgers in this formerly *Unionist city* were not likely to share their water or their wells with Pemberton's parched troops.

The lack of water rations in the Confederate trenches would prove lethal in Vicksburg's heat when their soldiers were limited to one cup of water per day for the last three weeks of June. During the last week of the Siege, water rations were reduced to one-quarter cup per day, far short of the recommended 13 cups per day in 2023.

War on the Loess Bluffs

Union forces were introduced to the loess bluffs in the Spring of 1862. RAdm. David Farragut realized that his naval forces and several thousand Union soldiers under Brig. Gen. Thomas Williams were no match for Vicksburg's fortified heights.

U.S. Army strategists recognize today that Vicksburg's loess heights alone gave its defenders a 10-times advantage over attacking infantry.

Maj. Gen. William Sherman would test 13,000 Confederates on the severe Chickasaw Bluffs north of Vicksburg with his 30,000 soldiers on December 29, 1862. Half of Sherman's battlefield was almost impassable Mississippi-Yazoo Delta backwater swamp. His assault force was quickly bogged down in the face of vicious enemy fire, obstacles, and marsh.

His force was gravely rebuffed with 1,776 casualties. True to the Army's 10:1 ratio regarding attacks on Vicksburg's heights, the Confederacy suffered but 187 losses. The loess hills took 85 percent of Union troops engaged, more than double the losses of the *Charge of the Light Brigade* in the Crimean War. Sherman's Col. John DeCourcy was a Crimean War veteran.

It was RAdm. David Porter's turn at Grand Gulf, Mississippi, on April 29, 1863. After a six-hour bombardment pounded Brig. Gen. John Bowen's high forts and higher trenches with thousands of shells, Porter instructed Grant to go with *Plan B*. The Navy's most powerful gunboats were no match for Grand Gulf's Bowen-designed lofty emplacements.

The loess hills highlighted two weaknesses of the *City Class* ironclads: gunboat artillerists could not elevate their guns higher than five degrees and their wooden decks made them vulnerable to plunging fire from higher elevations.

Thermopylae Revisited

It was ironic that Grant would land at Bruinsburg, Mississippi, on April 30, 1863, with the ***largest amphibious operation*** since Xerxes invaded Greece in 480 B.C. Xerxes was stymied by an infinitely smaller army of 300 Spartans who used the narrow Thermopylae Pass to their advantage.

The road Grant chose to move his army away from his beachhead at Windsor Plantation, the Rodney Road, was a seven-foot-wide sunken road created by years of narrow wagons degrading the road down to depths of up to 30 feet. Soldiers remembered the road being so narrow that four soldiers marching abreast would often rub their shoulders against the banks.

The Rodney Road of 1863 required eight hours to pass a Union Corps of 14,000. *(ALB)*

Vastly outmanned at Port Gibson, Bowen could replicate the advantage of the Spartans. He used the sunken roads and wicked terrain surrounding Magnolia Church to squeeze John McClernand's XIII Corps, neutralizing its advantage in size and artillery. With a force of 8,000, Bowen was able to contain a force of 23,000 all day until finally overwhelmed and out of ammo.

After his experience in Claiborne County's unforgiving terrain, Grant remarked, *"If Port Gibson was this bad, how bad then will Vicksburg be?"* He and his soldiers would pay dearly for a lack of local terrain intelligence.

Grant's three Corps departed Young's Point, Louisiana, without a siege train or mortars, with just a handful of military engineers, and with an army devoid of experience in siege tactics and operations.

Grant's engineering shortfall before the Gibraltar of the Confederacy would cost him and his Army 30 precious days and many additional lives in the blazing, unforgiving dusty ovens at Vicksburg.

"No Greater Topographical Puzzle"

In September 1862, Maj. Samuel H. Lockett, Vicksburg's chief engineer, was assigned to develop Vicksburg fortifications. On reviewing opportunities to protect the eastern rear of the city, he found an alien, badly broken landscape of virgin forest and spotty cleared hilltops. Lockett exclaimed, "*No greater topographical puzzle was ever presented to an engineer.*"

This caustic mission evaluation came from a man who had graduated college at age 16 and then attended the U.S. Military Academy, graduating second in his class. He would later invent engineering equipment and serve as a professor of engineering at Louisiana State University and the University of Tennessee.

Lockett was twice offered the U.T. presidency, managed major international engineering efforts, designed the pedestal for the Statue of Liberty, and supervised the raising of the Statue itself. Lockett was one of the best of his day. He was the man to take on the loess hills of Vicksburg.

After studying the terrain for about 45 days, Lockett used the terrain's advantage by building, on the highest points, nine heavy forts, nine miles of triangulating trenches on snaking ridges, hundreds of yards of natural and man-made obstructions, and wide, denuded killing fields.

He filled the trenches of the unapproachable fortress with 30,000 Confederates with British Enfield rifles, deadly out to 500 yards. Veterans would describe trying Vicksburg and Lockett's maze as 54 days of *murder, massacre, slaughter,* and *suicide.*

Vicksburg: Worse Than Sevastopol

Sherman's XV Corps was the first to arrive at Vicksburg on May 18, 1863. Most of Grant's remaining army was still gingerly feeling its way into the chasms around Vicksburg that day.

Grant had to convince Sherman to repeat his worst nightmare, loess heights that devoured his force at Chickasaw Bayou just to the west five months earlier. Sherman was unconvinced of success but obeyed.

The Confederate bastion, the Stockade Redan, had an eight-foot-high log wall and bristled on a suicidal hill on the city's prophetic Graveyard Road.

On May 18, the fort hid the fact that it was briefly devoid of a Confederate force. Some suggest that the Union army could have taken Vicksburg in two hours if the weakness had been visible to Grant

On May 19, Sherman's soldiers had survived four days on meager forage, fought their way from Jackson to Vicksburg, and pontooned the Big Black River on a hot, 50-mile march. They would advance with *one tired division*.

In order to reach the Confederate works, these hungry, exhausted soldiers were forced to climb 10-story precipices covered with jungle vegetation, pulling each other up, grabbing vines and saplings, and using bayonets as mountain-climbing instruments. They would face *two fresh Confederate divisions*.

Once they had reached the base of the Confederate bastion, they struggled in the soft loess soil, greatly disturbed by bombardment and construction. The dirt shifted like deep flour under them. The soil was complemented by abatis, chevaux-de-frise, deep trenches, and sharpened bamboo stakes.

Sherman, a master of the study of terrain, claimed Vicksburg to be worse than the dreaded Sevastopol in the Crimean War. He only agreed to the assault because Grant believed that Pemberton's forces were whipped from previous Campaign defeats and would immediately surrender.

Rather than an all-out attack, Sherman limited his advance to a *reconnoiter in force*. A full-scale assault would follow on May 22.

Two suicidal assaults on the fortified heights on May 19 and May 22 failed, costing Grant 4,141 soldiers and the Confederates about *one tenth* that.

Grant issued the order on May 25th to launch **the most extensive siege in American history**.

The loess soil, loosened in battle, would help hide the Union's carnage of two massacres. Left spoiling in the hot Mississippi sun for seven days, the stench was so bad by May 25 that both armies wanted to surrender.

Decaying remains up to 10 feet deep were finally covered by both armies where they lay for three miles, ten stories high along the Confederate works during a burial truce and enemy social on May 25.

Approach-trench diggers would lament about uncovering previously buried remains throughout the Siege. Post-traumatic stress syndrome, then known as *dying of a soldier's heart*, was being dished out by the wagonloads.

Living and Dying in Loess

The loess soil played several crucial roles in the siege. Its light weight and ability to stand without support on a 90-degree angle allowed 100 Union soldiers to dig 100-yard-long trenches, 8-feet by 8-feet, in a single day.

Citizens seeking refuge from over 150,000 large-caliber artillery rounds thrown into the city hid in relative safety in caves on the loess hillsides. For $30 in Confederate currency, a citizen could contract for a laborer to dig a cave for a family of two in what would be known as *"Prairie dog Town."*

Because the Army and Navy targeted precious Vicksburg livestock, industrious stock owners hid them in caves, some big enough to hold 200 people.

The soil's dry nature provided a somewhat cooler though claustrophobic dwelling. These earthen bombproofs greatly reduced deaths among Vicksburg's townspeople.

The soil also made for relatively easy digging of 13 large, zigzagging Union Approach trenches, parallels, and galleries facing Confederate forts. A crater would be opened in the forts by exploding a ton of black powder under each of them as part of Grant's massive final assault planned for July 6, 1863.

The Battle of the Crater at the 3ᵈ Louisiana Redan, June 25, 1863.
Note the free-standing loess walls and the proximity of trenches to the enemy.
From artwork by A.E. Mathews, 31ˢᵗ Ohio Volunteers. (Missouri Historical Society)

Loess soil confounded XVII Corps engineer Capt. Andrew Hickenlooper on the Jackson Road. Hickenlooper's challenge – the loess soil was not listed in his West Point Engineer Manual soils detonation chart. He was forced to *guesstimate* the amount of gunpowder needed to open a massive hole in the Confederate 3ᵈ Louisiana Redan on June 25.

Some suggested that he used too much powder; some, not enough. Either way, his resulting 40-foot-wide, 20-foot-deep crater was insufficient, leaving the hole with an uncollapsed crest in its rear.

Maddening Dust Everywhere

Loess is essentially compacted dust. Soldiers, whether marching or working, were always covered in sweaty dust. There are many tales of soldiers unable to distinguish friend or foe, all colored yellow by the loess.

A long march during the Mississippi drought of 1863 meant that soldiers were marching many hours in loess dust over their shoes. A force's strength could be determined at a distance by the enemy by the size of the force's trailing, rising dust cloud.

A marching formation would stretch considerably as soldiers backed away from each other to avoid eating the next man's dust. Reminiscent of the Oklahoma dust bowl, the maddening dust found its way into everything.

Because loess soil meant that the area lacked natural lakes or ponds, Grant's army was forced to find and haul in 37,000 gallons of fresh water a day for his initial attack group at Vicksburg.

Grant learned that many Confederates were getting their fresh water from a local natural spring or *seep*, *Glass Bayou*. Grant ordered latrines and dead animals placed on the pristine stream. By the time the siege ended, 19,000 of 30,000 Confederates were sick in hospitals. Glass Bayou was covered in green, bubbling ooze. Grant had employed germ warfare.

Overcoming Loess

The Northwestern soldiers used loess soil to their advantage to create their safe spaces. A favorite feature was the *gabion*, a stick-and-vine basket filled with lightweight trench diggings to create walls. Sherman personally demonstrated the gabion-building process to some of his unskilled troops.

Grant had 220 artillery pieces that needed to be moved into positions, some as tall as 10-story buildings. Savvy troops bound themselves in leather, in multiple pods of 300, and muscled the artillery up and into position. If an artillerist failed to chock the wheels on his piece, he and his team might end up chasing it into the gorge and wrestling it back into position.

The soft loess Confederate fortifications barely survived the day-and-night bombardment of 400 Union artillery pieces firing up to 100 rounds each daily for almost two months. One Confederate soldier lamented that the nice, high trench he had at the start of the Siege was now waist high, eroded by constant bombardment.

In the end, the fatigue of daily maintaining damaged Confederate fortifications was overwhelming to the sick, starving soldiers who eventually had insufficient usable earth to be used in the repairs.

The up-and-down life in the Vicksburg canyons was so exhausting that one soldier admitted that he was too tired to leave his trench, climb down for his supper, and climb back up.

Miserable Confederate soldiers were rarely allowed to leave their trenches to bathe, where they remained covered in lice, chiggers, and ticks. They were aware that a Union soldier might step into the space they vacated on break.

John Logan's loess trench and Coonskin Foster's tower on the Jackson Road in 1863.
Image from Frank Leslie's Illustrated Newspaper in June 1863.

The photo above shows the essence of the Union soldier's trench experience at Vicksburg. Quickly constructed, large trenches that did not generally require wooden support, easily shaped steps, and the famed gabion baskets forming the shooting line were trademarks of Vicksburg's Union battlements. Spades and picks were as readily available and as important as rifles.

For living quarters, Union soldiers created *shee-bangs*, two-man makeshift dugouts covering nine miles of 10-story yellow bluffs. Each shee-bang

supported four soldiers, two on the firing line or working while two rested inside, i.e., a *hot bunk*.

Soldier shee-bangs in front of the Shirley House, **often confused with citizen caves**, are shown at left. Switchback walks allowed soldiers to climb the extreme cliffs to their abode.

The 47-day loess-hills Siege of Vicksburg would be **the worst Siege ever inflicted on American citizens**.

The photograph at left is from the *Photographic History of the Civil War*, 1911.

PART II
The Voices Echoing from the Bluffs

The origins of more than 200 key political, military, and public figures 1500 to 1854

Mississippians in Frederick C. Triebel's *The Last Stand* on the Mississippi State Memorial, Vicksburg National Military Park. *(GJMC)*

PART II
The Voices Echoing from the Bluffs

US/CS indicates a soldier who participated against his native state.
Civilians are identified. All others are military personnel who will appear later.

1500

Hernando de Soto is born in Badajoz, Spain.
Spanish explorer and first European to see the Mississippi River.

1643

Nov 22 René-Robert Cavelier, Sieur de La Salle, is born in Rouen,
France.
French explorer.

1649

Henri de Tonti is born in Gaeta, Italy.
French explorer.

1655

Antoine Crozat, Marquis de Chatel is born in Toulouse,
France.
First proprietary owner of French Louisiana.

1658

Mar 5 Antoine de la Mothe, sieur de Cadillac, is born in
Saint-Nicholas-de-la-Grave, France.
French explorer. Founder of Detroit.

1667

Jan 30 Jean-Francois Buisson de Saint-Cosme is born in Lauzon,
Quebec, Levis, Canada.
Canadian missionary.

1671

Apr 21 John Law is born in Fife, Scotland.
*Scottish economist and entrepreneur (Mississippi Company and Company of
the West).*

1680

Feb 23 Jean-Baptiste Le Moyne de Bienville is born in Montreal, Canada.
Governor of French Louisiana multiple terms.

1686

Feb 27 Étienne Perier is born in Brest, France.
Governor of French Louisiana, 1726-1733.

1695

Antoine Simon Le Page Du Pratz is born in Holland.
French historian.

1730

George Johnstone is born in Dumfriesshire, Scotland.
First governor of British West Florida.

1746

Jul 23 Bernardo de Galvez is born in Madrid, Spain.
Colonial governor of Spanish Louisiana and Cuba.

1747

May 30 Don Manuel Luis Gayoso de Lemos is born in Porto, Portugal.
Governor of Spanish Louisiana, 1797-1799.

1748

Jul 29 Francisco Luis Hector, Baron de Carondelet, is born in Noyelles-sur-Selle, French Flanders, France.
Governor of Spanish Louisiana and West Florida, 1791-1799.

Aug 1 Samuel Gibson is born in South Carolina.
Founder of Port Gibson, Miss.

1750

James Willing is born in Philadelphia, Pennsylvania.
Leader of Continental raids in the Mississippi valley.

1751

Mar 16 President James Madison is born Port Conway, Va.
Signed the Act of Statehood for Mississippi.

1754

Jan 24 Andrew Ellicott is born in Buckingham, Pennsylvania.
Military surveyor of the Mississippi Territory.

1755

Apr 6 Capt. Isaac Guion is born in New Rochelle, N.Y.
U.S. military representative in the Natchez District.

1756

Peter Bryan Bruin is born in Winchester, Va.
Founder of Bruinsburg, Miss.

1759

Jun 17 Elias Toutant-Beauregard is born in New Orleans.
Commandant of Spanish forts. First commandant of Fort Nogales.
Relative of Confederate general Pierre Gustav Toutant-Beauregard.

1765

Feb 4 Robert Fulton is born in Little Britain, Lancaster Co., Pa.
Inventor of the first functional steamboat.

Dec 8 Eli Whitney, Jr., is born in Westborough, Mass.
Cotton gin inventor.

1766

Mar 17 Rev. Newitt Vick is born in Virginia.
Founder and namesake of Vicksburg.

Dec 10 Joseph Emory Davis is born in Wilkes County, Ga.
Warren County, Miss., pioneer and brother of Jefferson Davis.

1767

Mar 15 Andrew Jackson is born in Waxhaws, Carolinas.
Bruinsburg trader and U.S. President who removed the Choctaw and
*   Chickasaw from Mississippi.*

1771

Nov 10 Rev. Tobias Gibson is born in Pickens Co., S.C.
Father of Mississippi Methodism.

1772

Apr 16 Elizabeth Clark *(Vick)* is born in Virginia.
Wife of Rev. Newitt Vick.

1781

Dr. Rushworth Nutt is born in Northumberland Co., Va.
"Petit Gulf" cotton hybridizer and agricultural and mechanical genius.

1786

Jul 13 Winfield Scott is born in Dinwiddie County, Va. **(US)**

1789

Thomas Redwood is born in England.
Founder of the Carthage community in the 1840's, later named Redwood.

Apr 8 Rev. John Lane is born in Fairfax Co., Va.
Developer of the city of Vicksburg.

1792

Mar 12 Hartwell W. Vick is born in North Carolina.

1794

May 5   James Shirley is born in Goffstown, N.H.
Dartmouth graduate and wartime owner of the Shirley House.

1795

Honore P. Morancy is born in Santo Domingo.
Considered the most important person in early Vicksburg.

1798

Jun 12   Samuel Cooper is born in Hackensack, N.Y. **(CS)**
C.S. Adjutant General, highest ranking C.S. officer.

1799

Mar 8   Simon Cameron is born in Maytown, Pa.
U.S. Secretary of War.

1800

Turpin Green Atwood is born in Providence, R.I.
*A prominent U.S. cotton gin pioneer, he opens a gin factory on
N. Washington St. in Vicksburg before the war.*

May 9   Abolitionist John Brown is born in Torrington, Conn.

1801

Jul 1   James Glasgow Farragut is born in Campbell's Station,
Tenn. **(US)**
*He changes his name to David to honor his adopted father, David Porter.
He is the adopted brother of David Dixon Porter and William "Dirty Bill"
Porter, key naval officers on the Mississippi River.*

1802

Jan 3   Andrew Gallatin McNutt is born in Rockbridge Co., Va.
Progressive early Miss. governor, U.S. Senator, and Vicksburg resident.

Jul 1   Gideon Welles is born in Glastonbury, Conn.
U.S. Secretary of the Navy.

1804

Aug 15   Samuel Moore Pook is born in Boston, Mass.
U.S. naval architect and designer of the City-Class ironclads.

Oct 5   Robert Parker Parrott is born in Lee, N.H.
Ordnance designer, specifically, the Parrott Rifle cannon.

Nov 13   Theophilus Hunter Holmes is born in Sampson Co., N.C.

1806

Apr 10   Leonidas Polk is born in Raleigh, N.C.
*Episcopal bishop who lays the cornerstone for Christ Church in Vicksburg.
Also, a Confederate general known as the "Fighting Bishop."*

Sep 12   Andrew Hull Foote is born in New Haven, Conn.

1807

Jan 16	Charles Henry Davis is born in Boston, Mass.
Feb 2	Joseph Eggleston Johnston is born in Farmville, Va.
Apr 7	Francis Wilkinson Pickens is born in Togadoo, S.C.
	War governor of South Carolina. Alternate date: 1805.
Aug 24	Charles Ferguson Smith is born in Philadelphia, Pa.

1808

Mar 10	William David Porter is born in New Orleans, La. **(US)**
	Brother of David Dixon Porter. Known as "Dirty Bill." Adopted brother of David Glasgow Farragut.
Jun 3	President Jefferson Finis Davis is born in Fairview, Ky. **(CS)**
	The only Confederate president.
Dec 29	President Andrew Johnson is born in Raleigh, N.C. **(US)**
	Serves as Vice-President under Lincoln.

1809

Feb 12	President Abraham Lincoln is born in Hodgenville, Ky.
Sep 14	Sterling Price is born in Prince Edward Co., Va.
Nov 13	John Adolphus Bernard Dahlgren is born in Philadelphia, Pa.
	Ordnance designer, specifically, the Dahlgren cannon.
	Dr. Hugh Shiell Bodley is born in Lexington, Ky.
	Martyr in Vicksburg's effort to rid itself of notorious gamblers.
Dec 24	Henry Augustus Walke is born in Princess Anne Co. Va. **(US)**

1810

Jan 1	Charles Ellet, Jr., is born in Bucks County, Pa.
Aug 6	Judah Philip Benjamin is born in the Christiansted, D.W.I.
	C.S. cabinet member. First practicing Jewish U.S. senator.
Oct 13	James Shedden Palmer is born in Elizabethtown, N.J.

1812

Feb 13	Samuel Phillips Lee is born in Fairfax Co., Va. **(US)**
May 12	John Alexander McClernand is born in Breckinridge Co., Ky.
Aug 8	John Rodgers is born in Havre de Grace, Md.
Dec 4	Elias Smith Dennis is born in Newburgh, N.Y.

1813

	Thomas Neville Waul is born in Sumter County, S.C.
Jan 20	Jacob Gartner Lauman is born in Taneytown, Md.

1814

Mar 6 Sarah Knox Taylor (*Davis*) is born in Vincennes, Ind.
Knoxie is the first wife of Jefferson Davis.
She is the sister of Richard Taylor and daughter of Zachary Taylor.

Aug 10 John Clifford Pemberton is born in Philadelphia, Pa. **(CS)**

Nov 16 Michael Kelly Lawler is born in County Kildare, Ire.

Dec 19 Edwin McMasters Stanton is born in Steubenville, Ohio.
U.S. Secretary of War.

1815

Adeline Quincy (*Shirley*) is born in Boston, Mass.
Mistress of the Shirley House.

Jan 16 Thomas R. Williams is born in Albany, N.Y.

Jan 18 Richard Yates is born in Warsaw, Ky.
War governor of Illinois.

Apr 15 Henry Wager Halleck is born in Westernville, N.Y.

Apr 26 Andrew Jackson Smith is born in Bucks County, Pa.

Jun 15 Martin Edwin Green is born in Fauquier County, Va.

Jul 13 James Alexander Seddon is born in Falmouth, Va.
C.S. Secretary of War.

Nov 29 Stephen Augustus Hurlbut is born in Charleston, S.C. **(US)**

1816

Isham Warren Garrott is born in Ansonville, N.C.

Jan 18 Lloyd Tilghman is born in Claiborne, Md. **(CS)**

Jan 30 Nathaniel Prentice Banks is born in Waltham, Mass.

Aug 3 John Eugene Smith is born in Bern, Switzerland.

Nov 26 William Henry Talbot Walker is born in Augusta, Ga.

1817

Feb 7 Leroy Pope Walker is born in Huntsville, Ala.
First C.S. Secretary of War.

Mar 17 Braxton Bragg is born in Warrenton, N.C.

May 27 Isaac Newton Brown is born in Caldwell Co., Ky. **(CS)**

Sep 21 Carter Littlepage Stevenson is born in Fredericksburg, Va.

1818

Jan 3 Emma Warren Harrison (*Balfour*) is born in Charles City, Va.
Mistress of the Balfour House, she publishes her Siege of Vicksburg diary.

Mar 10 George Wythe Randolph is born at Monticello, Va.
C.S. Secretary of War, he is Thomas Jefferson's grandson.

1818 (Cont.)

Mar 23	Don Carlos Buell is born in Lowell, Ohio.
Apr 22	Cadwallader Colden Washburn is born in Livermore, Me.
May 28	Pierre Gustave Toutant-Beauregard is born in St. Bernard Parish, La.
Sep 28	James Richard Slack is born in Bucks County, Pa.
Oct 18	Edward Otho Cresap Ord is born in Cumberland, Md.
Nov 5	Benjamin Franklin Butler is born in Deerfield, N.H.
Nov 22	Samuel Gibbs French is born in Harrison Township, N.J. **(CS)**
Dec 4	William Wing Loring is born in Wilmington, N.C.
Dec 12	Paul Octave Hebert is born in Plaquemine, La.
Dec 13	Mary Todd (*Lincoln*) is born in Lexington, Ky. *First Lady and wife of Abraham Lincoln.*

1819

	Benjamin Montgomery is born into slavery in Loudon Co., Va. *Joseph Davis' mechanical genius and dreamer of an all-black city.*
Jan 14	Frederick Steele is born in Delhi, N.Y.
Mar 22	William Wirt Adams is born in Frankfort, Ky. **(CS)**
Sep 6	William Rosecrans is born in Delaware Co., Ohio.
Sep 9	Martin Luther Smith is born in Danby, N.Y. **(CS)**

1820

Jan 24	John Milton Thayer is born in Bellingham, Mass.
Jan 26	Edward Crawford Washington is born in Franklin Co., Pa. *He is George Washington's great-nephew.*
Feb 8	Tecumseh Sherman is born in Lancaster, Ohio. *As an adopted Catholic, he is required to have a Christian name. He is named William by his adopted Ewing parents on St. William's Feast Day.*
Mar 13	Louis Hebert is born in Bienville Parish, La.
May 23	James Buchanan Eads is born in Lawrenceburg, Ind.
Aug 8	Winfield Scott Featherston is born in Murfreesboro, Tenn.
Sep 14	Thomas Kilby Smith is born in Boston, Mass.
Sep 17	Earl Van Dorn is born in Port Gibson, Miss. *He is Andrew Jackson's great-nephew.*
Oct 11	Alfred W. Ellet is born in Bucks County, Pa.

1821

	Edward Higgins is born in Norfolk, Va.

1821 (Cont.)

Jan 16	John Cabell Breckinridge is born in Lexington, Ky. **(CS)**
Jan 29	Isaac Ferdinand Quinby is born in Morristown, N.J.
Feb 19	Francis Preston Blair, Jr., is born in Lexington, Ky.
Apr 19	Mortimer Dormer Leggett is born in Ithaca, N.Y.
Jun 6	John Dunlap Stevenson is born in Staunton, Va. **(US)**
Jun 13	Gustavus Vasa Fox is born in Saugus, Mass. *U.S. Asst. Secretary of the Navy.*
Jul 6	Edmund Winston Pettus is born in Limestone Co., Ala.
Jul 13	Nathan Bedford Forrest is born in Chapel Hill, Tenn.
Sep 6	Alvin Peterson Hovey is born in Mount Vernon, Ind.

1822

Mar 16	John Pope is born in Louisville, Ky.
Apr 27	Hiram Ulysses Grant is born in Point Pleasant, Ohio. *He is erroneously enrolled by his sponsor as Ulysses Simpson Grant. West Point officials require him to keep the name appearing on his Congressional sponsorship.*
May 21	Dabney Herndon Maury is born in Fredericksburg, Va.
Nov 22	Nathan Kimball is born in Fredericksburg, Ind.

1823

Jan 4	Peter Joseph Osterhaus is born in Koblenz, Germany.
Jan 29	Franklin Kitchell Gardner is born in New York City. **(CS)**
Aug 4	Oliver Perry Throck Morton is born in Wayne Co., Ind. *Indiana war governor and mentor to Abraham Lincoln.*
Aug 17	James Henry Burton is born in Shenandoah Spring, Va. *Armorer. Creator of the Burton Bullet, the modified conical .577 Minie ball.*
Sep 24	James Madison Tuttle is born in Summerfield, Ohio.
Dec 28	Thomas Alexander Scott is born in Franklin Co., Pa. *U.S. Asst. Secretary of War.*

1824

Jan 13	Seth Lanyard Phelps is born in Parkman, Ohio.
Feb 24	John Crawford Vaughn is born in Monroe Co., Tenn.
Feb 28	John Creed Moore is born in Hawkins Co., Tenn.
May 5	Thomas Welsh is born in Columbia, Pa.
May 16	Edmund Kirby Smith is born in St. Augustine, Fla.
May 31	Charles Leopold Matthies is born in Bromberg, Prussia.

1824 (Cont.)	
Dec 17	Manning Ferguson Force is born in Washington, D.C.
Oct 4	Eleanor Boyle Ewing *(Sherman)* is born in Lancaster, Ohio. *William T. Sherman's adopted sister and wife, Ellen.*

1825	
Jul 11	John Adams is born in Nashville, Tenn.
Nov 3	William Watson Smith is born, place of birth unknown.

1826	
Jan 26	Julia Boggs Dent *(Grant)* is born in St. Louis, Mo. *Wife of Ulysses S. Grant.*
Jan 27	Richard Taylor is born in Jefferson County, Ky. *Son of Zachary Taylor and brother of Sarah Knox Taylor Davis.*
Feb 9	John Alexander Logan is born in Murphysboro, Ill.
May 7	Varina Ann Banks Howell *(Davis)* is born in Natchez, Miss. *Second and surviving wife of Jefferson Davis. First Lady, C.S.A.*
Jul 6	John Irvin Gregg is born in Bellefonte, Pa. **(CS)**
Jul 8	Benjamin Henry Grierson is born in Pittsburgh, Pa.
Aug 10	Randal William McGavock is born in Nashville, Tenn.
Oct 31	Hugh Boyle Ewing is born in Lancaster, Ohio. *William Sherman's adopted brother and brother-in-law.*
Nov 17	John McArthur is born in Erskine, Scotland.

1827	
	Samuel DeGolyer is born in Fondasbush, Fulton Co., N.Y.
	Joseph Anthony Mower is born in Woodstock, Vt.
Mar 17	Martha *Pattie* Thompson *(Pemberton)* is born in Norfolk, Va. *Wife of John C. Pemberton.*
Jul 28	William Edwin Baldwin is born in Statesburg, S.C.
Sep 22	John Grubb Parke is born in Chester County, Pa.
Sep 27	Hiram Rhodes Revels is born in Fayetteville, N.C. *The first black U.S. Senator, he filled Jefferson Davis' seat.*
Oct 14	William Milo Stone is born in Jefferson County, N.Y.

1828	
	Ely Samuel Parker is born on the Seneca Tonawanda Reservation, N.Y.
Jan 28	Thomas Carmichael Hindman is born in Knoxville, Tenn.
Jul 16	Robert Brown Potter is born in Schenectady, N.Y.
Aug 12	John Horace Forney is born in Lincolnton, N.C.

1828 (Cont.)

Sep 8	Seth Maxwell Barton is born in Fredericksburg, Va.
Sep 24	Frederick Edward Prime is born in Florence, Italy.
Nov 8	Giles Alexander Smith is born in Jefferson County, N.Y.
Dec 5	John Eaton, Jr., is born in Sutton, N.H.

1829

	Leon Dawson Marks is born in West Feliciana Parish, La.
Jan 30	Alfred Cumming is born in Augusta, Ga.
Jun 17	John Summerfield Griffith is born in Montgomery Co., Md. **(CS)**

1830

Jan 8	James Lockhart Autry is born in Hayesborough, Tenn.
Feb 6	Marcellus Monroe Crocker is born in Franklin, Ind.
Mar 20	Eugene Asa Carr is born in Hamburg, N.Y.
Jul 22	William Sooy Smith is born in Tarlton, Ohio.
Oct 1	Jeremiah Cutler Sullivan is born in Madison, Ind.
Oct 30	John Stevens Bowen is born on Bowen's Creek, Ga.

1831

Feb 2	John Aaron Rawlins is born in Galena, Ill.
Apr 12	Grenville Mellen Dodge is born in Danvers, Mass.
Apr 22	William Sillman Hillyer is born in Henderson, Ky.
Jun 8	Thomas J. Higgins is born in Riverlequerre, Canada.
Aug 19	Stephen Gano Burbridge is born in Georgetown, Ky.
Sep 3	States Rights Gist is born in Union, S.C.

1832

	James M. Swords is born in Portsmouth, Ohio. *Editor of the Vicksburg Daily Citizen and, after the war, the Vicksburg Daily Herald.*
Mar 30	David Humphreys Todd is born in Lexington, Ky. **(CS)** *Confederate brother of Mary Todd Lincoln.*
Jun 1	Patrick White is born in Sligo, Ire.
Jul 26	George Boardman Boomer is born in Sutton, Mass.
Sep 25	William Le Baron Jenney is born in Fairhaven, Mass.
Dec 22	Edward Hatch is born in Bangor, Maine.

1833

Sep 22   Stephen Dill Lee is born in Charleston, S.C.
*Founding president, Vicksburg National Military Park (VNMP)
Commission and Mississippi State Agricultural and Mechanical College.*

Nov 3   Edward Dorr Tracy, Jr., is born in Macon, Ga.

1834

Mar 22   Francis Asbury Shoup is born in Franklin County, Ind. **(CS)**

Mar 24   John Wesley Powell is born in Mount Morris, N.Y.

Oct 1   Francis Marion Cockrell is born in Warrensburg, Mo. **(CS)**

Nov 29   Thomas Edwin Greenfield Ransom is born in Norwich,
Conn.

1835

Oct 1   William Hicks Jackson is born in Paris, Tenn.

1836

Feb 6   Thomas Oliver Selfridge, Jr., is born in Charlestown, Mass.

Aug 27   Mary Ann Webster (*Loughborough*) is born in New York City.
Author of "My Cave Life in Vicksburg."

1837

Feb 17   Francis Jay Herron is born in Pittsburgh, Pa.

Mar 14   William H. Tunnard is born in Newark, N.J. **(CS)**
Sergeant and biographer of the 3ᵈ Louisiana Infantry.

Jul 6   Samuel Henry Lockett is born in Virginia.

Aug 10   Andrew Hickenlooper is born in Hudson, Ohio.

Sep 2   James Harrison Wilson is born in Shawneetown, Ill.

1838

Sep 27   Lawrence Sullivan *Sul* Ross is born in Bentonsport, Iowa
Territory. **(CS)**
Founding president of Texas State Agricultural and Mechanical College .

1841

Nov 3   William Titus Rigby is born in Red Oak Grove, Iowa.
*VNMP Resident Commission until his death after over three decades of
service. VNMP Association lobbyist, park developer, and champion.
The Architect of the Vicksburg National Military Park.*

1842

Oct 26   Charles Floweree is born in Fauquier County, Va.
Treasurer, 1895 Vicksburg National Military Park Association.

1843

Jan 29   President William McKinley is born in Niles, Ohio.
Signed the act establishing the Vicksburg National Military Park.

Dec 25   Jennie Irene Hodgers is born in Clogherhead, Co. Louth, Ire.
A soldier with the 95th Illinois known as Priv. Albert D. J. Cashier.

1844

Mar 24   John F. Merry is born in Peninsula, Ohio.
Initiated national efforts to preserve the Vicksburg battlefield.
Recognized as the Father of the Vicksburg National Military Park.

1847

Jan 11   Thomas Clendinen Catchings is born in Brownsville, Miss.
Local Mississippi Congressman who sponsored the VNMP Act of 1899.

May 21   Isaiah Montgomery is born into slavery at Davis Bend, Miss.
His father, Benjamin, is plantation manager, inventor, and merchant.

1849

Dec 29   Orion Perseus Howe is born in Hiram, Portage Co., Ohio.

1850

May 30   Frederick Dent Grant is born in St. Louis, Mo.
The General's son who accompanies him as a lad on the Vicksburg
Campaign.

1854

Jun 8   William Tecumseh *Willie* Sherman, Jr., is born in San
Francisco, Cal.
As the mascot of the 13th U.S. Infantry, he will be known as "Sgt. Willie."

PART III
"Claim It, Name It, and Tame It"

*Native, foreign, and pioneer cultures
ebb and flow seeking permanence
12,000 B.C. to 1860*

Explorer Hernando de Soto encounters the region's inhabitants in May 1841.
Adapted from William H. Powell's 1855 oil painting in the U.S. Capitol Rotunda.

PART III
"Claim It, Name It, and Tame It"

12,000 B.C.

The first nomadic people enter what is now Mississippi.
They focus on a broad range of food sources.
Toward the period's end, they cultivate and domesticate plants.

6,000 to 0 B.C., the Archaic Period

The *Yazoo, Tunica, Koroa, Tioux* and *Ofogoula* settle the area.
Hunting small game, including deer, becomes their focus.
As the climate warms, they become semi-nomadic and
   sedentary.
Evidence of regional trade appears.

1,700 to 1,000 B.C., the late Archaic Period

Earthen circles and mounds appear just west of the Mississippi.
The *Poverty Point* site supports trade and ceremonial needs.

200 B.C. to 300 A.D., the region's Woodland Period

Settlements on high ground are preferred to floodplains.
Small, conical burial mounds appear.

Long-distance exchange of goods and materials is occurring.
An egalitarian society considers all members equal.
Introduction of the bow and arrow increases population.
Monumental earthworks and burials of dead are widespread.
Pottery, cord making, and fabric decorations appear.

700

The rise of the *Natchez* civilization occurs.

1000, the Mississippian Period

The society is typically organized into *chiefdoms*.
Agriculture (corn, beans, and squash) sustains them.
This subsistence method is a *revolutionary*.
Giant mound complexes rise, one with 89 mounds.

1540

Native populations subside and move to interior lands.
Hernando de Soto wants to colonize North America within a few
  years.
If successful, his family will be given a large grant of land.

1541

May 8 Hernando de Soto's expedition sees the Mississippi River.
He encounters the *Tunica* province of *Quizquiz*.
De Soto claims great portions of North America for Spain.
Spain's King Carlos V is only interested in Florida and the
  Continent's west coast.

1543

Disease and native political unrest are left in the Spanish wake.

1600

Indigenous Delta societies collapse due to drought and disease.

1650

2,000 members of four tribes remain in the lower Yazoo Delta.

1682

The *Quapaw* occupy the Delta.
The combined Tunica and Koroa occupy the Yazoo's mouth.
The great Tunica have been reduced to 900.

Mar 24 Explorer Robert Cavalier LaSalle visits present-day Delta, La.

Apr 9 LaSalle claims the river's valley, *La Louisiane*, for France.

1685

English from Charles Town connect with area *Chickasaw*.
Explorer Henry de Tonti arrives seeking LaSalle's colonists.

1690

The Chickasaw absorb several Mississippi Valley groups.
These include the *Taposa, Ibitoupa*, and *Chakchiumas*.

1699

Jesuit priest Antoine Davion's party meets the *Yazoo* people.
He briefly remains with them at the Yazoo River's mouth.

1700

Apr 1 Chevalier de Tonti is warmly received by the *Natchez*.
The last of the Mound Builders have *"miles of cornfields."*
The area is *"thickly set with great Natchez towns."*

The *Tioux* from the Pearl River seek refuge with the Natchez.

1702

Dec 31 The first shipments of northern copper have made their way to the Gulf of Mexico.

Jean-Francois Buisson becomes a missionary to the Natchez.
Five tribes unite after pressure and attacks from the Chickasaw.
The alliance: *Tunica, Koroa, Ofogoula, Yazoo,* and *Chakchiuma.*

1704

20 requested prospective brides arrive in the Louisiana colony.
They bring plague that kills 22 settlers.

1705

The Chickasaw are selling Tunica, Quapaw, and Koroa slaves.
The market is the South Carolina slave trade.
1,000-2,000 are being sold.

15,000 northern bear and deer hides are shipped to the Gulf.
Commercial exploitation of river resources starts a tragic trend.

1706

The Tunica are relocating to the lower Red River.
The Chickasaw and Choctaw are divided along the Yazoo –
Choctaw to the east; Chickasaw, west to the Mississippi.

The Chickasaw favor England; the Choctaw favor the French.
English traders are also making inroads with the Natchez.

The Petticoat Insurrection
Unhappy French women want to return to France.

1712

Antoine Crozat is given a royal trade monopoly in Louisiana.

1713

Antoine de Mothe, Sieur de Cadillac, is Louisiana's governor.
Jean Baptiste de Bienville is demoted to lieutenant governor.

Crozat establishes the first trading post among the Natchez.

1715

The *Yamasee War* erupts across the South over native slaves.

The Chickasaw protect the British traders; the Choctaw do not.

1716

French *Fort St. Pierre* is established on the Yazoo River.
Lt. Sieur de La Boulaye is the area's first *authority*.
Pierre Le Blond de La Tour has 60 tobacco workers.

1716 (Cont.)

Fort Rosalie is established by Bienville at Natchez.

1717

Crozat surrenders his charter for failure to thrive.
John Law's *Company of the West* picks up the royal monopoly.

1718

Bienville moves Louisiana's colonial capital to New Orleans.

1720

John Law's *Mississippi Company* experiences a *bubble burst*.
The Chickasaw interrupt French Mississippi River traffic.
The French continue to pay for Chickasaw scalps.

1726

Corrupt Bienville is replaced by Etienne Boucher de Perier.

1729

Nov 28   *Natchez Chief 'Great Sun':*
"The French intend to seduce our women, to corrupt our nation,
to lead our daughters astray, [and] to make them proud and
lazy."

The Natchez rise up after a deterioration of French relations.
Hundreds of soldiers and citizens are massacred at Fort Rosalie.
A great many women, children, and slaves are taken prisoner.

French settlers are moving to *Bayou Pierre*, 35 miles north of
former Fort Rosalie.

Dec 11   Fort St. Pierre is destroyed by the *Natchez* people.
Survivors are helped downriver by the *Choctaw*.

1730

The French and Choctaw occupy the former Natchez Grand
Village.
An artillery battery is built on the site of *Great Sun's* house.

1731

Jan 30   Forces under Governor Périer blockade the Natchez fort.

Battles rage from Baton Rouge to New Orleans.

Feb 4   French forces destroy the Natchez stronghold.
450 women and children and 40 warriors are captured.

Captive *Natchez* are sent to New Orleans where many die.
Remaining Natchez are sold as slaves in Saint-Domingue (Haiti).
200 find refuge among the Chickasaw.

1731 (Cont.)

Feb 4   Other Natchez live among the Creek, Chickasaw, and Cherokee.
The Natchez, as a people, cease to exist.

A large Natchez remnant massacres Tunicas at their village.
The Tunica move downriver to Trudeau Landing for a while.

1736

The French and Chickasaw trade victories.
The Chickasaw finally win at Ackia and Ogoula Tchetoka.

1739

A Choctaw Civil War engages British-French trading factions.

1750

Plantations line the Mississippi from Natchez south.
Primary crops are tobacco, indigo, rice, and cotton.

1754

May 28   The French and Indian War begins.
The French and natives block British westward settlement.

1758

French ethnographer Antoine Simon Le Page Du Pratz wrongly
interprets the *Ojibwe's Misi-ziibi* as *Ancient Father of Rivers*.
It actually means *long river*.

1762

Sep 15   Signal Hill, Newfoundland, is the last battle of the French and
Indian War.

Nov 23   Louis XV secretly cedes the Louisiana colony to Spain.

1763

Oct 10   The *Treaty of 1763* ends the French and Indian War.
Spain cedes eastern French Louisiana to Great Britain.
Spain will retain the western half of Louisiana.

Oct 17   The 1763 Proclamation forbids settling former French lands.
British West Florida is an exception to this restriction.

Migrants from New England enter the Natchez region.
Migration continues even after Spain's capture of the area.

Andrew Turnbull gets a grant for lands in future Warren County.

1765

British Gov. George Johnstone holds congresses with the
Choctaw, Chickasaw, and Creek to create commissioners and
establish trade and a justice system.

1770

500 settlers inhabit the Natchez District.

1773

400 Eastern families settle from Bayou Pierre northward.
Loosa Chitto (Big Black River) settlers are the Company of Military Adventurers (CMA) from Connecticut.
Loosa Chitto in Choctaw means big swamp.

John Stowers arrives penniless but determined.
They settle on the first high ground 25 miles east of Grand Gulf
   on the north side of the Loosa Chitto.

*A musket and a sack each of flour and corn can sustain a single
   pioneer a month in the Mississippi forests.*

1774

CMA's Phineus Lyman has 20,000 acres on Bayou Pierre.
He has 100 New England families prepared to settle it.
The few who come get grants of their own instead.

1775

Apr 19   The American Revolution begins.
The first homes appear in the future Warren County.

1776

Mar 1   Britain orders a blockade of colonial ports.

Jul 4   The Declaration of Independence is signed.
Tobacco is growing well in the district around Natchez.

1777

Jan 1   Bernardo de Galvez is named Louisiana's colonial governor.

Apr 1   Galvez closes New Orleans to British trade.

1778

The Royal Navy's blockade has shut down area economies.
Farmers have no way to market their products.
Credit and crops are failing.

Feb 19   The America Revolution and its impacts enter the area.
Cont. Navy Capt. James Willing's troops capture Natchez.
Galvez cooperates, wanting West Florida for Spain.
Willing sacks plantations, then hides below the Spanish line.

Natives are raiding homesteads, driving out area settlers.

Only John Stowers remains on the Loosa Chitto.

1779

Sep 21 Spain declares war on England.
Galvez captures British forts, including Natchez.
Natchez is under Spanish control.

1783

Sep 3 *The Treaty of Paris* gives Britain's lower half of what will
  become *Mississippi* to Spain.
Most Loosa Chitto settlers are now at *Fort Panmure* at Natchez.
European life begins to stir again in the area north of Natchez.

Migration begins again.
Spain grants an empire tobacco monopoly to West Florida.
Tobacco is now the mainstay of the Natchez District.

1785

Mar 22 The U.S. will hold negotiations with natives in Hopewell, S.C.
Commissioners will set the Southern indigenous policies.
They nullify Spanish influence among the tribes.

Homesteaders live by extensively exploiting local resources.
Slash-and-burn agriculture can clear several acres daily.
They mainly participate in local and regional markets.

White settlers are again on high ground along the Loosa Chitto.
The place **Nannachehaw** is 25 miles upriver.
An abundance of land lures young whites, stripping area labor.

Nov 28 Cherokee chiefs and warriors sign the Hopewell Treaty.
They call the worthless treaty papers *"Talking Leaves."*

1786

Jan 3 Choctaw medal chiefs and captains sign at Hopewell, S.C.

Jan 10 A small delegation of Chickasaw sign the Hopewell Treaty.
Nowhere in the treaties do the tribes agree to give up lands.

1787

Nov 3 Manuel Gayoso de Lemos assumes control at Natchez.
His command is the *new Natchez District*.

Dec 30 Spain is giving colonization grants for the Natchez District.
Peter Bryan Bruin claims land at Bayou Pierre.

1788

Dec 29 Bruin's home is on an ancient mound near Bayou Pierre.
A river landing bears his name, *Bruinsburg*.

Dec 31 Samuel Gibson has established a river port on Bayou Pierre.
It bears his name, *Port Gibson*.

1789

Nov 30   Bayou Pierre produces 97,000 lbs. of tobacco.
Cole's Creek near Natchez produces over three times that.

The Natchez District has 2,000 whites and 1,000 blacks.
Most of the blacks are enslaved.
Doing business in the area requires a trip to Natchez.

1790

The Choctaw approve a Spanish fort at *Los Nogales* for Governor Gayoso.
Los Nogales is 40 miles north of Bayou Pierre.
Louisiana governor Baron de Carondelet approves construction.
30 carpenters are hired from Natchez for the month's labor.
The fort and 60 acres overlook Tuscumbia Bend *(present-day Vicksburg)*.

Daniel Burnet has a sawmill on his land on Bayou Pierre.

A settlement at the Loosa Chitto's mouth has 200 citizens.
About 300 flatboats annually pass *Grand Gulf* downbound.
Free black Eleanor *Nelly* Price owns a trading store there.

Settlers sell farm products to *Fort Nogales* construction
   workers, early forms of *commercial farming*.
Tobacco is slowly giving way to cotton as the regional cash crop.
Farm profits may be used to buy a slave to help grow cotton.

1791

Masons replace wooden Fort Nogales structures with brick.
Fort Nogales takes its final form.
John Turnbull operates a Spanish-approved trading post
A fort communications road is built to Grand Gulf.
Nelly Price and Turnbull trade mostly with the Choctaw.

Turnbull brings the first enslaved people into the area.

1792

Jan 1   Sixty soldiers man Fort Nogales.
Customs collection officers are stationed at the fort.

Mar 13   Margaret Turnbull adds to her father John's grants.
She becomes the **first "*Warren County*" landowner**.

Jun 1   The 1792 Census is the first to report area crops and livestock.
The largest Loosa Chitto holding is 20 head.
The top hog farmer boasts 140.
Only half of the households own a horse.

1792 (Cont.)

Ohio Valley agricultural products are flooding lower river
   markets, pressuring and unsettling local farmers.
Court debtor actions threaten Natchez District commerce.

A starting homestead requires a gun, axe, some spades, maybe
   a cow and a plough.
A family head can tend 6-7 acres of corn and peas, a vegetable
   garden, a small orchard, a drove of hogs, and a herd of 30
   cattle.

1793

Feb 28   Gayoso's livestock laws are the first in the region.

1794

Jan 17   Andrew Jackson and Sarah Donelson marry in Natchez.
   Jackson operates a trading post on the bayou at Bruinsburg.

Natchez butcher and tanner Ebenezer Dayton owns pens and a
   slaughterhouse at Los Nogales.

Wildlife is sparse on the Loosa Chitto and at Los Nogales.
The Choctaw are dying of hunger and raiding the area.
Trading thousands of area furs has come back to destroy them.

1795

Oct 27   The *Treaty of San Lorenzo* grants free Mississippi navigation.
   Spain gives up Natchez and other key river forts.

Natchez is struggling to finds its economic niche.

Lumber and barrel staves are lucrative for Natchez.
Residents sell 1,134 *cane tacky* Texas mustangs.
3,000 Spanish Opelousas cattle from Louisiana are sold.
The area is limited by the lack of powerful, two-way river vessels.

Large herds of cattle are raised for sale in a regional market.
Lower river markets prefer fresh beef over northern salt beef.

John Barclay introduces the cotton gin at Natchez.
Residents quickly contract mechanics to construct others.

Most Loosa Chitto families own no slaves.
A Loosa Chitto address is given in *miles upriver from the
   mouth.*
Agriculture and animal husbandry have stagnated.

1796

Commercial staples production ends the isolated pioneer life.
A decline in the game-hide trade increases raising livestock.

1796 (Cont.)

Oct 2   Jacques Rapalje takes a Census of Nannachehaw.
Resident surnames: Stowers, Rapalje, Brashers, Antilton (sp.),
Cunningham, Cooper, Griffin, Myers, Cole, Fraser, Steel,
Moss, Erwin, Perry, Bowles, Machristy, Hyland, Calhoun,
Fortner, Eastman, Miller, and Marshall.

1797

Feb 1   Tensions rise with Spain as Americans settle the treaty area.
Spanish peach trees planted on area hills are now in full bloom.

May 29   Gayoso de Lemos is cheered, toasted as the Spanish depart.

Jun 9   Capt. Isaac Guion is enforcing the *Treaty of San Lorenzo*.
The Spanish have no right to occupy the region.
Surveyor Andrew Ellicott defiantly raises the American flag.

Jun 19   Ellicott arrives at Fort Nogales.

Jun 20   Ellicott dines with creole Cmdt. Elias Toutant-Beauregard.

1798

Mar 31   Commandant Beauregard has abandoned Fort Nogales.
Fort Nogales counts *16 or 17* inhabitants.
Andrew Glass, notorious highwayman, is among the group.

Apr 7   The Mississippi Territory is created.
The fort is renamed *Fort McHenry* for Secretary of War James
McHenry.
The surrounding community is named W*alnut Hills.*
Natchez, with a population of 1,200, is the territorial capital.

Dec 31   Andrew Glass operates a Natchez Trace way station, *McRaven*.

1799

Nov 22   The Methodist Hopewell congregation is led by circuit minister
Rev. Tobias Gibson, the father of Mississippi Methodism.

1800

Commercial farmers extend from the southern Big Black River
to Walnut Hills.
Cattle is sold to soldiers and regional bureaucrats.
Herding requires a minimum of labor, 30 cattle per hand.
120 cattle require two slaves, or a man, woman, and child.
Big Black cattlemen are the region's first slaveholders.

1801

Dec 17   The Choctaw give up Walnut Hills in the *Treaty of Fort Adams*.
The Mississippi Territory receives 2.6 million acres of land.
The Choctaw receive $2,000 and three sets of blacksmith tools.

1801 (Cont.)

Dec 17   In the *Treaty of Fort Adams*, the Chickasaw receive $700.
Some chiefs receive *secret* payments.

1802

Feb 1   The Mississippi Territorial capital relocates to Washington,
Miss., 13 miles northeast of Natchez.

1803

Apr 30   France sells Louisiana to the United States (*Louisiana Purchase*).
Napoleon believes it will strengthen the U.S. against England.
He sees the U.S. as the appropriate country to develop it.

Dec 20   The U.S. flag is raised over New Orleans.
Port Gibson is chartered, 22 years before Vicksburg.

Dec 31   60 Tunica are the only natives living near Mint Springs Bayou
under Fort McHenry.

1805

Nov 16   The *Treaty of Mount Dexter gives the* Choctaw $48,000.
The Mississippi Territory receives 4.1 million acres.

1808

All former British grants not settled are voided.
Only Spanish grants are recognized.

1809

Dec 22   Warren County, Miss., is created by the Mississippi legislature.

1810

Walnut Hills lacks women for homesteading.
In Walnut Hills, males tend to marry local indigenous women.

Men are focused on money crops, e.g., cattle and cotton.
Single men are growing cotton in place of a family.

Women are engaged in domestic production.
Homes are sufficient in bundles of cotton and spinning wheels.
Women fuel a local trade in cloth and other home goods.
Bartering is a mainstay.

The population of Warren County has exploded to 1,114.

1811

Mar 25   The *Great Comet* strikes fear in area residents.

Dec 16   A severe earthquake, epicentered at New Madrid, Mo., strikes.
Furniture shakes and dishes rattle as far south as Natchez.

1811 (Cont.)	
Dec 31	Rev. Newitt Vick, a Methodist, has arrived at Walnut Hills. He plans to build a cotton port, a plantation, and a church.

1812	
Jun 12	The United States declares war on Great Britain. The 10th Mississippi departs under Brig. Gen. Ferd Claiborne.
	Their pioneer life no longer feasible, cattle herders turn to cotton. Patterns of citizen cooperation are breaking down. Struggles for scarce resources are frequently turning violent.

1814	
Dec 24	The *Treaty of Ghent* ends the War of 1812. The Industrial Revolution is getting underway. The nation and states focus on transportation improvements.
	America's status in the world and its economy is strengthening. Waves of inventions are changing the national way of life. Mississippi is at the forefront of applying innovations. A one-party system means limited political strife.

1815	
	Warren County hamlets are called *neighborhoods,* named for their primary family.

1816	
Jan 27	Mississippi completes its survey of the Territory. Land is available for $2 per acre. *Hartwell W. Vick buys the first land, 375 acres, in Walnut Hills.*
	The Great Migration brings the world's citizens to the Mississippi Territory. *"The crops are certain; contentment is on every face. "In nine days, we saw 4,000 people coming into the Territory."*
	Individuals depend on extended *family networks*. Older men with legal control marshal family resources for power. This major societal change is the basis for *southern patriarchy*.

1817	
Mar 1	President James Madison approves Mississippi's statehood.
Jul 7	47 delegates meet to draw up Mississippi's constitution.
Aug 15	Delegates sign Mississippi's new state constitution. Political power shifts from Natchez to Mississippi's farmers.
Dec 10	Mississippi is the 20th state admitted to the Union.

1818

Mar 3   Hartwell Vick buys 225 more acres in Walnut Hills.
The most important person around is Honore P. Morancy.
He is postmaster and an extensive planter at Milliken's Bend, La.

Dec 30   Joseph E. Davis is a partner in 7,000 acres north of the Big
Black River on the Mississippi River.

1819

Aug 5   Rev. Newitt and Elizabeth Vick die of yellow fever minutes apart.
They are buried on his *Open Woods* Plantation.
He leaves land in the city center for a public building.
John Lane, Vick's son-in-law, becomes the city planner.
The *Vicksburgh* community will be named for its founder.

1820

Jan 1   Natchez is the undisputed metropolis of Mississippi.

Jul 1   The population of Warren County is 2,693, up 140% since 1810.

Oct 18   The Choctaw give up half their land in the *Treaty of Doak's Stand*.
The western half surrendered includes the lower Yazoo Delta.

Cotton production and Choctaw lands improve Walnut Hills life.
The area has grown from a *river village* to *vibrant community*.

There is increased demand for a Vicksburgh *port*.

Dec 30   Newly arriving Jewish families are meeting in homes.

1823

Apr 25   John Lane advertises "lots for sale in *Vicksburgh*."

1824

Apr 30   The U.S. General Survey Act will improve Mississippi River
navigation.

Dec 31   A Vicksburgh road to Clinton is complete.
John Lane has sold 30 lots in Vicksburgh.

1825

Jan 19   *Vicksburg* drops the 'h' and receives its state charter.

Cotton prices are fluctuating upward.
A lack of river system infrastructure and warehouses are the
only limitations to the growth of the cotton industry,

May 4   Dr. William B. Bay owns land two miles northeast from
Vicksburg on the Jackson Road, future site of the *Shirley
House*.

1826

Mar 31   John Lane has told the Probate Court, *"68 lots have been sold."*

1828

Lane is almost singlehandedly building Vicksburg.
He is developing with money intended for Newitt Vick's children, his nieces and nephews.

700 steamboats are plying the Ohio and Mississippi rivers.
The indigenous people call them *"boats that walk on water."*

1830

The small clusters of rural homes have disappeared.
New large farms and plantations have spread across the area.

The first antebellum mansion, *Anchuca*, is built in Vicksburg.

Oakland College opens near Rodney, Miss.

Dr. Rush Nutt and Smith Coffee Daniell are key Oakland benefactors.

At left, the Chapel of Oakland College, now Alcorn State University. The staircase is from the burned *Windsor* mansion.

Alcorn State University image.

1830 (Cont.)

Feb 22   Lots are advertised by Clinton, Miss., speculators for *Manchester*.

Sep 27   The Choctaw surrender their remaining lands in the *Treaty of Dancing Rabbit*.
Upper Yazoo Delta lands are exchanged for Oklahoma lands.
This treaty is part of Andrew Jackson's *Indian Removal Plan*.

Dec 6   Andrew Turnbull purchases land for Skipwith Landing.
The property, 50 miles north of Vicksburg, is perfectly located.
Leasing peaks at over $20,000 per year ($654,000 in 2023$).

1831

Sep 16   Citizens are concerned about wandering off-season vagabonds.
The local paper calls *"to citizens of Vicksburg"* for more militia.

Dec 25   7,000 Choctaw and 1,000 slaves have walked the *Trail of Tears*.

Dec 31   The Vicksburg & Clinton Railroad is a chartered line.

1832

Feb 25   A Choctaw spokesman:
*"We as Choctaws rather **chose to suffer** and be free, than to live under the degrading influence of laws, which our voice could not be heard in their formation."*

Oct 26   A new state constitution is approved in Convention.
It eliminates ownership of property as a requirement to vote.
The legal system no longer favors the landed aristocracy.
The state prefers popular democracy and economic opportunity.

1833

Dec 28   All lots have been sold in the town of *Manchester*.
The town includes a bank, two hotels, and businesses.

John Lane builds a home on Crawford Street.

The John Lane home, built 1833.
Photo 2011 by Janie Fortenberry, Photography with a Southern Accent.

1834

Oct 2   Vicksburg organizes to beat the Natchez Railroad to Jackson.
Planters' Bank of Mississippi is Vicksburg's first.

The Kangaroo is the most notorious den in Vicksburg.
Natchez-Under-The-Hill is the only more infamous hangout.

1835

Jul 4   William Bobb has a new Greek revival home on Crawford Street.

A crowd from *The Kangaroo* upsets a city July 4th affair.
Dr. Hugh Bodley leads citizens to arrest them and is killed.

1835 (Cont.)

Jul 4   Vicksburg citizens hang five *Kangaroo* perpetrators at Clay and Farmer streets.

Nov 10   30,000 bales of Big Black-and-beyond cotton reach Vicksburg.

1836

Jan 1   The Warren County seat is at Warrenton, south of Vicksburg.

William Bobb sells his home to Martha Vick Willis for $22,000. Dr. Bay sells his Jackson Road property to T.H. Goodall.

1837

Jan 1   Warren County is startled when its seat is suddenly in Vicksburg. Records were moved in the darkness to avoid *the opposition*.

Aug 1   Nicholas Gray buys T.H. Goodall's land for his *Wexford Lodge*.

1838

Nov 1   Vicksburg's first locomotive, the *Commercial*, makes a first run to the Big Black River, a year behind Natchez's *Mississippi*. Passengers include Vicksburg's Alexander McNutt, governor.

The locomotive *Mississippi*, the state's first locomotive.
As displayed at the Museum of Science and Industry, Chicago, Illinois.

1839

Feb 15   Alexander McNutt signs the *Married Women's Property Act.* The act allows women to own property *in their own name.* This is the **first legislation of its kind in the United States.** It protects women money from their husband's losses.

Dec 31   A railroad bridge on the Big Black River is complete.

1840

Cedar Grove mansion is built by John Alexander Klein.
Klein is known as Vicksburg's *Prince of Commerce*.
His wife, Elizabeth B. Day Klein, is William T. Sherman's niece.

1841

The town of *Manchester* is renamed *Yazoo City*.

The Anshe Chesed Jewish congregation is formed.
The name means *Men of Kindness*.

1842

Jul 15   Thomas E. Robins is building a Vicksburg castle: *Belmont*.
The building materials have been shipped from England.

Dec 31   Planters' Bank of Mississippi has failed.

1843

Jun 7   James Hagan, editor of the *Vicksburg Sentinel*, dies in a fight.
His killer is well-known Natchez leader Daniel Adams.
Adams' brother is the equally successful *William Wirt Adams*.

The affair spawns the *Anti-Dueling Society*.
Jefferson Davis is a proponent of ending the vice.

The founder of the society is Davis' nephew, Thomas Robins.
Robins is, in fact, a very frequent duelist who is mentioned in
Charles Dicken's book, *American Notes*.

1844

Jan 23   Issaquena County is created.
Issaquena means *deer creek*.

Jul 31   Old Man River goes out for one of his walkabouts.
The 1844 flood ravages the lower Mississippi valley.
95% of Delta planters fail to make a pound of cotton.
*"Any demand for debt payment is a **clear case for pistols**."*

1845

Jan 1   Vicksburg products are reaching national and world markets.
A *city of the elite*, Vicksburg is itself considered a world market.

Jul 5   Moved to action by the 1844 Flood, a Mississippi River
Improvement Convention is held in Memphis, the **first-ever
multi-state meeting for river solutions**.

1846

Conferences in Memphis and Cincinnati seek flood solutions.

1847

Jan 1   Flood control starts to get a serious foothold in Warren County.

1847 (Cont.)

County levee protection will cost Joe Davis $1,796 ($65,000 in 2023 dollars).
He believes that changing river hydraulics will hurt Davis Bend.
Court actions give him temporary relief.

Dec 13   Jeff Davis attacks trespassing canal diggers on Davis Bend neck.
He believes that they are trying to speed river flood runoff.
Like Joe, he believes it will increase their damages.

Jefferson Davis mobilizes his slaves:
"I was the only Confederate to ever arm Negros against white men."

1849

Dec 31   Nicholas Gray has sold his Jackson Road home to Ben Johnson.

Irish account for 44% of all foreign-born city workers.

1850

Aug 21   Thomas Redwood's *Carthage* has two stores and a post office on Skillikalia Bayou below Snyder's Mill.

1851

Mar 22   Ben Johnson sells his Jackson Road home to James and Adeline Shirley from New Hampshire.
Her maiden name is *Quincy* of the renowned Boston family.

Dec 10   Turpin Green Atwood, a premier Southern cotton gin maker, and his brother William have opened a gin and hardware factory, as well as a shipping warehouse, on North Washington Street in Vicksburg.

1852

Jan 14   The Steamer *George Washington's* explosion destroys the Grand Gulf wharf and kills many.

1854

Oct 15   Ground is broken for the Vicksburg, Shreveport, and Texas RR.

1856

Jun 17   Martha Patience Vick Willis dies.
Her son, Capt. John, Vicksburg Southrons, lives in the home.

1858

Jun 10   Davis slave Ben Montgomery is denied a patent for his invention, a new acclaimed propellor for boats in shallow water.
He is denied because a slave cannot submit for a U.S. patent.
Jefferson Davis' attempts to intervene for Montgomery fail.

1858 (Cont.)

Aug 17   Issaquena cotton and corn crops are destroyed by flood.

Nov 25   A rail system connection to New Orleans is complete.

Dec 8   Antonio Genella has the finest emporium between New Orleans and Memphis at 1108 Washington Street.

1859

Dec 31   The new Warren County Court House is complete.
Bavarian Max Kuner has installed the clock in the tower.

1860

Most of Vicksburg's inhabitants are simply *passing through*.
Only one in four have been residents for the last 10 years.
Only 39% of the 1850 household heads still remain in 1860.
Half of the county's 8,000 residents live in or near Vicksburg.
Vicksburg is Warren County's only municipality.

Vicksburg is now a remarkably *cosmopolitan* town.
Foreign-born from 17 nations are 25% of the free population.
Over 80% of those are from Ireland, England, or Germany.
For every four white laborers in Vicksburg, there are three slaves.

Jul 1   The city's largest slaveholder is Abraham Reading's Foundry.
He employs 28 men, 2 women, and 10 children.
Most city slaves serve in homes, offices, shops, and stores.

Oct 12   Six nuns of the Sisters of Mercy arrive in Vicksburg to start a Catholic school, escorted by Father Francis Xavier Leray, the namesake for their new school.

Oct 15   Warren County declares its new Court House *complete*.
The wharf is crammed with steamboats, barges, and pirogues.
Individual opinion, not Southern aristocracy, rules in the city.

Oct 18   70 boys and girls enroll at the *St. Francis Xavier Academy*.
The *Sisters* have been in Vicksburg for but **three days**.

CONVERSION TO 2023 DOLLARS

1800	*$23.88*
1805	*$25.71*
1810	*$24.46*
1815	*$19.54*
1820	*$25.71*
1825	*$30.39*
1830	*$32.70*
1835	*$34.19*
1840	*$34.58*
1845	*$39.58*
1850	*$38.57*
1855	*$34.58*
1860	*$36.25*
1865	*$18.46*
1900	*$35.93*

Source: CPI Inflation Calculator, officialdata.org

PART IV
The Sounds of Seeds Being Sown in Discord

New seeds, inventions, and an
ancient scourge gin a
"Cotton Rush"
5,000 B.C. to 1860

A harvest of cotton in the lower South.
From a Library of Congress vintage image.

PART IV
The Sounds of Seeds Being Sown in Discord

5,000 B.C.
Cotton fiber and cloth are produced in today's central America.

3,000 B.C.
Cotton becomes fabric in the Indus River Valley (Pakistan).

2,500 B.C.
Gossypium barbadense is grown in the Western hemisphere.
This is a form of short-staple cotton.

500 A.D.
Short-staple cotton is grown in the southwestern (Sonoran) desert.

1718
The French allow African slave importation at Biloxi.

1719
John Law's *Company of the West* brings the first slaves to Biloxi.
His slaves bring yellow fever.

1724
Louisiana's *Code Noir* sets slavery rules and relationships.

1763
May 8 The French and Indian War ends.
Under British rule, institutionalized slavery is set to increase.
Large numbers of Jamaican slaves are destined for Natchez.

1771
Aug 22 A slave revolt begins in Haiti.

1773

The Connecticut Company of Military Adventurers arrives.

A Loosa Chitto (Big Black River) settlement is created 25 miles north of its mouth at the Mississippi *(near today's old Hankinson's Ferry site).*

1784

Jul 14 The American War for Independence ends.

Tobacco production is down 75%.
Slaves are in excess in the tobacco colonies.
Eastern farmers are growing more food.

1787

Jul 13 *The Northwest Ordinance* bans slavery north of the Ohio River.
Very little cotton is being grown in the United States.

Sep 17 39 of 55 delegates sign the Constitution of the United States.

One delegate refuses to sign the Constitution because it codifies and protects slavery and the slave trade.
Many refuse to sign because it does not contain a Bill of Rights.

Three states *threaten to secede* if the slave trade is not allowed.
Slave importation is granted in the original states *until 1808.*

1789

Nov 1 Profits from subsistence farming might be used to buy a slave.
Extracting cotton seeds by hand limits the speed of production.
Cotton production is limited to coastal zones *(seacoast cotton).*

1790

Jan 1 Louisville, Ky., is a major slave market for former tobacco slaves.
More valuable excess black males are *"sold down the river."*
Most represent broken black families.
About 1 million slaves will follow this route after 1808.

1793

Loosa Chitto farmers now grow 100-200 lbs. of seedless cotton.
This cotton, for homestead use, requires less than an acre.
Cotton helps maintain a struggling pioneer lifestyle.
Households contain spinning wheels to make thread.

The few slaves owned by local pioneers are farm helpers.
Slaves are also available from Louisiana and Caribbean markets.

1794

Mar 14   **COTTON RUSH CATALYST 1**
Eli Whitney's cotton gin is patented.
A ginner can now deseed 50 pounds per day, rather than 1.
Labor for picking, rather than ginning, limits cotton
  production.

Jun 17   Jean St. Malo, slave organizer, is executed in New Orleans.

1795

Apr 30   **The first commercial cotton is grown in Mississippi.**

John Barclay brings the cotton gin into the Natchez
District.
Pioneers prefer *free time and recreation* to laborious cotton
  production.

Eli Whitney's world-changing cotton gin.
On display at the Eli Whitney Museum in Hamden, Conn.

1799

Benjamin Steele and Anthony Glass operate the first
cotton gin in the Walnut Hills area.
The gin is in the Loosa Chitto settlement near Jacques Rapalje.

1800

1 Jan   The Mississippi Territory's population: 8,850.
White, 5,179; free black, 182; slave, 3,489.

1800 (Cont.)

Jul 15 Primary local cash crops are indigo and tobacco.
A healthy farmer can cultivate 5-6 acres of cotton.
A family with several hands can grow 10 acres of corn and 15-18 acres of cotton.

Cotton farmers only add slaves to protect their own *free time*.
Adding mature sons increases cotton production possibilities.

Dec 31 Millions of pounds of cotton produced in Mississippi – None.
Heavy cotton production involves economic risks to pioneers.
Creole and *Tennessee Green* hybrids are poor producers.

Slaves may still purchase their freedom or be freed by owners.

1803

Apr 30 **The Louisiana Purchase is executed by Jefferson.**
Jefferson dreams of white, self-sufficient, yeoman households
farming moderate acreages, scattered across a wide expanse.

1804

Jan 1 The Haitian slave revolution ends with a free Haiti.
Sugar production moves to the *German Coast* of Louisiana.

Feb 21 **COTTON RUSH CATALYST 2**
Welshman Richard Trevithick shows off his *steam locomotive*.
Trains can reduce cotton shipping costs from $4 to $1 a bale.

Apr 22 Free Haitians massacre nearly all whites, 3,000-5,000.
The massacre puts Southeastern planters on high alert.

1806

Sep 15 Local New England settlers are growing quantities of cotton.
They are having success turning their cotton into thread.

1808

1 Jan Congress abolishes the foreign slave importation and trade.
Slaves must come from Louisiana or former colony markets.

1809

Dec 22 The Mississippi Territory establishes Warren County.

1810

1 Jan The Mississippi Territory's population: 40,352.
White, 23,024; free black, 519; slave, 17,088.

South Carolina is producing half of the nation's cotton.
The cotton industry is beginning a westward expansion.

1811

Jan 1   A few scattered buildings dot the new Warren County
             waterfront.

Jan 8   500 Louisiana *German Coast* sugar plantation slaves revolt.

Jan 11   Charles Desiondes, Louisiana slave revolt leader, is captured.

Oct 11   **COTTON RUSH CATALYST 3**
             The steamboat *New Orleans* departs Pittsburgh, Pa.
             Owner Nicholas Roosevelt is Teddy Roosevelt's grandfather.
             It is the first steamboat to ply the Mississippi River.

Dec 16   The New Madrid, Mo., earthquake violently shakes the region.
             The *New Orleans* must turn away refugees for lack of supplies.

Dec 19   **The *New Orleans* passes by Warren County.**

Dec 20   The *New Orleans* docks in Natchez.
             An industrious planter has a *test* single bale of cotton onboard,
             the first movement of cotton by steamboat.

1812

Jan 10   **COTTON RUSH CATALYST 4**
             Great Britain is importing 75% of U.S. cotton.
             Cotton is 41% of U. S. exports.
             Cotton is fueling northern industry, rail, and shipbuilding.

             The *New Orleans* completes its journey to New Orleans.
             Annual upriver commerce is still only 20 barges annually.

Apr 25   The General Land Office is created to disperse native lands.

1814

Dec 30   **COTTON RUSH CATALYST 5**
             Francis Lowell's power looms appear in Walthall,
             ** Mass., allowing weavers to keep pace with spinners.**
             Lowell's mills turn raw cotton into 50,000 miles of cloth yearly.
             The eastern textile mills flourish as a hot market for cotton.

1815

Feb 15   The War of 1812 ends.
             Slaves had participated on both sides.
             Promises of emancipation and equality do not materialize.

             Warren County's Joseph Davis owns just two slaves.

Nov 30   Dr. Rushworth Nutt, an agricultural and mechanical genius, has
             established Laurel Hill Plantation near Rodney, Miss.

1816

Apr 27   The *Tariff of 1816* protects textile mills from cheap British cloth.

Davis buys three more slaves for his 500 Cole's Creek acres.

1817

Oct 15   Davis has added 450 more acres to his Cole's Creek plantation.
His equal treatment of blacks and whites sets him apart.

17 steamboats are plying the Western waters.

1820

Mar 2   Thomas Jefferson: *"The Missouri question is the national knell."*
The *Missouri Compromise* admits one *free* and one *slave* state.
Missouri is slave; Maine is free.

National tensions are temporarily cooled.
Slave owners want no more anti-slave laws.
Anti-slave factions want no expansion of slavery.

Apr 30   Growers are using the more productive *Mexican* cotton hybrid.

Slaves may be rented to other families, even for odd jobs.
Idle slaves may work for others to earn *spending money*.

Dec 30   69 steamboats are in operation, their capacity doubling.
A steamboat allows a round trip, even in low water.
The vessels carry heavy cargo, equipment, and passengers.
Plantations and landings begin to crowd the Mississippi River.

A Vicksburg road to Clinton has reached the Big Black River.

The Navy is patrolling the coast of Africa to intercept slave ships.
Atlantic slave trade is considered piracy, *punishable by death*.

1821

Jan 12   Cotton planters struggle to maintain their standard of living.
They plant even more cotton, accelerating slavery.
White labor is being lured away by offers of cheap land.

1822

Dec 10   Mississippi now requires legislative approval to free a slave.
The possibility of slave self-manumission has ended.
The increase in the state's freed blacks is greatly slowed.

1825

Oct 1   Socialist Francis Wright has started *Nashoba* in Tennessee.
She senses that slave owners would free socially capable slaves.

1825 (Cont.)

Oct 1   Robert Owen, author of *A New View of Society,* inspires Wright. Wright: *"Educate slaves and colonize them in Haiti or Africa."*

Jun 24   Joe Davis meets Robert Owen, impressed by his concepts.
Davis and Owen have a nine-hour interaction.
Davis is inspired to use Davis Bend as a *manumission model.*

1830

Jan 1   Mississippi's population: 136,621.
White, 70,443; free black, 519; slave, 65,659.

May 28   **COTTON RUSH CATALYST 6**
The Indian Removal Act is signed into law by Andrew Jackson.
Mississippi takes jurisdiction over Choctaw/Chickasaw lands.
Massive amounts of land become available for development.
Lands are generally free of worry regarding indigenous people.

Sep 27   *The Treaty of Dancing Rabbit Creek* removes the Choctaw by 1833.

Dec 31   **Steamboats carry the most freight on less water than any other boats in world history.**

1831

Aug 21   The *Nat Turner Revolt* begins in Southampton Co., Va.

Sep 30   Davis and Natchez friends favor tariffs and condemn opponents.

Nov 17   The Mississippi Colonization Society aims to plant freed slaves in Liberia.
Many freedmen buy slaves and start their own cotton operations in Africa.

1833

Jan 1   Mississippi's enslaved total is 65,000, up 20-fold since 1800.

        COTTON RUSH CATALYST 7
Dr. Rushworth Nutt perfects *Petit Gulf* cotton at Rodney, Miss.
His Laurel Hill strain crosses *Mexican* and *Tennessee Green.*
Nutt's cotton hybrid will fuel the *Cotton Rush.*
The hybrid is easier to pick and more disease resistant.

The Flush Times – The concomitant boom in land, cotton, and slave markets will mark the next three decades.

Nov 10   Mississippi cotton production is a whopping 33 million lbs.

1833 (Cont.)

Dec 31 The *Forks of the Road* slave market is open in Natchez.
It has been developed by John Armfield and Isaac Franklin.
The market is capitalizing on the difference in low slave prices in
 Virginia and Maryland versus high prices in the Deep South.

1834

Aug 1 **Great Britain's Slavery Abolition Act takes effect**.
800,000 are freed in the Caribbean, South Africa, and Canada.

Nov 1 1,200 steamboats are in operation in the U.S.
Grand Gulf is third in Mississippi cotton handling.
Vicksburg and Natchez lead the market.

1835

Oct 15 Cotton is 15 cents a pound, about $5.12 a pound in 2023 dollars.

Dec 31 Railroad service is available from Grand Gulf to Port Gibson.
Vicksburg is feeling the pressure to open rail service.
Rail competitors enjoy four times less the cost of moving cotton.

1836

Horse- or mule-powered gins produce 400 lbs. daily, up 10
 times over manual methods.

Tobacco farms are failing due to exhausted soil and low sales.
Virginia planters are dumping their slave inventories South.
120,000 tobacco slaves are sold into the lower South this year.
Whites are moving South to capitalize on the cotton trade.
Joseph Davis purchases Benjamin Montgomery at the Forks in
 the Road Natchez slave market.

1837

An abolitionist charged with writing false passes for Vicksburg
 slaves gets 20-30 lashes.
A hardened attitude toward slaves reduces slave colonization.

May 10 England, weary of U.S. cotton financial risks, raises interest rates.
Failing banks and sinking cotton prices define the Panic of 1837.
Half of banks fail, businesses close, and unemployment explodes.
The model for cotton production tumbles like a deck of cards.
Slaves cannot be liquidated like other property. They starve.
The South exports 2/3 of U.S. exports but only consumes
 1/10 of its imports.

Nov 22 Grand Gulf, Vicksburg's competitor, processes 37,000 bales this
 year.

1839

Oct 8   COTTON RUSH CATALYST 7
Rush Nutt's steam-powered gins produce 4,000 lbs. of clean cotton daily.
This is 10 times the animal-driven systems.
Likewise, a steam compress can produce 5 to 10 bales daily.
Joe Davis is one of the first users of this new technology.

Cotton success is measured in bales per hand per acre.

1840

Jan 1   Mississippi's population: 375,651.
White, 179,074; free black, 1,366; **slave, 195,111.**
Enslaved now exceed the free population.

Oct 22   Warren County produces over 32,000 bales of cotton this year.
County production is second in the state.

Dec 31   The Vicksburg & Clinton RR is running to Clinton.

1842

Sep 17   Joe Davis has reversed his view and is now condemning tariffs.

Davis is educating his slaves and supporting their trade with lines of credit.
Ben Montgomery has his own plantation store at Hurricane.
His black and white customers spend up to $1,000 per year, $33,000 in 2023 dollars.)

1843

Oct 31   High cotton production and the continuing effects of the national Panic of 1837 have held cotton prices to 6 cents per pound.

1846

May 31   Cotton is now exhausting Southeastern soil.
Southwestern expansion is needed to preserve the industry.
Large quantities of idle slaves cannot simply be *"let go."*
Agronomy becomes the source of contention: *slave or free soil.*

The revised *Cotton Trap Cycle* — *Acquire fresh land to employ our slaves to make more cotton to pay our debts.*

Planters pray the Mexican War will open up Southwest lands.
Expansionists want to claim all of Mexico.
Some would like to obtain the island of Cuba and other places.

Jun 1   The Vicksburg & Meridian RR is the state's east-west railroad.

1846 (Cont.)

Aug 8   U.S. Rep. David Wilmot (Free Soil Party, Pa.*)* adds a rider to the Appropriation Bill.
It prohibits slavery in any land acquired from Mexico.
The Southern blowback is quick and fierce.

1847

Feb 15   The Wilmot Proviso is amended to include **all** acquired lands.
Rep. Lewis Cass (D, Mich.): *"Leave it to the people to decide."*

Most local teamsters who drive cotton wagons are slaves.

1848

Feb 2   The War with Mexico ends.
The *Treaty of Hidalgo* gives the U.S. 55% of Mexican territory.
Future Southwest and Midwest states become U.S. territory.

1849

May 7   A Jackson bipartisan meeting considers *Southern positions*.

Oct 1   Slavery proponents cry,
"Slaveholders must populate the Southwest quickly!"
Wilmot Proviso-style laws are considered intolerable.

Oct 10   John Quitman (D), *Father of Secessionism*, is Mississippi's governor.

Dec 31   49,000 bales of cotton are sent to Vicksburg by rail.

1850

Jan 1   Mississippi's population: 606,526.
White, 295,718; free black, 930; **slave, 309,878**.
Free blacks decline with the strengthened Fugitive Act.

Jul 15   Senator Henry Clay (Whig, Ky.) seeks to avert a sectional crisis.
The *Compromise of 1850* calms the *Wilmot Proviso* crisis.

Quitman calls for a special Mississippi *secession* session.
Quitman's opponent is U.S. Senator Henry Foote (D), a Unionist.

Sep 18   The *Fugitive Slave Act* is strengthened to return escaped slaves.
Northerners resent direct involvement in protecting slavery.
This issue causes more ill will than all the others.

Nov 2   Jefferson Davis calls for state conventions to decide their future.
He believes Congress has compromised Southern legal rights.
Yazoo County: *"Secede if the Fugitive Slave Act is repealed."*
Davis favors resistance over secession or a Confederacy.

1851

Jan 1 There are 3.2 million slaves in 15 slave states.
1.8 million of them are producing cotton.
50% of slave sales involve breaking up a family.

High prices for slaves makes it difficult for non-slaveowners to buy into the cotton game.
High-priced land also puts a strain on first-time yeoman farmers.

Jul 5 The *California Gold Rush* is improving Southern economics by pumping more wealth into the system.

Sep 1 Narciso Lopez is executed for his role in attempting to overthrow the Spanish government in Cuba.
Cotton planters had hoped to gain land for cotton production and slavery.
Jefferson Davis prefers Cuba over American territories for slavery and cotton expansion.

Sep 5 Rev. Jeremiah Chamberlain, founding president of Oakland Agricultural College at Lorman, is murdered on campus.
Slavery supporter George Briscoe is a leading subject
Anti-slavery ministers are at risk in their very pulpits.
Area circuit minister Rev. F.M. Logue is wounded twice for preaching the release of educated, trained slaves on their 21st birthday.

Sep 30 Mississippi's Nashville-Convention delegates have voted *Union*.
The vote is 57% percent *against* secession.
Secessionist Quitman pulls out of the gubernatorial race.
Thoughts of an immediate Mississippi secession subside.

Nov 4 Democrat Davis loses in his bid to be Mississippi's governor.

Dec 1 Mississippi produces 194 million lbs. of cotton, six times that of 1833.
Mississippi's enslaved rises to 310,000, five times that in 1833.

1852

Mar 20 Harriet Beecher Stowe's *Uncle Tom's Cabin* is published.
The book sells 300,000 copies the first year.
Lincoln: "... the book that started this great war."

1854

May 30 The *Kansas-Nebraska Act* rekindles the slavery battles.
The *Missouri Compromise* is dissolved.
For the first time, slavery will be voted on by the states.

1854 (Cont.)

Jun 1 *Lincoln opposes the Kansas-Nebraska Act and will use it to launch the Republican party.*

Overinvestment in slaves, over production of cotton, and overreliance on credit is making area planters vulnerable. Planters are in that dangerous debt cycle of buying slaves to grow more cotton to buy more slaves, and on and on.

Jun 8 The Gadsden Purchase creates the Southwestern U.S. border. The lands provide a route for an intercontinental railroad.

1856

May 21 Abolitionist raids in Lawrence, Kans., create a bloody border war.

May 23 Sen. Preston Brooks thrashes Sen. Charles Sumner in chamber. Sumner had inflamed Brooks in his recent anti-slavery speech.

Jul 12 William Walker proclaims himself president of Nicaragua. Southern planters are hopeful a cotton industry with slaves can take root there.

1857

Mar 6 The Supreme Court *Dred Scott* decision fans national flames. Freed blacks are declared not American citizens. The Louisiana Purchase states' ban on slavery is deemed unconstitutional. Congress nor Territories have the right to ban slavery.

May 1 William Walker is captured *(rescued)* by the U.S. Navy, ending his brief reign in Nicaragua and hopes of a cotton colony there.

May 26 The sons of Dred Scott's owner, Peter Blow, buy his freedom. The action sets off celebrations in the North.

Jun 26 Lincoln speaks out against the Dred Scott decision in Springfield. The decision has tightly polarized the country. *It accelerates Lincoln and his Republican Party.*

Oct 16 John Brown captures Harper's Ferry Arsenal in Virginia. He intends to start a slave rebellion and free Virginia slaves. *Mississippi is on high alert for slave reactions.* Mississippi expands its state militia.

Nov 20 Davis approves of Cuban statehood but opposes California's.

Mississippi: *"Secede if an abolitionist is elected president."* Davis: *"If an abolitionist is elected, call for the gods of battle."*

1858

Jan 1   Henry Vick's *Vick's Hundred* seed is a very popular cotton strain.

Feb 27   Mississippi and Louisiana legislatures consider reopening the slave trade.
The measure fails as it threatens to break Southern solidarity.
Some illegal slave trading still occurs.

Jun 16   Lincoln gives his *House Divided* speech in Springfield, Ill.
He has just accepted his party's nomination for the U.S. Senate.

1859

Oct 31   *Red Jack* is given 20 years in the Mississippi prison for forging passes for Vicksburg slaves.

1860

Jan 1   **Mississippi is the richest state in the nation.**
Vicksburg is the commercial center of Mississippi.
75% of Southern cotton is grown with 150 miles of Vicksburg.

Haller Nutt, Rush's son, owns 43,000 acres and 700 slaves.
His home *Longwood* is under construction in Natchez.

David Hunt of Natchez owns 25 plantations and 1,000 slaves.
He is one of 12 millionaires in Natchez, placing Mississippi first in the millionaire population.
He is known as *King David*.

Aug 12   Talk of secession is hurting Warren County's economy.
Land values, credit, and loans are all negatively impacted.

Nov 5   South Carolina governor W.H. Gist orders 10,000 rifles from U.S. arsenals before the Presidential election.

Nov 6   Lincoln is elected President of the United States.
Only 37 free blacks are living in Vicksburg, a drastic drop.

Nov 9   *The Mississippian: "The deed is done; disunion is the remedy."*

Nov 10   James Chestnut (D, S.C.) is the first to exit the U.S. Senate.

Dec 3   South Carolina seats are empty in Congress.

Dec 16   South Carolina appoints 16 *compromise* delegates.

Dec 17   U.S. Senator Ben Wade (R, Ohio) fires back, *"No compromise!"*
The First Baptist Church of Columbia, S.C., hosts the Secession Convention.

Dec 20   1:30 p.m. – South Carolina unanimously secedes.
An independent Republic of South Carolina is formed.

First Baptist Church, Columbia, S.C., becomes the cradle of the Confederacy.
Library of Congress photo from Encyclopædia Britannica, brittanica.com.

1860 (Cont.)

Dec 20 The U.S. Senate establishes a *"Committee of Thirteen"* to examine plans to save the Union, including extending to the Pacific Ocean the line established by the 1820 Missouri Compromise, prohibiting slavery north of the 36th parallel.

1860 cotton shipments to England total 3.8 million bales.
Cotton is 65% of the Gross National Product.
75% of Federal revenue is derived from the cotton trade.

Dec 31 Warren County has 6,896 white residents and **13,763 enslaved.**
A slave, in 2023 dollars, may be worth $20,000-$150,000.
3.5 million slaves are valued at $10 to $15 trillion in 2023 dollars, the South's wealth and power, rentable, sellable, or usable as collateral.
Cotton is 11 cents a pound.
A good hand can pick $797 of cotton per day, 2023 dollars.

1861

Jan 4 President James Buchanan calls for a national day of prayer and fasting regarding the national crisis.

Jan 7 A Secession Convention convenes in Jackson.

1861 (Cont.)

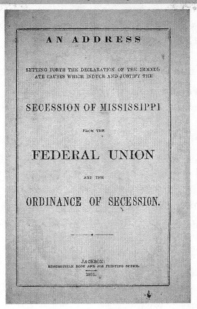

Jan 7   *Mississippi's position:*
"Our position is thoroughly identified with slavery."

Jan 9   Delegates vote 83-15 in favor of Mississippi leaving the Union.
Vicksburg and Natchez delegates vote *Unionist* to avoid impacts
   to the cotton economy. One voter is absent.
Mississippi becomes the second state to secede.

Davis cries at his desk in the Senate, realizing what is in
   store for the South.
*"I know those people. They will destroy the South to reunite
   the country."*

Jan 21   Jefferson Davis gives an emotional farewell to the U.S. Senate.

Jan 31   Virginia, still in the Union, calls for a *Peace Conference*.

Apr 12   Confederates fire on Fort Sumter.

May 1   The South aims to coerce France and England into supporting it.
2.5 million bales of cotton are burned to create a shortage.
The strategy is labelled *Cotton Diplomacy*.
England is equally concerned about Northern wheat and corn.
They need both sides.

Confederate States of America - Mississippi Secession

A Declaration of the Immediate Causes which Induce and Justify the Secession of the State of Mississippi from the Federal Union.

1861 In the momentous step which our State has taken of dissolving its connection with the government of which we so long formed a part, it is but just that we should declare the prominent reasons which have induced our course.

Our position is thoroughly identified with the institution of slavery – the greatest material interest of the world. Its labor supplies the product which constitutes by far the largest and most important portions of commerce of the earth. These products are peculiar to the climate verging on the tropical regions and, by an imperious law of nature, none but the black race can bear exposure to the tropical sun. These products have become necessities of the world, and a blow at slavery is a blow at commerce and civilization. That blow has been long aimed at the institution and was at the point of reaching its consummation. There was no choice left us but submission to the mandates of abolition, or a dissolution of the Union, whose principles had been subverted to work out our ruin.

That we do not overstate the dangers to our institution, a reference to a few facts will sufficiently prove.

The hostility to this institution commenced before the adoption of the Constitution, and was manifested in the well-known Ordinance of 1787, in regard to the Northwestern Territory.

The feeling increased until, in 1819-20, it deprived the South of more than half the vast territory acquired from France.

The same hostility dismembered Texas and seized upon all the territory acquired from Mexico.

It has grown until it denies the right of property in slaves and refuses protection to that right on the high seas, in the Territories, and wherever the government of the United States had jurisdiction.

It refuses the admission of new slave States into the Union and seeks to extinguish it by confining it within its present limits, denying the power of expansion.

It tramples the original equality of the South under foot.

It has nullified the Fugitive Slave Law in almost every free State in the Union and has utterly broken the compact which our fathers pledged their faith to maintain.

It advocates negro equality, socially and politically, and promotes insurrection and incendiarism in our midst.

It has enlisted its press, its pulpit, and its schools against us, until the whole popular mind of the North is excited and inflamed with prejudice.

It has made combinations and formed associations to carry out its schemes of emancipation in the States and wherever else slavery exists.

It seeks not to elevate or to support the slave, but to destroy his present condition without providing a better.

It has invaded a State and invested with the honors of martyrdom the wretch whose purpose was to apply flames to our dwellings, and the weapons of destruction to our lives.

It has broken every compact into which it has entered for our security.

It has given indubitable evidence of its design to ruin our agriculture, to prostrate our industrial pursuits, and to destroy our social system.

It knows no relenting or hesitation in its purposes; it stops not in its march of aggression, and leaves us no room to hope for cessation or for pause.

It has recently obtained control of the Government, by the prosecution of its unhallowed schemes, and destroyed the last expectation of living together in friendship and brotherhood.

Utter subjugation awaits us in the Union, if we should consent longer to remain in it. It is not a matter of choice, but of necessity. We must either submit to degradation, and to the loss of property worth four billions of money, or we must secede from the Union framed by our fathers, to secure this as well as every other species of property. For far less cause than this, our fathers separated from the Crown of England.

Our decision is made. We follow their footsteps. We embrace the alternative of separation; and for the reasons here stated, we resolve to maintain our rights with the full consciousness of the justice of our course, and the undoubting belief of our ability to maintain it.

The Warren County Court House is a statement of Vicksburg's place of power, prominence, and prosperity in the Cotton Rush. *(GJMC)*

PART V
Many Voices Marching Toward Common Glory

Citizens and Soldiers Follow
A Linked Destiny to Vicksburg
1802-1865

Missouri's Union soldiers above and Confederate soldiers below at Vicksburg by Victor S. Holm on the Missouri State Memorial, Vicksburg National Military Park. Missouri had 27 Union and 15 Confederate regiments and units at Vicksburg. *(GJMC)*

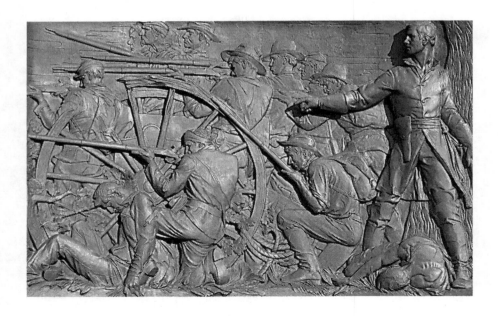

A
Prelude to National Dissolution
1802-1860

1802

Mar 16   The U.S. Military Academy (USMA) is established at West Point, N.Y.

1810

Dec 17   David Glasgow Farragut is commissioned a midshipman.

1824

Jul 4   Samuel Emory Davis dies having left everything to son Joseph.
With low prospects, Jefferson Davis chooses a military career.

Sep 20   Jefferson Davis is a plebe at West Point.

1826

Dec 25   Davis is arrested for his role in the USMA *Egg Nog Riot*.
He avoids a court martial.
Generally, he defies discipline and is, at one time, court-martialed for drinking.

1827

Dec 30   Joseph Davis' 5,800-acre home is on Davis Bend, Miss.
"Hurricane" is named for a tragic tornado that wrecked the place and killed his nephew.

1828

May 1   Jefferson Davis is graduating 23^d of 33 at the USMA.
He is seen as combative, very pugnacious, and insubordinate.
Vicksburg Operations Classmates: None noted.

1829

Feb 2   David Dixon Porter is appointed a midshipman at age 16.

Jul 1   Davis is under Col. Zachary Taylor in the Michigan Territory.
His inherited slave, Jim Pemberton, is accompanying him.

1832

Feb 18   The northern winters are extremely hard on Davis.
The resulting pneumonia will create lifelong bronchial issues.

Apr 6   The Black Hawk War breaks out.
Davis is home on furlough.
He essentially misses the Black Hawk War.

Apr 21   Abraham Lincoln is captain of the 31st Illinois militia.
He does not participate in battle but buries the dead.

Aug 6   Lincoln finishes 8th of 11 in a bid for the Illinois General
Assembly.

Aug 27   Sauk leader Black Hawk surrenders at today's Prairie du
Chien, Wis.
Davis will escort Black Hawk to St. Louis for detention.

1833

May 16   President Jackson appoints John C. Pemberton to the USMA.
His roommate is **George Meade**, also of Philadelphia, Pa.
Both will command in key Confederate defeats on the same day.

1834

Aug 4   After mixed results, Lincoln is elected to the General Assembly.

1835

Jun 17   Davis marries Sarah Knox Taylor, daughter of Zachary Taylor.
His brother-in-law is Richard Taylor.

Jun 30   1st Lt. Davis resigns after a February court-martial.
He was charged with **insubordination**.

Sep 15   Sarah Davis dies of malaria, three months after their marriage.

Nov 15   His wife dead and he unemployed, Davis becomes a planter.
Brother Joe has given him the use of 800 acres of Davis Bend.
He is a new resident of Warren County, Miss.

1836

Aug 1   Lincoln is reelected to the Illinois General Assembly.

Oct 10   Pemberton has made poor grades in *engineering* and *tactics*.

1837

Feb 1   Pemberton survives USMA dismissal proceedings on drinking
and ethics issues.

May 1   Pemberton is graduating 27th of 50 in his USMA class.
Vicksburg Operations Classmates:
U.S., Thomas Williams. C.S., Braxton Bragg, W.H.T. Walker.

Jul 1   Pemberton is promoted to 1st lieutenant.

1838

Jan 24 Pemberton fights at Loxahatchee, Fla., in the Seminole Wars.

May 15 Carter L. Stevenson is graduating 42^d of 45 at the USMA.
Vicksburg Operations Classmates:
U.S., A.J. "Whiskey" Smith.
C.S., P.G.T. Beauregard (2^d in class), Alexander Reynolds.

Aug 31 The Jeff Davis home *Brierfield* is under construction.
It is Davis' first effort at architectural design.

1839

Jan 23 Separated from his ill father by his present assignment,
Pemberton regrets ever having entered West Point or the
Army.

May 15 A reluctant Hiram Ulysses Grant departs home for the USMA.
At registration, his name is entered as Ulysses Simpson Grant

Dec 3 Lincoln is admitted to practice in the U.S. Circuit Court.

1840

May 1 William Sherman is graduating 6th of 42 in his USMA class.
Vicksburg Operations Classmates:
U.S., none noted.
C.S., Paul Octave Hebert, Trans-Mississippi Dept.
(1st in class).

1841

Feb 27 David Dixon Porter is promoted to lieutenant.

1843

May 1 Grant is graduating 21st of 39 in his USMA class.
Vicksburg Operations Classmates:
U.S., Charles Hamilton, Isaac Quinby, Frederick Steele.
C.S., Samuel French.

1845

Feb 26 Jefferson Davis marries Varina Banks Howell at her home.

Oct 10 The U.S. Naval Academy is established at Annapolis, Md.

Dec 8 Jefferson Davis, a strict *constructionist*, is elected to Congress.
He supports states' rights and a reduction of tariffs.
He opposes the creation of a national bank.

1846

May 3 Grant, hearing Matamoros, Mexico, cannon:
"I am sorry that I enlisted."

May 9 Gov. Albert Gallatin Brown calls up 28 Mississippi companies.

1846 (Cont.)

May 11   Davis votes for the war with Mexico.

May 13   Congress approves the war with Mexico.

Jun 1   17,000 men gather at Vicksburg for the Mexican War.
Only one Mississippi regiment is requested, angering the
   Mississippians.

The *1st Mississippi Rifles* is commanded by Jefferson Davis.
Davis' influence obtains the *1841 Rifle* for his men.
It is later known as the *Mississippi Rifle.*

Aug 3   Lincoln is elected to the U.S. House of Representatives as a
   Whig.
He is known during this term for his opposition to slavery.

Sep 30   Grant is promoted to 2ᵈ lieutenant.

1847

Jan 31   The *2d Mississippi Rifles* regiment has 1,037 men at Vicksburg.

Feb 23   Jeff Davis is heroically wounded repulsing Mexican lancers.
Braxton Bragg's artillery saves the day at Buena Vista.

Jun 30   The heroic 1st Mississippi Rifles regiment has mustered out.
Davis is considered a hero of the Mexican War.

Sep 12   Joseph E. Johnston leads a regiment at Chapultepec.

Sep 13   Lt. Pemberton escorts Lt. Grant to see Maj. Gen. William Worth.
Grant receives brevets for two battles.

Sep 23   Pemberton's gallantry at Monterey earns him a captain's
   brevet.

Dec 6   Jeff Davis is selected to fill Mississippi's vacant Senate seat.

1848

Jan 24   Gold is discovered at Sutter's Mill, Cal.
The gold is the first discovered in the Sierra Nevada mountains.
William T. Sherman bites the first piece, confirming it is gold.

May 30   The Mexican War ends.

Jul 4   Sherman's gold-proving expedition arrives at Sutter's Mill.
He is accompanied by Military Governor Richard Mason.

Aug 22   Grant marries Julia Boggs Dent, daughter of a slave owner.
Grant will himself own and free one slave, William Jones.

Dec 1   Pemberton departs for San Antonio, Tex., to join Gen. Worth.

The New Orleans firm of Marcy and Zeigler is building Davis'
   new home, *Brierfield.*
The $10,000 home is valued at $390,000 in 2023 dollars.

1848 (Cont.)

Dec 5 President James Polk launches the *Gold Rush with Sherman's gold, sent by special courier for Polk's state of the union talk.* **Sherman is a catalyst for the world-changing event.**

Dec 31 John Dahlgren is employed in the U.S. Navy Ordnance Bureau.

1849

Mar 21 Lincoln exits politics and returns home to practice law.

1850

Jan 2 Sherman departs California on the steamship *Oregon.*

Jul 1 Frederick E. Prime graduates 1st of 44 in his USMA class.
His placement makes him, in essence, the *engineer of the year.*
Vicksburg Operations Classmates:
U.S., Eugene Carr.
C.S., none noted.

Sep 27 John Pemberton is promoted to captain.

1851

Jan 1 James and Adeline Shirley buy *Wexford Lodge* and 60 acres.

Mar 31 The USMA expels John Stevens Bowen for a year for not reporting a violation of the ethics code.

Wexford Lodge, also known as the Shirley House after 1850.
(NPS/Larry Brewer)

1852

Apr 16 The new Davis home *Brierfield* on Davis Bend is complete.

1852 (Cont.)

Jun 1 John Horace Forney is graduating 22[d] of 43 at the USMA.
Vicksburg Operations Classmates:
U.S., Henry W. Slocum, Charles R. Woods.
C.S., none noted.

Aug 17 Grant's 4th Regiment passes through California's Golden Gate.

1853

Mar 4 Judah Benjamin is the first practicing Jewish U.S. Senator.

Mar 7 Jeff Davis is appointed Secretary of War by Franklin Pierce.

Jun 16 John Bowen graduates 13th of 52 at the USMA.
Vicksburg Operations Classmates:
U.S., James McPherson (1st in class), William Sooy Smith,
    Alexander Chambers.
C.S., none noted.

Nov 15 The Royal Small Arms Factory in Enfield, England, is producing
the Pattern 1853 rifled musket, capable of *hitting a body* at
500 yards and beyond.

Dec 31 The Louisiana Seminary of Learning & Military Academy is
authorized by the legislature near Pineville.

1854

Apr 11 Grant posts his resignation the day he is promoted to captain.

Jul 1 Stephen Dill Lee graduates 17th of 47 at the USMA.
Vicksburg Operations Classmates: None noted.

Jul 31 Grant's resignation takes effect.
He has been threatened with court-martial.

Sep 27 The *Arctic,* rammed by the *Vesta,* quickly sinks, inspiring
Charles Ellet's interest in ram-vessel wartime applications.

1855

Mar 3 Congress approves Davis' idea of using camels in the Army.

Jul 24 Capt. David Dixon Porter on the *U.S.S. Supply* is in Italy
enroute to Africa to buy camels for the Army.

Aug 4 Porter and Maj. Henry Wayne are near Tunis to buy camels.

Dec 1 The Army is adopting James Burton's new conical bullet.
The bullet is an elongated Claude-Etienne Minié bullet.
The bullet has been developed under Secretary of War Davis.
Despite Burton's role, the bullet is still called the *Minié Ball.*

1856

Feb 15 Porter's *U.S.S. Supply* departs Africa with 33 camels.

1856 (Cont.)

Apr 26 Porter's ship of camels and handlers arrives near Indianola, Tex.

Aug 27 Davis' camels arrive at Camp Verde, Tex., for testing.

1857

Jan 30 Porter returns from Africa with 41 more camels.

Mar 4 Davis returns to the Senate, ending his time as War Secretary.

Dec 23 Grant pawns two gold watches to afford Julia's Christmas gifts.

Dec 30 Sir Joseph Whitworth is producing an extremely accurate rifle.
The rifle, carried in a special case, costs **$1,000 in gold**, or
$35,000 in 2023 dollars, and weighs 38 lbs.
The *target rifle* is capable of hitting its mark a mile away.

1858

Jan 10 The Davises have the largest law library east of the Mississippi.

Jun 16 Lincoln receives the Republican U.S. Senate nomination from
Illinois.
He gives his "House Divided" speech, launching his party.

Nov 22 The *U.S.S. Hartford (below)* is launched.
It is the last hoorah of the wooden warships.

(USNHHC)

1859

Feb 10 Sherman is practicing law with the firm of Sherman, Ewing, &
McCook in Leavenworth, Kans.

Mar 29 Grant signs manumission papers for his slave William Jones.
Grant will be the last president to own a slave.

Aug 2 Sherman is hired as superintendent, Louisiana Seminary of
Learning, and chair of engineering, architecture, and drawing.
The school is to be styled after the Virginia Military Institute.

Nov 8   John McClernand is elected to the Congress from Illinois.

1860

Jan 2   The Louisiana State Seminary of Learning & Military
Academy opens, Professor William T. Sherman presiding.

May 18   Lincoln is nominated for U.S. President in Chicago, Ill.

Jun 28   Brig. Gen. Joseph E. Johnston becomes Army Quartermaster.
Sen. Jeff Davis supported his friend Albert Sidney Johnston.

Aug 7   Grant is upbeat after many slumps.
"I hope soon to be above the frowns of the world."

Nov 6   Whig Unionists carry Warren County.
Lincoln does not appear on Southern ballots.

Nov 9   Lincoln is elected 16th President of the United States.

Nov 15   The sheet music *"Dixie"* is selling 500 copies per day.

Dec 15   Sherman predicts correctly, dreading disunion:
"I look for the first collision to be at Charleston.
South Carolina will fall far astern."

"The war will be fought on the Mississippi River."

Dec 20   1:30 p.m.–South Carolina secedes.

Families are dividing at the highest levels.

Mary Todd Lincoln will lose brothers in the Confederate Army.

B
A Nation Asunder Organizes For War
1861

January 1861

9   Mississippi secedes from the Union.

10 Florida secedes.
Louisiana state troops seize the local arsenal at Baton Rouge.
Sherman, in charge of the arsenal, is greatly distressed by events.

11 Alabama secedes from the Union.

13 Vicksburg batteries fire on the *suspicious* steamer *A.O. Tyler.*

18 Sherman requests to be released immediately if Louisiana secedes.
"I will remain loyal as long as one state supports the Constitution."

19 Georgia secedes.

20 Mississippi troops seize Fort Massachusetts on Ship Island, Miss.

21 Sherman resigns his post at the Louisiana State Seminary.
Sherman to wife Ellen: *"I feel no desire to take a hand in a war."*
Davis delivers his emotional farewell address to the U.S. Senate.
The Mississippi Congressional delegation withdraws, Davis last.

23 The *Vicksburg Whig:*
"It is the duty of patriots to follow the state, whatever its course."
Earl Van Dorn is made a brigadier general in the Mississippi Militia.

25 *Windsor*, one of the South's grandest homes, is nearly complete.
The Smith Daniell family owns 21,000 acres and over 300 slaves.

26 Louisiana becomes the 6th state to secede.
Davis is installed as major general over Mississippi state forces.

February 1861

1   Texas secedes over the objections of its iconic governor Sam Houston.

9   Davis, a moderate, is appointed Confederate provisional president.
The Confederate White House is in Montgomery, Ala.

February 1861 (Cont.)

9   Jefferson Davis will build a nation while fighting for its survival.
Van Dorn is appointed major general of state troops, replacing Davis.

10   Davis receives his Presidential appointment at his *Brierfield* home.
He is distraught but accepts the post out of a strong sense of duty.

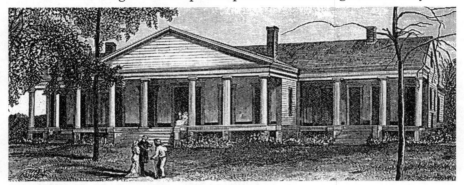

Brierfield, 1863, the home designed by Jefferson Davis.
From "House Divided," The Civil War Research Engine at Dickinson College, Carlisle, Pa.
https://hd.housedivided.dickinson.edu/node/39865

February 1861 (Cont.)

11   Davis' train stops at Vicksburg enroute to Montgomery.

President Davis gives his first address.
*"I struggled earnestly to maintain the Union and the constitutional
equality of all states but our safety and honor required us to
dissolve our connection with the United States.*
*"I hope that our separation may be peaceful. But whether it be so or
not, I am ready, as I have always been, to redeem my pledges to
you and the South by shedding every drop of blood in your cause."*

14   Davis is delivering 25 whistlestop speeches to *one continuous
ovation.*

16   Davis arrives in Montgomery, Ala., to great fanfare.
"The time for compromise has past," he says in a mood of defiance.

3ᵈ Lt. James L. Autry joins the 9ᵗʰ Mississippi in Holly Springs, Miss.

18   Davis takes the oath of office as President of the Confederacy.
Each of the first seven seceded states will receive a Cabinet member.

20   Sherman departs his beloved Louisiana Seminary for New Orleans.

21   Leroy Pope Walker becomes the first C.S. Secretary of War.

25   Judah Benjamin is appointed Confederate Attorney General.

26   Davis signs the act creating the infrastructure of the C.S. Army.

February 1861 (Cont.)

27 The North has 88% of the nation's industry.
Ships, 11 times that of the Confederacy; iron production, 15 times;
locomotives, 24 times; firearms, 32 times.
Sherman loves the South but chastises friends for "taking on the
world's largest industrial power in your own backyard when the
South doesn't even have a factory to make shoes."

March 1861

1 P.G.T. Beauregard and Braxton Bragg are the first C.S. generals.
Joe Johnston is incensed at Davis for being passed over several times.
"You have tarnished my fair fame as a soldier and a man."

Johnston says his Army Quartermaster post gives him rank by law.
Davis: "The Quartermaster post was staff, not field command."
A huge argument ensues.

2 Davis allows the Congressional generals list to stand.
Davis shows his disdain for being told what to do.

4 Abraham Lincoln is inaugurated President of the United States.
Gideon Welles is named U.S. Secretary of the Navy.

8 U.S. Senator John Sherman arranges a White House introduction to
Lincoln for brother William.

16 Earl Van Dorn enters the Confederate Army as a colonel of infantry.

Texas governor Sam Houston is removed for not swearing allegiance
to the Confederacy. His son will help defend Vicksburg.

April 1861

1 The United States is a generation behind in naval technology.
The Army engineering component is deficient: 43 officers and 100
enlisted.
Union military strength is 16,400.

8 At a tense Cabinet meeting, Davis gives the Fort Sumter ultimatum.
"Yielding any part of our country would weaken it in global eyes."

11 Van Dorn is given command of Confederate forces in Texas.

12 **Confederate forces begin an attack on Fort Sumter, S.C.**

Smith Coffee Daniell II of *Windsor* dies of yellow fever at age 34.

13 Fort Sumter surrenders.

15 Lincoln declares a *State of Rebellion* exists.
His call for 75,000 troops dampens Vicksburg's *Unionist posture*.
Lincoln's move produces in Jefferson Davis a *war president*.

Grant is nominated to raise a volunteer company in Galena, Ill.

April 1861 (Cont.)

15   Kentucky's governor: *"Our troops will not oppose Southern states."*
Tennessee's governor echoes similar sentiments.

Israel Pemberton tells brother John to stay with the Union.

16   Lincoln calls for a blockade of Southern ports.

17   Virginia, the most populous Southern state by far, secedes.
Pemberton casts a vote for secession.

Joe Johnston is the highest-ranking U.S. officer to resign.
He accepts a brigadier rank and command at Harper's Ferry, Va.

19   Grant rides 14 miles to Hanover, Ill., to recruit volunteers.

Pemberton's last U.S. order is to hold steamers on the Potomac.

20   The captured Norfolk Navy Yard yields the South 1,200 cannon.

21   600 U.S. volunteers leave Chicago to protect Cairo, Ill.

22   David Dixon Porter is promoted to commander.

Pemberton is being pressed on both family sides to choose a side.
He cannot and will not attack Norfolk, Pattie's home.
Pemberton's brothers, Andrew and Clifford, join the Union army.
The country is widely shattering at the family level.

23   Davis sends cannon to Missouri to capture the Federal arsenal there.
The guns are hidden in crates marked *marble*.

24   John Pemberton resigns from the Union army.

26   Pemberton departs for Richmond, Va.

29   Illinois governor Richard Yates offers Ulysses Grant a post as an aide
to the adjutant general.

Davis prefers a defensive strategy against the North.

30   The *McRae*, New Orleans' first gunship, is the converted *Habana*.

31   Confederate funding is made available for 10 converted gunboats.

May 1861

4   After impressing Governor Yates, Grant commands *Camp Yates*.

6   Arkansas secedes.

8   Pemberton is made a Virginia artillery lieutenant colonel.

John McClernand's wife Sarah, Mary Todd Lincoln's dear friend, dies.

9   New Orleans shipyards are busy converting packets to gunboats.

10   Militia Col. John Bowen surrenders at Camp Jackson, Mo.
His captor is *Col. Frank Blair* who he will fight again at Vicksburg.

May 1861 (Cont.)

13   Sherman: *"The Mississippi River will be a **grand theater of war**."*

14   Sherman rejoins the Army as field commander of the new 13th U.S. Infantry.

15   Joe Johnston wants to abandon Harper's Ferry, Va.
Davis and Lee want the arsenal held.
Johnston argues it is indefensible and doesn't want to waste troops.
Davis exposes his *Supreme Commander* side, ordering it held.

     The notorious Confederate privateer *Calhoun* begins its service.

     John Pemberton is named colonel in the Virginia artillery.

17   McClernand joins the Army as brigadier general of volunteers.
Sherman and Grant are also on that list.
Sherman outranks Grant.

20   North Carolina secedes.
Kentucky declares its neutrality.

21   Winfield Scott finalizes the *Anaconda Plan* to strangle the South.

24   A Grant offer to serve in the regular Army is *lost in the system*.

     Navy designer Samuel Pook reports to Capt. John Rodgers at Cairo, Ill., for *"special duty."*
James Eads plans to convert steamboats into ironclads with Pook.

26   The Confederate capital begins its move to Richmond, Va.

June 1861

1   Lee to Johnston: *"To give up Harper's Ferry would be depressing."*

     Very quickly, Pook has drafted plans for Eads' seven ironclads.
The gunboats will carry the monikers *"Pook's Turtles"* or *"smoke pots."*

4   Grant is posted as a colonel of an Illinois volunteer regiment.

7   Rodgers to Welles: *"Three gunboats are needed to protect Cairo."*

8   Tennessee secedes.

     Rodgers buys the steamers *Lexington*, *Conestoga*, and *A.O. Tyler*.
No one has ever converted steamers of such size into war vessels.
Three wooden-laminate timberclads are required by month's end.

     Their construction is by authority of the Army, not the Navy.
The ironclads are considered *floating artillery barges*.

     Secretary Welles to Rodgers: *"You had no authority to buy boats."*
Welles: *"The Navy has no officers to command the gunboats."*

11   War Sec. Simon Cameron to Welles: *"Gen. Scott supports Rodgers."*

June 1861 (Cont.)

12	Rodgers to Welles: *"Gen. George McClellan approved my purchases."*
13	Adj. Gen. Sam Cooper okays Johnston's abandoning Harper's Ferry. A dismayed Davis deems Johnston's action premature and hasty. *The issue opens a fissure between Cooper and Davis.*
15	Pemberton becomes a major in the Confederate Artillery Corps. 12,000 Western U.S. troops are garrisoned at Cairo.
17	Grant takes command of the 7th Illinois, the future 21st Illinois. Pemberton is promoted to brigadier general.
18	The U.S. Sanitation Commission is created to aid soldiers.
23	The raising of 500,000 Union volunteers is approved.
25	Davis creates Department No. 2, the Western Department.
28	Grant's regiment, to a man, decides to stay in *if under his command.*
30	Sherman receives his brigade.

July 1861

1	100,000 C.S. troops are armed, most with shotguns or squirrel rifles.
3	Grant moves his regiment toward Quincy, Ill., in his first march.
7	The 21st Illinois calls 11-year-old favorite Fred Grant *"Colonel."*
11	Grant crosses the Mississippi into Missouri to hold bridges and rail.
13	Now in enemy territory, Grant sends Fred home.
15	John McClernand introduces a Bill for money and men for the war.
18	The Army requests bids to construct James Eads' ironclad gunboats.
21	Beauregard is appointed full general in the Confederate Army.
	Sherman impresses Lincoln at First Manassas. Davis rallies soldiers there: *"I am President Davis. Follow me!"*
22	The recruitment of 500,000 Union soldiers, with full Army veteran benefits for wounded or disabled, is passed.
23	Davis, before a crowd, takes credit for *saving Bull Run*. Beauregard says that his poor supplies kept him from pressing on and taking Washington, D.C. *Animosity is now building between Davis and Beauregard.*
24	John Pope adds four regiments to Grant's command.
27	George McClellan is given command of the Army of the Potomac. McClellan's gunboat project oversight falls to John C. Fremont.
28	Joe Johnston calls rank when Lee assigns an adjutant to Johnston.
31	Grant is promoted to brigadier general of volunteers by Lincoln.

July 1861 (Cont.)

31 Samuel DeGolyer has been captured at Bull Run directing artillery.

August 1861

1 Gustavus Vasa Fox is appointed Assistant U.S. Navy Secretary.

3 At Julia's behest, Fred Grant returns to the front lines.

4 Capt. David Todd, Mary Lincoln's brother, commands the
Confederate Harwood and Ligon prisons in Richmond.
Samuel DeGolyer is Todd's prisoner after Bull Run.
They will fire their guns at each other at Vicksburg's Great Redoubt.

Fremont is arbitrarily using ironclad funds for artillery and mortars.
A shortage of gunboat funds means their decks will not be armored.
Bids are opened for ironclad construction. Eads is low bidder.

5 *The U.S.S. Mound City, Cairo,* and *Cincinnati* will be built at Mound
City, Ill.
The U.S.S. St. Louis, Carondolet, Louisville, and *Pittsburg* will be
built at Carondolet, Mo.

Without cotton revenue that is 75% of Federal intake, Lincoln
signs the Revenue Act to collect income taxes to fund the war.

7 Sherman is promoted to brigadier general of volunteers.

The Maryland legislature adjourns, leaning toward neutrality.
Federal troops and police arrest pro-Secession legislators there.
With Maryland as a border state, **Washington D.C. remains
inside the Union instead of the Confederacy**.

12 Lt. Seth L. Phelps arrives in Cairo with the three new timberclads.
The delivery is late due to carpenter foul-ups during construction.

20 After conflicts with Fremont and lagging schedules, Rodgers
resigns the ironclad project.
Capt. Andrew Hull Foote is named construction superintendent.

23 Funds for the *C.S.S. Arkansas* and *Tennessee* are authorized.

24 The construction of the ironclad *Arkansas* in Memphis is ordered.

31 Grant is given command of the District of Southeast Missouri.

The C.S. Congress has promoted Davis' favorites over Joe Johnston.

September 1861

2 Grant arrives in Cairo, Ill.

3 Grant occupies the Paducah & Southland RR near Paducah, Ky.

4 Leonidas Polk orders Gideon Pillow to take Columbus, Ky.

5 Grant learns that Polk is considering taking Columbus.

	September 1861 (Cont.)
5	Polk captures Columbus and blocks the river, fortifying the bluff. *Polk's very costly strategic error will end Kentucky's neutrality.* **The Confederacy will lose the gateway to its heartland.**
6	Foote at St. Louis commands construction of the *brown water navy*.
7	Grant occupies Paducah.
10	Albert Sidney Johnston is to command the Western Department.
15	A.S. Johnston assumes command of the huge area west of the Alleghenies.
18	A.S. Johnston sends Simon Buckner to fortify Bowling Green, Ky.
20	Scott's original deadline for completing *16* ironclad gunboats passes.
25	Judah Benjamin is appointed the second Confederate Secretary of War.
28	Samuel DeGolyer is promoted to major.
30	Davis travels to Centreville, Va., for a war conference.

	October 1861
1	Davis talks war strategy with Beauregard, Johnston, and G.W. Smith. Maj. Gen. Smith: *"Victory in Virginia wins all; losing here loses all."*
	Davis is unwilling to bleed resources from other states any further. He is already getting complaints from state governors. **He does not have the authority to nationalize state troops.**
	Attention shifts to the West.
	Grant's asks Julia: *"What would you think of my taking Fred on my campaign?"*
10	Scott's next deadline for completion of the ironclad gunboats passes. Foote avoids boat-naming ego issues, naming them after cities. Hence, they will be called *"City Class"* ironclads.
	Fremont wants Ead's *Submarine No. 7* to be the *U.S.S. Benton*. He purchases the *New Era* for conversion into the *U.S.S. Essex*.
14	A floating drydock battery, the *C.S.S. New Orleans,* is commissioned.
15	William A. Lake dies in a duel with Henry Cousins Chambers. They are opponents for the Confederate Congress. Lake is a prominent Vicksburg citizen and landowner. His daughter Mary is Mrs. Duff Green.
17	Sherman discusses his Kentucky needs with Cameron in Louisville. *Cameron's brother James died at Bull Run serving under Sherman.* Sherman needs 60,000 to defend Kentucky. For an offensive, he would need 200,000, he says.

October 1861 (Cont.)

18 Cameron to press at Harrisburg, Pa.: *"Sherman is absolutely crazy."*

21 Cameron's trip memorandum does not mention the *"crazy"* phrase.

28 John McClernand resigns his seat in the House of Representatives.

30 Missouri is admitted to the Confederacy but does not secede.

November 1861

1 Sherman's estimate for 200,000 troops is rebuffed as excessive.
Newspaper accounts are making him a laughingstock.
Sherman: *"I am riding a whirlwind, unable to guide the storm."*

Grant is authorized to go downriver to demonstrate in Missouri.

3 New general-in-chief McClellan asks Sherman to *clarify his situation.*

5 Sherman is notified that Don Carlos Buell will replace him.
Grant is ordered to demonstrate near Belmont, Mo.

6 Grant embarks 3,000 soldiers, headed for Belmont.

Sherman is asked to send McClellan *daily reports* from Kentucky.
Sherman is under close and mistrustful scrutiny at the top level.
Asst. War Secretary Thomas Scott: *"Sherman is gone in the head."*

Davis is elected to a six-year term as Confederate president.
No Southerner has his political or military experience.
Alabama fire-eater William Yancey:
"The man and the hour have met."

7 Grant's first battle is a draw at Belmont against Gideon Pillow.
McClernand is Grant's second in command.
Grant cheats death twice on the field and on his boat.

The floating barracks *C.S.S. Red Rover* is acquired to support the
floating drydock battery *C.S.S. New Orleans.*

8 Sherman's wife Ellen is called to Louisville, Ky., by Capt. Frederick
Prime.

9 Ellen writes to John Sherman of his brother's physical and mental
state and history.

Kentucky is admitted into the Confederacy with 20% enslaved.

10 The *C.S.S. General Polk* arrives near Columbus ahead of the fleet.

14 Buell arrives and Ellen leaves Sherman to continue with his duties.

15 The steamer *New Era* begins conversion to the *U.S.S. Essex.*

18 68 of Kentucky's 110 counties pass an Ordinance of Secession.

21 Connecticut and Massachusetts troops depart for Ship Island, Miss.

November 1861 (Cont.)

23   The *C.S.S. Tuscarora* accidentally burns in the river at Helena, Ark.

29   Pemberton is ordered to the defenses of Charleston, S.C.

30   Union and Confederate gunboats skirmish at Columbus, Ky.

December 1861

3   The U.S expedition to Ship Island, Miss., occupies the island.

9   Media reports:
"Sherman's illness has removed him from command."

10   Kentucky is the 13th state admitted to the Confederacy.

11   The Cincinnati *Commercial* declares Sherman *insane*.

The *C.S.S. New Orleans* and *Red Rover* arrive near Columbus, Ky.

The *C.S.S. New Orleans*, the drydock battery.
From the Philadelphia Enquirer, November 4, 1862.

12   Sherman pours out his heart and rationale to adopted father and father-in-law Thomas Ewing.
John Sherman and Ellen launch a campaign and potential legal action.

13   The *Commercial* retracts its Sherman article point by point. Unfortunately for Sherman, the damage is already done.

15   Pemberton is learning from Lee, e.g., using rail to move forces. Lee provides wisdom that Pemberton will apply at Vicksburg.
"Holding your line is more important than areas in your front."

23   DeGolyer resigns his commission due to gaps in his training while he was absent.

30   John Rawlins: *"Grant's accusers are false and with malice."*

C
Emerging Heroes and Hurdles
1862

January 1862

1 Pemberton's forces beat back an incursion on the Coosaw River, S.C.

Capt. Thomas O. Selfridge is aboard the *U.S.S. Mississippi* near Biloxi, Miss.

Henry Halleck, sensing political issues, may give Sherman a second chance.

4 Sherman admits contemplating suicide for the past few weeks.

7 The floating battery *C.S.S. New Orleans* chases Federal gunboats away.

Battle of Lucas Bend, Ky., January 11, 1862

11 The ironclads *U.S.S. St Louis* and *Essex* deploy on the Mississippi.
The *C.S.S. cottonclads Ivy, Jackson,* and *General Polk* are engaged.
These are the **first Union ironclads in battle.**
The battle is one of the **last major roles for the outclassed timberclad warships.**
No casualties are reported in the brisk contest.

14 Cameron, the new Minister to Russia, is replaced by Edwin Stanton.
The new War Secretary Stanton is a good friend of the Ewing family.
Lincoln appreciated Thomas Ewing's help with the *Trent Affair*.

Pemberton is promoted to major general.

15 Construction issues and finding crews have delayed the ironclads.

The *U.S.S. Cairo* is commissioned at Mound City, Ill.
The *U.S.S. Carondolet* is commissioned at Carondolet, Mo.

16 The *U.S.S. Louisville* is commissioned at Carondolet.
The *U.S.S. Cincinnati and Mound City* are commissioned at Mound City.

January 1862 (Cont.)

23   The captured privateer *Calhoun* becomes the *U.S.S. Calhoun.*
C.S. Mansfield Lovell: *"The ship will prove a great Gulf Coast pest."*

25   The *U.S.S. Pittsburg* is commissioned at Carondolet.

26   Grant is feeling held back by Halleck in advancing on C.S. Fort Henry.

27   Lincoln is agitated and signs General Order (G.O.) No. 1:
"The Army and flotilla at Cairo must move by February 22^d.
  Officers who will not move will be removed."

29   Van Dorn assumes command of the Trans-Mississippi District.

30   Grant has 30,000 soldiers and seven new *City Class* ironclads.
Halleck: *"Grant, make preparations to take and hold Fort Henry."*

The *U.S.S. Monitor* is launched for trials in New York.
Eads' gunboats have already experienced naval battle.

31   The *U.S.S. St. Louis* is commissioned at Carondelet.

Lt. Isaac N. Brown, C.S.N., is converting four steamers into gunboats.

February 1862

2   Halleck to Grant: *"Move on Fort Henry."*
David Farragut departs Virginia on his new flagship, *U.S.S. Hartford.*

5   Confederates spot dense volumes of smoke approaching Fort Henry.
Andrew Foote tells his gunboats, *"It must be victory or death."*

Battle of Fort Henry, Ky., February 6, 1862

6   **The first shots are fired by ironclads on land fortifications.**
Fort Henry is evacuated.
Two Union gunboats are disabled; the *U.S.S. Essex* is heavily
  damaged. Cdr. William "Dirty Bill" Porter is wounded.
Casualties: K, killed; W, wounded; C, captured; M, Missing.
U.S., 32 gunboat crew, K/W
C.S., 15 fort personnel K, 20 W
"The U.S. flag is on the soil of Tennessee. It will never be moved."

The unfinished *C.S.S. Louisiana* is launched in New Orleans.

9   Davis admits that Confederate resources can't cover the needs.

10   Grant's 11-year-old son Fred joins him at the front for a few days.

11   Grant holds a very rare *council of war.*

Albert Sidney Johnston withdraws his army from Kentucky.
The Kentucky Confederate government goes into exile.

12   Grant to Halleck: *"We start this a.m. for Donelson in heavy force."*
Grant is 10 days ahead of Lincoln's G.O. 1 deadline.

February 1862 (Cont.)

Battle of Fort Donelson, Ky., February 14, 1862

13 Davis is preparing to pull Robert E. Lee back from South Carolina to Virginia and replace him with John Pemberton.

14 Grant attacks Fort Donelson and fails, investing the fort.
The naval assault is repulsed.

15 Sherman offers Grant his support, though Sherman outranks him.
"I have faith in you. Command me in any way." Grant is impressed.

Confederates attempt a poorly organized breakout at Fort Donelson.

Stonewall Jackson brings seven charges against William Wing Loring.
"His conduct is subversive of good order and military discipline."
Loring's court-martial is blocked by Davis.
Jackson threatens to resign unless Loring is removed.
Robert E. Lee: *"I have no room for this man in my Army."*
Loring is promoted to major general and sent to southwest Virginia.

16 Grant wants to accept surrender without embarrassing his enemy.
Charles F. Smith to Grant: *"Except only Unconditional Surrender."*
The moniker *"Unconditional Surrender"* Grant is born.
Fort Donelson's fall costs A.S. Johnston 12,000, a third of his force.
Two more Union gunboats are disabled. Their crews are *learning*.
Casualties:
U.S., 507 K, 1,976 W, 208 M
C.S., 327 K, 1,127 W, 12,392 C/M

Halleck takes credit for both victories, asking to command the West.
He calls for Buell, Grant, and Pope to be made major generals.
He does not congratulate Grant officially.

The *U.S.S. Cairo* is ordered to the Cumberland River.

17 Stanton brings Grant's promotion papers to Lincoln.
Lincoln: *"Southerners may think they are better than Western men. They will discover themselves in a grievous mistake."*
Lincoln knows full well who to credit for Forts Henry and Donelson.

The *C.S.S. Virginia* is commissioned at Portsmouth, Va.

18 Grant controls the Cumberland River.
Halleck orders Grant *not* to advance on Nashville, Tenn.

19 C.S. gunboats are sent north to cooperate with Polk near Kentucky.
Davis calls a two-day Cabinet conference at Centreville, Va.
A.S. Johnston is told to withdraw supplies and prepare for a retreat.

23 A.S. Johnston evacuates Nashville, Tenn.
Brown is ordered to burn his four gunboats under conversion there.

February 1862 (Cont.)

24 The *U.S.S. Benton* is commissioned from Eads' *Submarine No. 7*.

25 The City of Nashville falls to the Army of the Ohio.
The *U.S.S. Cairo* arrives at Nashville.

Battle of Island No. 10, February 28, 1862 – April 8, 1862

28 The Battle of Island No. 10 near New Madrid, Mo., begins.

The *U.S.S. Oneida* is commissioned.
Capt. Samuel Phillips Lee is commanding.

March 1862

1 Sherman joins the Army of West Tennessee, leading the 5th Division.

2 Polk, his position untenable, retreats from Columbus, Ky.

3 Pope's 26,000 assault New Madrid, Mo., fail, and lay siege.
Confederate gunboats are credited with stymying Pope.

Halleck to McClellan:
"Grant was away from his post without approval."

4 Pemberton commands the Department of South Carolina and
Georgia.

Union military and naval forces occupy Columbus, Ky.
**The first major C.S. Miss. River fortification falls without
a fight.**

6 Pope sends units to capture Point Pleasant south of New Madrid, Mo.

7 The *C.S.S. Virginia* is completed in Portsmouth's Gosport Navy Yard.

8 The two-day battle of the *U.S.S. Monitor* and *C.S.S. Virginia* begins at
Hampton Roads, Va.

9 After Halleck's jab about his absence without leave, Grant asks to be
relieved over confusion about messages he sent prior.

10 Grant is suddenly given new troops meant for Samuel Curtis.
Curtis is a personal friend of John McClernand.

The *C.S.S. Defiance* is the first of 14 in the La. River Defense Fleet.

11 Stanton to Halleck: *"Show evidence against Grant or stand down."*

McClellan is removed to command the Army of the Potomac.
Halleck is given command in the West, the Department of the
Mississippi.

DeGolyer is recommended to command the 8th Michigan Artillery.

13 A chastised Halleck to Grant: *"Take command. Do great things."*
Pope's newly arrived heavy artillery opens fire on New Madrid, Mo.

March 1862 (Cont.)

14 *Fort Thompson* is evacuated by Confederates at New Madrid.
Pope enters New Madrid, surprised that there is no opposition.
Island No. 10 is now completely cutoff.

John Bowen is promoted to brigadier general.
Pemberton's South Carolina command is made permanent.

15 Pope sets up batteries to bombard Island No. 10.
Union gunboats and mortar scows add to the bombardment.
Foote takes nine gunboats and mortars with 1,500 troops to
Hickman, Ky.

Davis is *acutely distraught* at Joe Johnston's recent retreat action.
He blasts Johnston for abandoning Centreville and its huge stores.
Davis let his friend A.S. Johnston pass over a similar Nashville action.
Johnston defiantly reminds Davis of his *inconsistency*.

17 Foote ties the U.S.S. *Benton*, *Cincinnati*, and *St. Louis* together to
attack.
Island No. 10 is teaching Foote about attacking superior fire power.

Grant steams to rejoin his army near Savannah, Tenn.
Grant writes to wife Julia that he *expects a big fight*.

18 Judah Benjamin is named the third Confederate Secretary of State.
George Wythe Randolph is appointed Confederate Secretary of War.

19 Pope to Halleck: *"I need Foote to run gunboats by Island No. 10 so
I can cross the Mississippi River into Tennessee."*
Island No. 10 has 6,000 troops and 75 heavy guns.

20 Foote responds to the Army request by running by Island No 10.

Grant wants a quick strike from Savannah, Tenn., to Corinth, Miss.
Halleck to Grant: *"Wait for Buell. Don't get drawn in."*

Albert Sidney Johnston is building his force to confront Grant.

21 John McClernand is named a major general for Fort Donelson action.

27 Sterling Price adds his Missouri State Guard into the Army of the
West.

29 The *C.S.S. General Price* visits Vicksburg on its way to Kentucky.

31 The *U.S.S. Cairo* arrives at Savannah, Tenn., Grant's headquarters.

April 1862

1 Albert Sidney Johnston has assembled 40,000 troops.

The *U.S.S. Cairo*, *Tyler*, and *Lexington* and Sherman go down the
Tennessee River to Eastport, Tenn.

April 1862 (Cont.)

1   42^d Illinois soldiers spike guns on the Tennessee side at Island No. 10.

2   Beauregard receives intel that Buell is moving to reinforce Grant.
     Grant is assembling, organizing, and reviewing his troops.

     Bowen accepts promotion to brigadier general.

3   C.S. forces begin the arduous march to Shiloh for an April 4th attack.
     Sherman to Ellen: *"I expect Confederates to await us at Corinth."*

4   Pope digs a cutoff chute on Wilson Bayou to bypass Island No. 10.
     The chute puts the Navy above Island No. 10, the Army below.
     The *U.S.S. Carondelet* makes a night run by Island No. 10 to cheers.

     A.S. Johnston is delayed due to bad roads and communications.

5   Johnston's attack is stalled another day by torrential rains.
     Grant: *"I have scarcely the faintest idea of an attack."*

     The *U.S.S. Cairo* arrives to defend the Cairo Naval Station.

The Battle of Shiloh, Tenn., April 6–7, 1862

6   A.S. Johnston surprises a relaxing Grant with a morning attack.
     Grant changes his tune to Buell: *"I have been looking for this."*
     Sherman is wounded twice; a nearby lieutenant is killed.
     Grant dodges death on the hot battlefield and is asked to move back.
     Cannonballs pass inches from both Sherman and Grant.

     John Bowen is badly wounded by an exploding artillery shell.
     A.S. Johnston receives a mortal wound; Beauregard steps up.

     Grant is pushed into a defensive posture, barely holding his own.
     Sherman to Grant:
     "Well, Grant, we've had the Devil's own day of it."
     Grant to Sherman: *"Lick 'em tomorrow though."*

     Beauregard wires Davis: *"Complete victory!"*

     The *U.S.S. Pittsburg* makes a night run past the batteries of Island
        No. 10, covering Pope's activities.

7   Don Carlos Buell arrives with reinforcements at Pittsburg Landing.
     The combined Union Army goes on the offensive.
     Grant's scabbard is shot away.
     Kentucky secessionist governor George W. John is killed.

     Shiloh proves the war will not be a *one-battle war.*
     The battle ends any chance for a national reconciliation.
     Multiple Southern military goals are ended.

After Shiloh, *"The South never smiled."*

April 1862 (Cont.)

7   **Shiloh Casualties,** *over a five-mile battlefield*:
U.S., 13,047
C.S., 10,699
Shiloh is the largest battle to that time on American soil.

8   Nathan Bedford Forrest is the last casualty at Shiloh.
He is shot attacking Sherman with empty pistols.

Davis declares to Congress *a great victory at Shiloh.*
Meanwhile, Beauregard has the Confederate Army in retreat.

Sherman court-martials four officers.
The 53ᵈ Ohio is disgraced.

Island No. 10 falls to *pre-Vicksburg tactics.*
The capture is the first of a lower Mississippi River position.

9   Grant is briefly hailed as the national *Man of the Hour* after Shiloh.
The *New York Times, Herald,* and *Tribune* declare victory!

10   Field reports have come in.
New York Tribune: "Grant's Army was surprised at Shiloh."
Halleck informs Grant that he will take Grant's command after
   Shiloh questions.

Lincoln tells detractors (Halleck): *"I can't spare this man. He fights."*
The Grant and Sherman bond is tightened.
Halleck's jealousy of Grant has percolated back up.

Welles thanks the Army's Western Gunboat Flotilla, particularly
   Henry Walke and William Hoel, for its contributions to date.

Work to strengthen the *U.S.S. Cairo's* pilothouse is completed.

Union forces attack Fort Pulaski near Savannah, Ga.
Pemberton declares it secure; it falls in the afternoon.
Fort Pulaski points out his *inability to assess military situations.*
Word is out that Pemberton is not doing a good job.

Davis weeps for the loss of his friend and idol, A.S. Johnston.
He wires five states to send all they can to Shiloh; he gets little.
The fallacy of confederated, independent states is hurting Davis.

11   Halleck arrives and takes command of Army of the Tennessee.

Severely wounded Confederate Shiloh soldiers arrive in Vicksburg.
Vicksburg gets its first up-close look at the very graphic face of war.

12   The Gunboat Flotilla departs for Fort Pillow, just north of Memphis.

13   The U.S. steamer *Planter* is stolen by a slave crew in Pemberton's
   theater and sneaks away to Union forces and surrenders.

April 1862 (Cont.)

13 Andrew Foote requests leave to have his wound properly treated.
Capt. Charles H. Davis is given *temporary* command of the Flotilla.
The Army transports follow the Flotilla to Fort Pillow.

As John Pope arrives, five cottonclad Confederate rams round the
bend.
The *U.S.S. Benton, Carondolet,* and *Mound City* pressure the rams.

14 The *U.S.S. Cairo* drifts into Plum Point with her mortar scows in tow.

15 Welles requests Hoel's full name so that he can promote him.

16 Davis signs the Confederate Conscription Act a year into the war.

Pope departs for Shiloh after Halleck withdraws from Fort Pillow.

17 Foote to Welles: *"10 Rebel gunboats at Memphis and 10 coming."*
Losing Pope hurts **the most successful inland naval campaign**.

The Capture of New Orleans, La., April 18 – May 1, 1862

18 Union mortar scows under David D. Porter open fire on New Orleans.

19 The *C.S.S. Mississippi, yet unfinished,* is launched in New Orleans.

20 Farragut sends two boats to cut the chain blocking the Mississippi.

21 The C.S. steamer *Alfred Robb* is captured on the Tennessee River.

22 The remaining two Louisiana river defense vessels go downriver to
bolster the forts.

23 Stanton: *"Did Grant or others cause the sad losses at Shiloh?"*
Grant is languishing as Halleck's deputy with nothing to do.

24 Farragut hoists red lanterns, signaling his crews to run by Forts
Jackson and St. Philip.

Pope arrives at Shiloh to join Halleck's Mississippi mission.

25 Farragut's Western Gulf Blocking Squadron takes New Orleans.

Injured Maj. Gen. Charles Ferguson Smith dies at Savannah, Tenn.
He was Grant's mentor, dear friend, and instructor at West Point.

The *C.S.S. Arkansas* is commissioned in Memphis, Tenn.

27 At Vicksburg, Joseph Davis and family evacuate Davis Bend.

Pemberton moves his headquarters to Charleston.
Pemberton and Brig. Gen. Roswell Ripley are in a running feud.
Ripley requests and receives a brigade of Va. and N.C. soldiers,
separating him from Pemberton.

28 Cut-off river forts below New Orleans surrender to Farragut's force.

April 1862 (Cont.)

28   Davis asks Congress for a three-year draft of war-age white men.

29   Farragut and 250 marines remove the state flag from City Hall.

Confederates abduct 15 Davis Bend slaves for fortification work.

30   Johnston ignores a Davis-Lee request to delay evacuating Yorktown, Va.
He then breaks communications with Richmond for a week.
"I could not consult with Davis without accepting his approach."
Johnston was hesitant to involve the Cabinet after public leaks.

Joe Davis moves all he can from Davis Bend to near Bolton, Miss.
Davis' remaining slaves ransack the island.

May 1862

1   Maj. Gen. Benjamin Butler's force takes command of New Orleans.
Sherman is promoted to major general of volunteers for Shiloh.

7   Farragut's *U.S.S. Iroquois* drops anchor at Baton Rouge, La.

The Fall of Baton Rouge, La., May 8, 1862

8   Baton Rouge falls to Union forces.

9   Foote gives Gunboat Flotilla command to Flag Officer Charles Davis.

10   Evacuated New Orleans regiments are repositioned at Vicksburg,
the 4th and 28th Louisiana, followed by 17th, 26th, 27th, and 30th.
Louisiana artillery is combined with Mellon and Balfour Mississippi
infantry.

The Battle of Plum Point, Tenn., May 10, 1862

10   The **first naval battle in the West** occurs four miles above Fort
Pillow.
The *U.S.S. Mound City* and *Cincinnati* are sunk by Rebel rams.

11   Lincoln gives the Navy the thanks of a grateful nation.

Union forces raise the *U.S.S. Mound City*, sunk the day before.

Foote: *"Seven Reb gunboats are 15 miles south of New Madrid."*

Foote hears John Pope's snide talk about the Navy at Island No. 10.

Davis overrules Pemberton's martial law declaration after Fort
Pulaski.

Grant to Halleck: *"My position differs little from one under arrest."*

The *C.S.S. Virginia* is scuttled by her crew on the James River, Va.

All of *"Pook's Turtles"* are still actively engaged on the Mississippi.

May 1862 (Cont.)

The Fall of Natchez, Miss., May 12, 1862

12   *Iroquois* Cdr. James S. Palmer demands the surrender of Natchez. Without troops, Mayor John Hunter surrenders without resistance.

Brig. Gen. Martin Luther Smith takes command of Vicksburg.
Limited fortification of the city begins.
3,600 soldiers are available for the city's defense.

13   Natchez is occupied by Union forces.

15   David Farragut returns to New Orleans, leaving Palmer in command.

16   The 6th Michigan is in action at Grand Gulf, Miss.

Charles Davis is miffed that Charles Ellet's rams are not *under the Navy.*
Ellet agrees to *cooperate* and not *go on his own missions.*

18   Farragut's fleet arrives at Vicksburg.
Palmer wants to destroy Vicksburg.
Cdr. Samuel Phillips Lee on the *U.S.S. Oneida* calls for its surrender.

Defiant Lt. Col. James Autry, Vicksburg post commander, is the son of Alamo martyr Micajah Autry.
"Mississippians don't know how to surrender or care to learn."
The passive mayor tells Cdr. Lee that he created no defenses.
A single cannon fires on Vicksburg, awaiting the city's response

19   Vicksburg forces total about 4,000 Louisianians and Mississippians.

20   As McClellan nears Richmond, Johnston refuses to brief Davis.
Lee's attempts to talk to Johnston also prove fruitless.
The Davis-Johnston relationship is affecting operations and trust.

22   Pemberton receives hypothetical questions from key citizens.
His response shows Pemberton is *willing to abandon Charleston.*

23   Governor Pickens fires back that Charleston must be the priority.
Lee is on Pickens' side.
Pemberton does not grasp Southern fanaticism to *The Cause.*

24   Farragut arrives at Vicksburg with 1,500 of Benjamin Butler's troops.

Vicksburg Is Under Fire, May 25, 1862

25   Farragut begins the bombardment of Vicksburg.
75% of the citizens take refuge far east of the city.

26   The *U.S.S. Richmond* and two transports appear at Grand Gulf, Miss.
The Brookhaven Light Artillery strikes the transport *Laurel* and quickly retires into the countryside.
U.S.S. Kimeo, Katahdin, and *Brooklyn* shell Grand Gulf in payback.
Grand Gulf surrenders and repays the Navy with wood and food.

May 1862 (Cont.)

26   A quick skirmish near Grand Gulf kills Maj. Frederick Boardman, 14th Wisconsin.

The Trans-Mississippi Department, C.S.A., is created.
Maj. Gen. Thomas C. Hindman is given command.

27   Vicksburg experiences Farragut's heaviest bombardment to date.

Pemberton announces he is abandoning batteries on Cole's Island.

28   Halleck is at Corinth after a month-long, mile-a-day Shiloh march.
He has entrenched every night of the march and took no losses.
His soldiers call him *"Old Brains."*

Sherman advances to within a mile of Corinth's main line.
Halleck refuses Grant's suggestion to encircle and trap Beauregard.

Lt. Isaac N. Brown commands the Yazoo City, Miss., Navy Yard.

29   Beauregard is using deception to sneak away from Corinth by rail.

The Fall of Corinth, Miss., May 30, 1862

30   C.S. deception delays Halleck, enabling a C.S. escape to Tupelo, Miss.
Johnston: ***"Losing Corinth has sealed Vicksburg's fate."***
Johnston is already washing his hands of Vicksburg, Davis' home.
The fall of Corinth also isolates the city of Memphis.
Fort Pillow's importance to the Union is greatly reduced.

Grant decides to quit the Army after the post-Shiloh drama.
Sherman presses Grant into a crucial decision to remain.

Farragut arrives in New Orleans.
He has completed **the Navy's most successful campaign**.

Butler's 1,500 soldiers remain in Baton Rouge.

Pemberton's army is being cannibalized for more important duties.

31   Johnston attacks isolated Union elements at Seven Pines, Va.
Johnston's plan is flawed in many ways, but briefly stalls the Union
advance.

Davis rides to the front and sees wounded Johnston riding to the rear.
Johnston is unconcerned about the pressure he is placing on Davis.
Davis confides to Lee that Lee will now command Johnston's army.

Kentucky elects a second Confederate governor, Richard Hawes.

June 1862

1   Davis replaces the wounded Johnston with Lee.
Lee will name Johnston's old command *Army of Northern Virginia*.
The rift between Johnston and Davis is becoming a chasm.

June 1862 (Cont.)

2   20,000 U.S. troops create a diversion to distract Pemberton's troops.

3   The last Confederate troops evacuate Corinth.

A raft built at Liverpool Landing near Satartia, Miss., closes Yazoo River traffic and protects hidden commercial steamboats.

Vicksburg's Maj. Gen. M.L. Smith orders cotton within 20 miles of Grand Gulf burned to keep it from U.S. capture.
850 Davis bales are burned, their net worth, $20.6 million in 2023 dollars at a war-inflated 1862 $1.50 per pound.

4   Arkansas is threatening to leave the Confederacy due to a lack of support from Richmond and a siphoning off of its soldiers to other states.

5   Charles Davis anchors his boats four miles upstream of Memphis.

The U.S.S. Winona reports a force of workers fortifying Grand Gulf.

Sherman visits a dejected Grant, pleading with him to stay.
Sherman uses his Shiloh turnaround, asking Grant wait for his.

The Battle and Surrender of Memphis, Tenn., June 6, 1862

6   **The *U.S.S. Cairo* opens fire first at Memphis.**
Ellet frustrates Davis by pushing his rams ahead of Davis' gunboats.
The damaged *U.S.S. Queen of the West* requires beaching.

A sharpshooter's bullet strikes Charles Ellet in the leg.
The Gunboat Flotilla and U.S. Rams devastate the Confederate Navy.
Memphis surrenders.

Grant writes to Sherman that he will remain in the Army.
Sherman: *"You can't stay away a week if armies are moving."*

7   The *C.S.S. General Polk* and *Livingston* escape to Haynes Bluff, Miss.

9   The Union Navy is engaged in *an affair* at Grand Gulf.

10   Sherman's prediction about Grant's turnaround comes true.
Halleck restores Grant's command of the Army of the Tennessee.
Sherman, in effect, has saved the war and the Union.

11   The captured *Alfred Robb* is the *Robb*, **the first U.S. *tinclad*.**

South Carolina governor Pickens' sends Davis a message of *"no confidence"* in John Pemberton.
"Pemberton does not possess the confidence of citizens or troops. Everyone has lost confidence and many suspect treachery."
Pemberton longs to return to Virginia to be near his family.

12   The *U.S.S. Cairo* is ordered to return to Fort Pillow, Tenn.

June 1862 (Cont.)

16 Secessionville, S.C., is Pemberton's largest battle to date.
6,500 Union soldiers attack his garrison of 500 but withdraw.
The battle exposes Pemberton's desire *to lead from the rear*.

17 Halleck gives Grant command of the District of West Tennessee.

The *U.S.S. Mound City* is tragically hit in battle at St. Charles, Ark.
Of her 175 crew, 82 are buried at the site. Only 25 are uninjured.

18 Sherman is serving as the military governor of Memphis.

G.W. Morgan defeats Carter Stevenson at Cumberland Gap, Ky.

20 Van Dorn commands Southern Mississippi and Eastern Louisiana.
He enhances the defenses around Vicksburg with 10,000 troops.

Farragut again steams from Baton Rouge for Vicksburg.

Braxton Bragg replaces Beauregard in the Western Department.

21 Brig. Gen. Thomas Williams departs for Vicksburg on transports.
Lincoln visits Scott who suggests Halleck as Army senior general.
Halleck sends Grant to Memphis to oversee the military district.

Col. Charles Ellet, Ram genius, dies of his Memphis wound.
Lt. Col. Alfred Ellet replaces his brother as Ram Fleet commander.

25 Farragut returns to Vicksburg with a larger fleet.
He also has Thomas Williams' 3,000 soldiers.
Williams is ordered by Butler to cut a canal through DeSoto Point.

John Bowen's brigade arrives in Vicksburg by train from Jackson.

26 Union mortars under Porter open fire again on Vicksburg.

RAdm. Andrew Foote dies of *Bright's Disease* from his wound.
Charles Davis is promoted to the flag-officer rank of commodore.

27 Porter shells the city ahead of Farragut's running of the batteries.
2:00 a.m. – Farragut runs his ocean-going ships by Vicksburg to link
with the Army's Western Gunboat Flotilla.
Farragut's fleet suffers a great deal passing the Vicksburg batteries.
He is dismayed when only half of his vessels pass, severing his force.

Young Vicksburg resident Lucy McRae on the threat to Vicksburg:
*"Vicksburg, however, put on her war clothes, and cannon were
rushed to the riverfront; forts sprang into sight in a short time."*

New England soldiers and 1,200 slaves begin a DeSoto Point canal.

Vicksburg's defenders are under direct command of Earl Van Dorn.

Mortar boats remain at Vicksburg with some Union vessels.

June 1862 (Cont.)

27 The *U.S.S. Monarch* and *Lancaster* are first into the Yazoo River.

Mrs. Alice Gamble is Vicksburg's first citizen bombardment death.

28 Farragut departs for New Orleans.

July 1862

1 Charles Davis and the Gunboat Flotilla link up with Farragut's vessels.
Davis: *"Vicksburg must surrender or be destroyed."*

10 Porter leads his mortar fleet downriver from Vicksburg.

11 Halleck is called to Washington as general-in-chief.
Grant takes command of west Tennessee and north Mississippi.

Congress honors the late Alfred Foote for his Western gallantry.

12 Johnston complains that the railroad system will cause him to fail.
Davis leaves him in position anyway.

Pemberton is excited about being recalled to Richmond near Pattie.
Unfortunately, the assignment falls through.

13 Rebel deserters reveal that the *C.S.S. Arkansas* is ready for action.

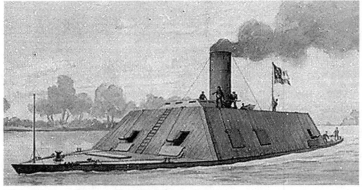

The *C.S.S. Arkansas* by R.G. Skerrett, 1904.
From the U.S. Naval Historical Center courtesy of the Navy Art Collection.

July 1862 (Cont.)

14 *C.S.S. Arkansas*, declared operational, departs Yazoo City, Miss.

New England soldiers are dying in droves in the canal swamps.

15 The *C.S.S. Arkansas*, under Isaac Brown, mauls Farragut's U.S. fleet.
The *U.S.S. Essex, Carondolet, Queen of the West, and Tyler* are engaged.

July 1862 (Cont.)

15 The *C.S.S. Arkansas* kills 13 U.S. sailors and wounds 36.
The *Arkansas* suffers 12 killed and 18 wounded.

A *"floating trash heap"* with an unskilled crew has shamed Farragut.
Farragut is *mortified* by the embarrassment to his fleet.
He seeks revenge on a vessel with *"mismatched engines."*

16 Grant takes command of the District of West Tennessee.

17 The *Second Confiscation Act* frees slaves of disloyal masters.
It allows *property* of disloyal citizens to be confiscated.
The Act forbids troops from returning slaves to their masters.

The *U.S. Militia Act* allows black inductions into military service.
It also provides for a state militia draft system.

Lincoln signs an act to create *National Military Cemeteries*.

21 Sherman arrives to command in Memphis.

22 The Dix-Hill Cartel sets prisoner exchange protocols.

Bowen is assisting with Vicksburg fortification designs.

The Federal Ram *Sumter* passes the Vicksburg batteries.
The *U.S.S. Essex* and *Queen of the West* attack the *C.S.S. Arkansas*
at Vicksburg.

23 Halleck is recalled to Washington to replace McClellan.

24 A falling river is forcing a Union withdrawal at Vicksburg.
Farragut's ocean-going vessels require higher stages.
Work on the DeSoto Point canal has stopped.

26 The bombardment of Vicksburg ends.
William's Ditch canal is abandoned; 600 graves are found.

27 500 blacks are found abandoned, overworked, and starving on
DeSoto Point.
The slaves did not receive their promised freedom for labor.

28 Davis takes the Flotilla to Helena, Ark., costing him his command.

30 Theophilus Holmes replaces the Trans-Mississippi Dept.'s Hindman.
The unpopular Hindman was removed at the request of citizens.

August 1862

1 Fox and Welles are lobbying for Navy command of the Army Flotilla.

3 The hastily repaired *C.S.S. Arkansas* departs for Baton Rouge.

Indiana's John Usher asks Lincoln for *"a special Vicksburg Army."*

4 Maj. Gen. John Breckinridge's Confederate force arrives at Baton
Rouge, La.

August 1862 (Cont.)
The Battle of Baton Rouge, La., August 5, 1862

5   Van Dorn orders an expedition to retake Baton Rouge.
Breckinridge only has 2,600 effectives when attacked.

Brig. Gen. Thomas R. Williams is killed in his successful charge.
"Dirty Bill" Porter with the *U.S.S. Essex* and *Sumter* repel infantry.

Casualties:
U.S., 383
C.S., 456

Mary Todd Lincoln's half-brother, C.S. Lt. Alexander Humphreys
Aleck Todd is killed at Baton Rouge.

Governor Pickens asks Davis to replace Pemberton with Beauregard.

Lloyd Tilghman is exchanged for Brig. Gen. John F. Reynolds.

6   After only 23 days of service, the struggling *C.S.S. Arkansas* is failing.
Her crew destroys her as she faces the approaching *U.S.S. Essex*.
The loss of the *Arkansas* ends Breckinridge's effort at Baton Rouge.

Bowen arrives nearby a day late, camping on the Comite River.

7   *C.S.S. Arkansas* survivors steal away from Nolan Plantation.

11   ***"The C.S.S. Arkansas was our last hope for the Mississippi
River."***

Farragut leaves Vicksburg behind him for deeper waters.
The lack of Army-Navy cooperation is being noted.
Split Army-Navy gunboat responsibilities spell a change.

12   Breckinridge falls back to a defensive position at Port Hudson, La.

15   New York press: *"Yazoo River water creates a River of Death."*

Bowen's brigade is ordered to Camp Moore near Tangipahoa, La.
Camp Moore is the largest and main training camp in Louisiana.

16   Davis asks Governor Pickens to have confidence in Pemberton.
He will detail an engineer officer to help him.

18   Benjamin Butler deploys to New Orleans from Baton Rouge.

Vicksburg sends 6,000 muskets to the Trans-Mississippi Dept.

20   Pickens rebuffs Davis' request to support Pemberton.
Southern bias against the Pennsylvania Confederate is obvious.

21   A brief U.S. attack on Haynes Bluff captures an old Spanish cannon.

22   Two Mississippians share their torpedo designs with the C.S. Navy.

23   Bowen skirmishes at Greenville, Miss., with soldiers and gunboats.

August 1862 (Cont.)

25   Missouri and Ohio units land again at Bolivar, north of Scott, Miss.

Recruitment of blacks soldiers in the South Carolina Sea Islands is approved.

28   John McClernand is approved for a leave of absence to recruit troops.

29   Gen. William N.R. Beall assumes command of Port Hudson, La.
Pemberton is relieved in South Carolina, replaced by Beauregard.

30   John Pope is defeated at the Second Battle of Bull Run.

Bragg's amazing rail movement via Mobile helps capture Richmond, Ky.

Davis vetoes Secretary of War Randolph's plan to trade cotton with Northern interests for Northern food and salt.
Randolph's relationship with Davis is weakened.

September 1862

1   Maj. Samuel Lockett begins a military terrain survey of Vicksburg.
"No engineer has been presented a greater topographical puzzle."
He begins a *choking point* raft on the Yazoo River at Snyder's Mill.
Scores of packets are yet hidden safely away in the Yazoo tributaries.

6   John Sidney Bowen is born to John and Mary at Camp Sterling Price at Milldale, a few miles northwest of Vicksburg.

8   The *U.S.S. Essex* is severely damaged by fire from Port Hudson, La.

The ironclad *U.S.S. St. Louis* is renamed the *Baron DeKalb*.
This is in anticipation of the Navy assuming ironclad command.
The U.S. Navy already has a *U.S.S. St. Louis* in service.

12   A fatal accident is caused by *Douglas the Camel* exciting a horse near Iuka, Miss.
The accident is the earliest mention of Douglas, mascot of the 43^d Mississippi Infantry.

Lt. Cdr. Thomas O. Selfridge, Jr., commands the *U.S.S. Cairo*.

17   Pemberton, now relieved at Charleston, is called to Richmond.
His replacement Beauregard finds Pemberton's fortifications *faulty*.
Pemberton did poorly in battlefield engineering at the USMA.

Hugh Ewing, distinguished at Antietam, joins Sherman's XV Corps.
Ewing is Sherman's adopted brother *and brother-in-law*.

The Battle of Iuka, Miss., September 19, 1862

19   Grant and William Rosecrans battle Sterling Price.

Grant has little tactical control over Rosecrans.

September 1862 (Cont.)

19   Reviews at Iuka are mixed, though declared a Union victory.
Reports of Grant's drinking surface.
The battle begins an enmity between Grant and Rosecrans.

22   Lincoln issues the preliminary Emancipation Proclamation.

Sherman is considered the *benevolent* governor of Memphis.
Porter is stunned when Welles assigns him a command in the West.

23   Brown is tasked to build a monster 300-foot ironclad at Yazoo City.
The Yazoo Navy Yard is hampered by a lack of building materials.

24   Sherman burns Randolph, Tenn., after a U.S. gunboat is fired upon.

Beauregard assumes command in Charleston.

28   The 33ᵈ Illinois is engaged in a skirmish at Friar's Point, Miss.

30   Self-promoting McClernand accompanies Lincoln to Antietam.

Porter's rapid, diverse fleet plan is reshaping naval warfare.

October 1862

1   Congress transfers the Western Gunboat Flotilla to the U.S. Navy.
The Flotilla is redesignated the *Mississippi Gunboat Squadron.*
Porter wants Ellet's independent rams rolled into a new entity.

Pemberton is promoted to lieutenant general to resolve issues with
   rank in the Western theater.
He is given the Department of Mississippi and East Louisiana, *one of*
   the most complex, difficult departments in the Confederacy.
Randolph: *"Your first priority is to defend your department.*
   You will report directly to the War Department."
Pemberton is caught between two bosses with different mindsets.

Earl Van Dorn will be Pemberton's cavalry chief.

Charles Davis is reassigned as Chief, U.S. Bureau of Navigation.
He is promoted to rear admiral to protect his reputation.

Grant assembles his army at Grand Junction, Tenn.

Bowen, Stevenson, and Loring replace Maj. Gen. Mansfield Lovell.

The Battle of Corinth, Miss., Oct. 3–4, 1862

3   Price and Van Dorn must hold Grant in lower Tennessee.
They combine and attack the rail crossroads at Corinth.

Price sees *Old Abe*, eagle mascot of the 8ᵗʰ Wisconsin, in battle.
"Capture or kill that bird at all hazards. I would rather get that
   screaming Yankee buzzard than capture a whole brigade."

October 1862 (Cont.)

4   Price and Van Dorn fail to retake Corinth.
    Bowen is livid at Van Dorn and Lovell's failure to expand advances.

    Casualties:
    U.S., 2,359
    C.S., 4,838

    McClernand holds a meeting with Lincoln at Antietam.

    Pressing England's support using *Cotton Diplomacy* has failed.
    England had stockpiled cotton during bumper crops just in case.
    Europe develops other cotton sources in Egypt and East India.
    Cotton prices are beginning to skyrocket in the United States.

5   John Bowen saves retreating Confederates from classmate James
    McPherson at Davis Bridge on Tennessee's Hatchie River.

    Maj. Gen E.O.C. Ord is seriously wounded.

6   Fox is pressing for Porter to command the Gunboat Squadron.
    Welles convinces Lincoln who considers Porter brash and impulsive.
    The choice is *unsatisfactory to many*; *his peculiar skills are needed.*

7   Rosecrans implores Grant to defeat the retreating Confederates.
    Grant returns to Corinth when he learns his friend Ord is wounded.
    The rift between Rosecrans and Grant is ever widening.

    Lt. Cdr. Selfridge completes repairs to the *U.S.S. Cairo* at Memphis.

8   Van Dorn's weary soldiers reach Holly Springs, Miss., after Corinth.

9   Pemberton arrives with his staff in Jackson, Miss.
    He is Samuel Cooper and Robert E. Lee's choice for Vicksburg.
    Asst. Adj. Robert Memminger: *"The whole department is in chaos."*
    Pemberton launches immediate improvements in the Department.

    Pemberton lacks confidence and is anxious to be near Pattie again.

10 C.S. governors are complaining about *their* troops being sent
    exclusively, it seems, to Virginia, while they lack troops at home.

14 Pemberton establishes his command at Jackson.
    Lockett is completing his topographical survey of Vicksburg.

15 Newly promoted RAdm. Porter takes command of the ironclads.
    Porter is known to be able to identify and solve problems, *whatever*.
    Porter presses for many *tinclads* for inland streams and a system of
    convoy and shipping protection against river raiders.

    McClernand is planning his *independent* Vicksburg command.
    He sends his proposal for a *Vicksburg Army* to Halleck.

19 Col. Mortimer Leggett: *"A hellish attempt is afoot to ruin Grant."*

October 1862 (Cont.)

20 Lincoln allows McClernand to recruit in Indiana, Illinois, and Iowa.
McClernand departs to recruit his Army to capture Vicksburg.
Lincoln's McClernand orders are not shared with Grant or Halleck.

21 Davis:
"We are at our maximum; the enemy is just building."

25 Grant commands the Department of the Tennessee.
Grant's force reaches 48,500.

Bowen celebrates his 33^d birthday at Lumpkin's Mill, Miss.
Vicksburg is Officially on Grant's Horizon

26 **Grant mentions Vicksburg to Halleck for the first time.**
Grant lays out the framework for Vicksburg's capture, if reinforced.

November 1862

1 Maj. Gen. Nathaniel Banks commands the Army of the Gulf.
Lincoln hopes that Banks can cure the ill will left by Benjamin Butler.

New Orleans may help test Lincoln's *10% reconstruction plan.*
New state governments with 10% male loyalty and no slavery.

Ellet is tasked to build and command the new quick riverine
response team, the Mississippi Marine Brigade (MMB).

2 Without a Halleck response, Grant moves to Grand Junction, Tenn.
Grant: *"The Campaign against Vicksburg has begun."*

Union forces capture Ripley and nearby Orizaba, Miss.

4 Grant arrives at Grand Junction, Tenn., with five divisions.
He headquarters in a large home, Hancock Hall.

5 Grant sends Charles Hamilton's cavalry toward Holly Springs.
Confederates retreat south to Abbeville, Miss., on the Tallahatchie.

6 Antietam's Stephen Dill Lee is promoted to brigadier general.
He is installed as Pemberton's artillery chief.

The Mississippi Central Railroad (MCRR) Campaign

8 Grant begins his Mississippi Central RR Campaign with 60-70,000.
Union cavalry skirmish at Coldwater, Old Lamar, and Hudsonville.

9 Grant asks about Union units passing Cairo (McClernand's army).

10 Halleck makes Memphis the center of **joint operations**.
Grant is confused and upset. Memphis is in *his* district.
Grant is not considering a role for the Navy.
Halleck fails to mention McClernand.

11 Grant wants Chaplain John Eaton to be Contraband *Superintendent.*
Eaton hopes to avoid working with camp contrabands (freedmen).

November 1862 (Cont.)

The Mississippi Central Railroad Campaign Theatre

11   Grant mentors to Eaton, *"I will take care of you."*
National freedmen policies are developing with Grant and Eaton.
Sherman is resisting using freedmen except as pioneer labor.

Nathan B. Forrest raids Jackson, Tenn., to wreck Grant's supply lines.

12   Joe Johnston advises Richmond that he is able to resume command.
Johnston is appointed to command the Department of the West.
He commands Pemberton and Bragg.
He has much responsibility but little authority.
His staff reports to Davis.

Johnston believes his armies need to be consolidated.
He believes that he needs the Trans-Mississippi Dept. combined with
     Pemberton's Department.
Davis' failure to approve a unified command will be a crucial error.
Pemberton and Holmes will be separated by the river and distance.

13   Holly Springs, Miss., falls to Grant's cavalry after a brief skirmish.
Grant orders Sherman with at least two divisions to Oxford, Miss.

Grant sets policies under Eaton to deal with contrabands in camp.
These discussions coalesce U.S. policies toward freedmen.

November 1862 (Cont.)

13   John Eaton plans a large contraband center at Grand Junction, Tenn.

John Pope is taking complete credit for Island No. 10 and Fort Henry. The Navy's Foote: *"Not a single shot was fired by the Army."*

14   Grant tells Sherman to prepare for a southward push.

The 2ᵈ Illinois Cavalry reports more skirmishing near Holly Springs.

15   A Corinth court of inquiry is brought by Bowen against Van Dorn.

Grant is ready to move on Vicksburg.

19   Pemberton is informed that he is now under Braxton Bragg.
Adj. Gen. Samuel Cooper tells Bragg that he *must help Vicksburg*.
Pemberton's commissary orders rations for 10,000 for five months.

20   Mary Bowen joins her husband at camp at Abbeville, Miss.
Mary Loughborough, also from Carondelet, Mo., is with her husband,
 Maj. James Loughborough.

Pemberton evacuates Abbeville 11 miles north of Oxford, Miss.

Porter and Grant meet and size each other up in Cairo, Ill.
Porter asks Sherman if Grant is considering a move on Vicksburg.
Sherman: *"If he is, he hasn't told me."*

21   Joe Johnston sends a large, diversionary raid to west Tennessee.

Randolph resigns when Davis reverses his Harper's Ferry decision.
Davis makes James Seddon his fourth Secretary of War in two years.

22   Porter orders the *U.S.S. Cairo* to Helena, Ark.

23   Thomas Weldon is building a Yazoo blocking raft at Haynes Bluff.
The Weldon Brothers built the Vicksburg and Raymond courthouses.
George Weldon was his partner in the company.

24   Isaac Brown recommends a Confederate barricade on the Yazoo Pass
 near Helena.

26   The Joseph Davis family settles at Fleetwood near Bolton, Miss.
He acquired the property from Thomas J. Catchings.

27   Grant's 40,000 depart Grand Junction, pushing Pemberton south.
Pemberton calls for 4,000 slaves to fortify Grenada, Miss.

Maj. Gen Alvin P. Hovey moves from Helena toward Grenada.
Maj. Gen. Cadwallader C. Washburn's 1,900 horse soldiers focus on
 Grenada and the railroads.
Charles Hamilton's Federal cavalry leaves Grand Junction.

Camp Vernon at the Tippah's mouth is deserted by the 33ᵈ
 Mississippi.

November 1862 (Cont.)

27 W.W. Loring is called to Jackson as Pemberton's second in command.
*With Johnston as his superior and Loring as his second in command,
Pemberton is doomed from the onset.*

28 The *U.S.S. Carondolet* and others arrive at Milliken's Bend, La.

Hovey, with cavalry and infantry, follows Washburn to Grenada.
U.S. Maj. Gen. John Logan breaks camp at LaGrange, Tenn.

29 Grant sets up headquarters at Holly Springs and Waterford, Miss.
Sherman reaches Wyatt, Miss., on the Tallahatchie north of Oxford.
Washburn reaches Mitchell's Crossroads near Charleston, Miss.

Griffith's Texas cavalry leaves Toby Tubby Creek just north of
Oxford to intercept Washburn.

Union artillery opens fire on Pemberton's line on the Tallahatchie.
Pemberton departs Jackson to meet Grant's southern incursion.

Numerous skirmishes are reported in the Holly Springs area.

30 Davis orders six black Union prisoners in Georgia executed.

Hovey's cavalry approaches Grenada.
Pemberton believes that his flank is threatened.

The 1st Indiana Cavalry burns the steamer *Half Moon* on the
Tallahatchie River.

December 1862

1 Union troops reach the line of the Tallahatchie River.
Pemberton abandons the Tallahatchie south for the Yalobusha River.

The 3d Michigan Cavalry is engaged at Oxford, Miss.

Louisiana refuses to send any more troops outside of the state.
"All 30 of our regiments are outside of Louisiana."

At Vicksburg, Maj. Gen. Martin L. Smith complains:
"There is no process for transporting or purchasing rations."

2 Confederates fall back to Oxford.
Union forces cross the Tallahatchie River unopposed.
Sherman to Grant: *"Rebels may be in retreat toward Grenada."*
Union troops take Oxford after a brief skirmish.

The Battle of Oakland, Miss., December 3, 1862

3 Grant moves to Oxford, Miss.

The Rebs are bivouacked near Springdale, south of the Yocona.
The 3d Louisiana hears artillery to the west.
Union forces are trying to swing around to Grenada.

December 1862 (Cont.)

3   Griffith's Texas cavalry attacks Washburn's 1,900 cavalry.
He successfully stops a Union flanking move.
Union forces do not continue, fearing a C.S. build up at Coffeeville.

Washburn now fears that he will be flanked and withdraws.
Pemberton's forces withdraw to Grenada at the same time.

4   Grant outlines his joint operation for Vicksburg to Halleck.
The *U.S.S. Cairo* departs for the Yazoo River.

The Union Army occupies Oxford, Miss.
Rebs stop at Coffeeville, Miss., and entrench along the Yalobusha.
Johnston to Bragg: *"Delay Grant by raids on his supply lines."*

Battle of Coffeeville, Miss., December 5, 1862

5   Brig. Gen. Lloyd Tilghman hides C.S. brigades and artillery on the
Water Valley road.
He ambushes Col. Theophilus Dickey's U.S. cavalry near Coffeeville.

Grant to Halleck: *"Pursuing the enemy. Captured and killed many."*
Concurrently, Grant's line of defense is collapsing at Coffeeville.
Dickey is pushed back three miles to the head of the U.S. column.
Dickey retreats to Water Valley.

Grant is defeated by *Tilghman and others paroled at Fort Donelson.*
The battle halts Grant's invasion as he pulls back to Oxford.
In Oxford, Grant and Sherman discuss using McClernand's Army.
Halleck directs Grant to have Sherman in Memphis by Dec. 20.

Federal cavalry is pressing the rear of Sterling Price's columns.
Skirmishes are the norm along the Union route in north Mississippi.

6   Porter's dream flagship *U.S.S. Black Hawk* is commissioned at Cairo.

7   Hovey returns to Helena, ineffective in destroying the MCRR.

Pemberton withdraws as Hovey threatens his communications line.

Van Dorn is replaced by Loring as infantry commander of 1st Corps.

8   The U.S. *Proclamation of Amnesty and Reconstruction* is issued.

Davis to Lee: *"I am going home to inspire my people.*
I will give up middle Tennessee to save Vicksburg."

Grant asks Sherman to spend the night to talk about Vicksburg.
Sherman will have a division and troops at Memphis and Helena.
The plan is for him to cross the Yazoo River near Vicksburg.

Halleck diverts McClernand's ally Samuel Curtis to Missouri.
Halleck is helping the Grant-Sherman team over McClernand.

The *U.S.S. Cairo* arrives at the Yazoo River, taking two days to recoal.

December 1862 (Cont.)

9 Grant tells Sherman:
*"I will hold Pemberton at Grenada or follow him to the gates of
Vicksburg."*
Halleck to Grant:
"Lincoln may insist on a separate Vicksburg commander."

10 Bragg orders Forrest to get going on Grant's supply-line raids.
Davis trains to Mississippi from Richmond on his *inspiration trip*.

11 Grant's quartermaster says he can't meet Grant's boat timetable.

Forrest departs Bragg to disrupt Union supplies and communications.

Selfridge requests that the *U.S.S. Cairo* be used for **minesweeping**.

12 Halleck orders Grant and Sherman to ignore McClernand, absorb his
troops, and move on Vicksburg.
Grant orders Sherman with one division to Memphis.
He is to organize, as he sees fit, ALL forces he finds at Memphis.
He is then to move down the Mississippi River as soon as possible.
*"And, with the cooperation of the gunboat fleet under command of
Flag-Officer Porter, proceed to the reduction of that place - as
your own judgment may dictate."*

The Mississippi Gunboat Squadron is clearing Yazoo River mines.
The *U.S.S. Cairo* is sunk in 12 minutes by two friction-primer mines.
Her sailors safely escape and retrieve what valuables they can.
The *U.S.S. Pittsburg* crushes the *Cairo's* chimneys to conceal her.

Sherman arrives in Memphis, excited and concerned.
"All this should be done before the winter rains."

Davis, in Murfreesboro, wants 9,000 Bragg soldiers for Vicksburg.
Johnston argues that the soldiers are badly needed in Tennessee, *a
typical Davis-Johnston impasse, which Davis always wins*.

John Logan's Camp Turnabout is on the Yocona River with 7,000.

13 Forrest arrives on the east bank of the Tennessee River.
The luxury steamer *New Uncle Sam* is now Porter's *U.S.S. Black
Hawk*.

14 Sherman to a friend:
*"My hobby always has been the Mississippi, and my faith cannot be
shaken that the possession of this great Artery will be the most
powerful auxiliary in the final steps that must restore the
Sovereign power of our Government."*

Grant thanks Halleck for showing confidence to Elihu Washburn.
Grant hopes that his good wing and division commanders will not be
outranked by McClernand's staff.

December 1862 (Cont.)

14 McClernand, 50, is away preparing to marry his deceased wife Sarah's 18-year-old sister.

Vicksburg corn is already $25 a barrel; flour, $80 a barrel; bacon, $1 per lb.; pork, 70 cents per lb. *Multiply 1863 prices by 36 to realize 2023 dollars, e.g. flour is $2,880 a barrel in 2023 dollars.*

15 Pemberton: *"The threat to the Yazoo Navy Yard is not significant."*

Forrest crosses the Tennessee at Clifton to divert Grant's attention. Grenville Dodge: *"No Rebs at Savannah. Check Forrest at Clifton."* Union pickets estimate Forrest's strength at 3,000.

The U.S. Quartermaster to Grant: *"I have 20 large steamboats and more coming."* Jesse Grant and Julia are at Walter House in Holly Springs.

Grant is unaware the rear of his army is in danger. 1,800 Confederate cavalry troopers cross the Tennessee River. The Kentucky-to-Mississippi rail line is critical to his operations.

17 Grant's G.O. 11 expels Jewish merchants from his camps.

Reports: *"10,000 C.S. cavalry and artillery are across the Tennessee River."* Forrest skirmishes with Union scouts.

18 Grant's order assuming overall operational command takes effect. Sherman, Porter, and McClernand *do not receive the order*. Sherman is two days from launching his operation. Porter arrives in Memphis on his flagship *U.S.S. Black Hawk*. McClernand is still honeymooning.

Porter's luxurious flagship, the *U.S.S. Black Hawk*.
(USNHHC)

December 1862 (Cont.)

18   Grant to Welles:
"McClernand is nowhere to be seen, but I will cooperate."

Grant, trying to trap Forrest, asks the Navy for more gunboats.
Grant: *"5,000-10,000 cavalry nearing our base at Jackson, Tenn."*
Grant to Dodge: *"Combine Corinth-Jackson forces to drive Forrest."*
Col. William Lowe is ordered from Fort Henry to stymie Forrest.

Jeremiah Sullivan: *"Reb numbers are 10,000 to 20,000 and rising."*
Grant: *"I expect a good report tomorrow."*
Just then, Grant's telegraph goes dead, a bad omen.

Battle of Lexington, Tenn., December 18, 1862

18   Forrest routs Col. Robert Ingersoll at Beech Creek.
He takes 140 prisoners, two 3-inch rifles, and other equipment.

19   Davis and Johnston travel from Chattanooga to Vicksburg.
Davis orders Carter Stevenson's division deployed to Pemberton.
Davis has overruled a miffed Johnston again.

Julia Grant, alerted by a C.S. colonel's wife, flees Holly Springs.
Van Dorn departs Grenada with 3,500 to attack Holly Springs.

Confederates are rampaging around Jackson, Tenn.
Forrest sends 600 infantry and two guns toward Jackson.

The 39th and 27th Ohio arrive by train.
Jeremiah Sullivan drives the Confederates back at Jackson, Tenn.

Van Dorn's Raid at Holly Springs, Miss., December 20, 1862

20   Halleck: *"The Vicksburg operation is under Grant's command."*
James McPherson asks to go along on Grant's Campaign.

Julia and Jesse Grant are now with Grant in Oxford.

Van Dorn's raid destroys Grant's supply depot at Holly Springs.
Grant's communications are severed for a week.
His army loses winter rations, clothing, and supplies for two weeks.
Forage for his horses is also lost.
Losses are estimated at $3 million, $108 million in 2023 dollars.
Grant and Eaton were together in conference during the raid.

Pemberton reinforces Vicksburg.
Davis, Johnston, and Pemberton are in Vicksburg.
Davis: *"This city must be held at all costs."*

Forrest orders tearing up 70 miles of rails and burning stations.
Confederates are threatening the main Union base at Trenton, Tenn.
Union scouts report Forrest closing fast in two columns.
Maj. James Fry surrenders to Forrest at Trenton, Tenn.

December 1862 (Cont.)

20 A Union soldier:
"If only Forrest's boots were in the road, we would retreat."

Grant pulls back to Grand Junction, Tenn.
Sherman departs Memphis with 32,000 troops, confident that Grant
  will be engaging Pemberton near Grenada as Sherman lands.
Frederick Steele awaits him at Helena, Ark., with reinforcements.

21 Davis and Johnston are inspecting the Vicksburg fortifications.
Davis asks Holmes for 10,000 Arkansas soldiers for Vicksburg.

A large Union convoy is reported moving south from Memphis.

Sherman and Porter learn of Van Dorn's raid but receive no recall.
James McPherson orders a retreat to Oxford.

22 Forrest paroles 400-500 Trenton prisoners.
He sends 800-900 to Columbus, Ky.
Forrest pushes toward Union City, another key rail hub.

Halleck wants Columbus, Ky., *Gibraltar of the West, held at all
  costs.*
Federal consternation has descended into terror.

Sherman assembles his army at Friar's Point, Miss., and departs.
All Union vessels are assembled at Friar's Point.

Johnston: *"Vicksburg is the usual defect in Confederate engineering.
  You put an army inside this ring and your whole Army will be
  trapped."*
Davis believes the city is impregnable.
The executive party inspects Haynes Bluff.

Grant reestablishes his headquarters at Holly Springs.
Sherman's command boat is the steamer *Forest Queen.*

23 Sherman gives his commanders hand-drawn maps and orders.
Union gunboats staged at Vicksburg enter the Yazoo River.
Grant writes to Sherman about his return to Grand Junction.
His missive will reach Sherman after his defeat at Chickasaw Bayou.

24 An inspection of troops is held for the Davis Presidential Party.
Jefferson Davis travels to Grenada.

A Christmas Ball is held at the Balfour House in Vicksburg.
The Lake Providence, La., outpost reports many Union steamers
  headed south.

Col. Phillip Fall canoes from DeSoto Point in a driving storm with
  the message telegraphed from Lake Providence for M.L. Smith.
Maj. Gen. Smith orders an evacuation of Vicksburg.

December 1862 (Cont.)

24   Sherman's expedition arrives at Milliken's Bend, La.

Pemberton redeploys another Grenada brigade to Vicksburg.

Davis' G.O. 111 will execute Ben Butler and his officers if captured. Captured black soldiers are to be turned over to state authorities.

The Yazoo River to Haynes Bluff is declared *clear of mines*.

25   3:00 a.m. – Drums roll to man defenses north of Vicksburg. Stephen D. Lee will defend from Chickasaw Bayou to Haynes Bluff.

The Union fleet is anchored at the mouth of Yazoo River.
A. J. *Whiskey* Smith wastes a day severing the Desoto Point railroad not knowing the railroad bridges were already washed out.
The precious day allows Pemberton to strengthen his force and lines.

Grant's army is spending Christmas along the Tallahatchie River.

Davis and Johnston review troops at Grenada.
Pemberton heads for Vicksburg to assume overall command.
Forrest departs Union City, Tenn., planning a destructive escape.

McClernand marries his teenage sister-in-law, Minerva Dunlap.
He intends for her to accompany him on *his* Vicksburg Campaign after the honeymoon.

26   Davis speaks to the legislature in Jackson to inspire the state.

Pemberton arrives at Smith's Balfour House headquarters.
Carter Stevenson's division is deployed to Vicksburg.
Johnston's staff is asked to help facilitate moving Grenada troops.

Sherman lands at Johnson's Plantation on the Yazoo River in sight of Chickasaw and Drumgould bluffs with 60 guns and four divisions.

27   Sherman organizes for battle and surveys the battlefield.
"There are many obstacles to overcome just for a fair fight."
Col. John DeCourcy's brigade pushes back the Confederate pickets.
DeCourcy is a veteran of the *Crimean War* and *Premier Baron of Ireland*.

Porter's second Squadron division proceeds up the Yazoo River.
The *U.S.S. Benton* and *Baron DeKalb* are removing mines.
The *Louisville* and *Cincinnati* are attracting Confederate attention.

Silent Haynes Bluff batteries suddenly blaze away at the *Benton*.
Lt. Cdr. William Gwin on the *Benton's* deck is drastically wounded.

Porter to Sherman: *"The Benton has been a good deal cut up. Keep it quiet. Don't let the Confederate gunners know."*

December 1862 (Cont.)

27 The U.S.N.'s **first hospital ship** is commissioned, *U.S.S. Red Rover.*
Nuns are aboard, the **first onboard female volunteers.**
Flag Officer Charles Davis:
*"No one but those who have witnessed it can comprehend the
sufferings to which our sick have been exposed by the absence of
proper accommodations on board the gunboats and by the
necessity for frequent and sometimes hasty change of place. The
arrival of the Red Rover will put a stop to all this."*

The first hospital ship, *U.S.S. Red Rover.*
Courtesy of the National Library of Medicine.

December 1862 (Cont.)

28 Pemberton's force arrives from Grenada, with Sherman unaware.

A blinding fog slows Union operations.
Sherman continues off-loading at Chickasaw Bayou.
The Chicago Mercantile Battery arrives almost last.

The 3ᵈ Louisiana departs Greenville for Vicksburg.
Van Dorn returns to base after a 500-mile Holly Springs expedition.

DeCourcy's soldiers fight through heavy abatis toward the enemy.
Heavy fire from Chickasaw Bayou bluffs halts his advance.
Sherman assigns George Morgan the next morning's assault.
Morgan: *"I will be on those hills 10 minutes after I'm ordered."*

New York Herald: "Deadly black snipers are fighting with the Rebs."

Maj. Gen. Morgan Smith is seriously wounded in the hip.
A.J. *Whiskey* Smith assumes command of his division.

Col. Allen Thomas' C.S. brigade on the right flank is pushed back.

McClernand arrives in Memphis with a new wife and *no army.*

December 1862 (Cont.)

28   Loring's insubordinate, troublemaking style manifests itself.
"I do not think much of our commander (Pemberton)."

The Battle of Chickasaw Bayou, Miss., December 29, 1863

29   7:30 a.m. – Sherman attacks Vicksburg's northernmost heights with 30,720 and 54 guns.
Cocky George Morgan calls Sherman to the front: *"It's hopeless."*
Sherman, grimly:
"We will lose 5,000 men before we take Vicksburg and we may as well lose them here as anywhere else."

His soldiers are marching through freezing swamps under heavy fire, confronting overwhelming abatis.
Despite their challenges, Union soldiers sing *"Dinner in Vicksburg."*
They face 12,792 Confederates dug in on a desperately elevated bluff.

Sherman's casualties are 80 percent of those engaged in the fray.
In Crimea, the Charge of the Light Brigade loss was only 40 percent.

Casualties:
U.S., 208 K, 1,005 W, 583 C/M
C.S., 57 K, 120 W, 10 M

Camp Loring is on Knight's Creek, Graysport Road, near Grenada.

McClernand finds the letter reducing him to Corps commander.

Porter agrees Ellet's *Lioness* will lead tomorrow to Haynes Bluff.

Holmes to Davis regarding his request for 10,000 soldiers:
"Arkansas soldiers will desert if they are sent east of us."
Davis' manpower mill is essentially tapped out.

Sherman's Chickasaw soldiers sleep among the frozen dead.

30   Fog ends Sherman's hope for a secondary Haynes Bluff landing.

Sherman to Grant:
"I reached Vicksburg at the appointed time, landed, assaulted, and failed."

Porter: *"This was the only time I saw Sherman unhinged. At every point, he encountered obstacles of which he had never dreamed."*

31   Forrest blocks Rosecrans reinforcements at Stone's River.
Bragg does not have Carter Stevenson's 9,000 sent south by Davis.
Lt. Col. James L. Autry, the 1862 hero of Vicksburg, dies there.

Forrest orders his men to Parker's Crossroads and takes a beating.

D
Forces Collide to Control the Key
January-August 1863

January 1863

1   Lincoln's Emancipation Proclamation *reunification offe*r expires.
    A provision enables *freed slaves to become soldiers.*
    Hundreds of Union soldiers protest on hearing the news.

   Sherman's soldiers, back on the boats, depart for Milliken's Bend.
    Critics say Sherman wasted the entire day of December 26.
    Sherman: *"I could have taken Vicksburg on Christmas Day had*
      it not been for Halleck's delays."

   Brig. Gen. Winfield Scott Featherston is transferred from Virginia
      to Mississippi.

   The price of cotton has soared to $1.89 per lb.
    An 1863 bale is worth $30,000 in 2023 dollars; a 2023 bale is $375.

2   McClernand arrives at Milliken's Bend on the steamer *Tigress*.
    Outranked, Sherman has no option but to meet with him.
    Union forces have completely evacuated Chickasaw Bayou.
    The Rebel band teases them, playing *"Come Out of The Wilderness."*

   Loring takes command of the 1st Division, Army of Mississippi.
    The 3d Louisiana reaches Snyder's Mill north of Vicksburg.

3   Porter, Sherman, and McClernand hold their first joint ops meeting.
    An irate McClernand berates both, making an enemy of Porter.
    He solidifies Porter's *mediocre* relationship with Grant.
    McClernand protests to Stanton regarding Grant's actions.

   Lt. Cdr. Gwin, *Benton* commander, dies from his wounds of the 27th.
    Sherman writes to Grant, accepting *full blame* for Chickasaw Bayou.

4   McClernand's G.O. 1: <u>He</u> commands the *Army of the Mississippi*.
    He departs with transports and gunboats for Arkansas Post.
    The expedition could eventually lead to the capture of Little Rock.

January 1863 (Cont.)

4   The Arkansas Post expedition will certainly help lift the morale after Chickasaw Bayou.

Halleck instructs Grant to revoke G.O. 11 regarding the Jews.
Most Jews have already departed.

Davis arrives in Richmond after his journey to Mississippi.

5   *Memphis Daily Appeal:*
"Pemberton has foresight in anticipating the enemy."
He also still has Van Dorn and his cavalry to see for him.
He has decimated both Grant and Sherman's operations.

Arkansas, originally a Unionist state, is agitated with Davis:
"Our soldiers signed up to protect Arkansas also."

7   Halleck: *"Richmond papers report a rebel victory at Vicksburg."*
Grant is anxious to hear of Sherman's fate at Chickasaw Bayou.

McClernand constantly advises Lincoln on strategy and staff.
McClernand to Lincoln:
"Halleck possesses no genius, justice, generosity, or policy."

8   McClernand's Arkansas Post expedition reaches the White River.

9   Grant closes his headquarters at Holly Springs, Miss.
McClernand's force at Arkansas Post unloads at Notrib's farm.
Welles: *"If the Army had cooperated, Vicksburg would be ours.
Halleck is good for nothing."*

A C.S. Soldier: *"Mississippi is so poor you can hear it groan at night.
The people resent our soldiers more than any state we've been in."*

10   Grant returns to Memphis.
Displeased, he exerts his authority over McClernand.
Grant moves vulnerable Grand Junction contraband to Memphis.
Eaton: *"Their terror of being left behind made them swarm over the
freight and passenger cars, clinging to every available space, and
even crouching on roofs."*

Porter's fleet drops anchor three miles south of Fort Hindman, Ark.

11   Porter's fleet silences the big guns of Fort Hindman.

12   Porter and McClernand capture Arkansas Post and Fort Hindman.
An angered Grant orders them back to Vicksburg.
Grant relaxes when Sherman explains their goal and cooperation.

Halleck authorizes Grant to relieve McClernand.
Chief of staff John Rawlins relieves McClernand of expedition lead.

13   The 13th U. S. Infantry is on the steamer *Silver Queen.*

January 1863 (Cont.)

13   McClernand's task force departs Arkansas Post.
Grant to McPherson:
"I am in command of the Vicksburg operation."

18   Grant consults with McClernand, Sherman, and Porter.

19   The Arkansas Post task force is enroute to Milliken's Bend.

20   Lincoln is anxious for a canal to bypass Vicksburg.
Sherman is confident that slaves and his troops can dig the canal.

21   Halleck gives Grant troops in Arkansas to man both sides of the river.
Pemberton does not control the forces on both sides.
Coordination between Pemberton and the Trans-Mississippi is poor.

The Arkansas Post task force arrives back at Milliken's Bend.
107 Union transports and 20 gunboats prepare to go to Helena, Ark.

Halleck notifies Grant that Lincoln immediately revoked G.O. 11.

Bowen's men briefly mutiny over drilling and discipline.
Martin Green and Elijah Gates cool them down.
His Missouri troops are considered the *best trained in either army.*

22   Sherman's troops begin excavating the DeSoto Point canal.
Sherman is not convinced of its utility.
Porter believes the project is *"ridiculous."*

23   McClernand:
"Vicksburg is cut off from waterborne resupply and reinforcement."

The 13th U.S. Infantry camps at Young's Point to help dig the canal.
C.S. scouts report 107 steamers and 14 gunboats northbound at
    Terrapin Neck 25 miles above Vicksburg.

The Vicksburg Commissary is reporting a shortage of beef.

Pemberton to Davis:
"Grant and Sherman are west of me to take Vicksburg."
Pemberton suspects a landing at Warrenton, the old county seat.

24   The 1st Minnesota Light Artillery arrives on the *Jeannie Deans.*

26   Joe Johnston is feeling useless, *"as though I've been put on a shelf."*

Grant departs Memphis for Vicksburg.
McClernand writes to Grant that his troops are sick *"to an alarming
    extent."*

Halleck wants the Vicksburg canal completed, as does Lincoln.
Grant thinks weather is against the canal venture.

28   Grant arrives at Young's Point, La., his new base of operations
    opposite Vicksburg.

January 1863 (Cont.)

29 Grant holds a council with his key players at Young's Point.
He meets with an indignant McClernand and takes command.
Grant: *"I find no Army or Navy confidence in McClernand."*
Grant keeps McClernand on *for the good of the service.*

Grant leaves the steamer *Magnolia* for Louisiana's spongy soil.

James H. Wilson is taking 500 troops north to Helena, Ark.
Wilson has been ordered to breach the levee at Moon Lake, Miss.

Sterling Price goes to Richmond, seeking a transfer back across the
   Mississippi.
Bowen learns that Price has returned to Missouri with only the state
   guard.
The amazing Missouri soldiers are still his to command.

Bowen is again given command of Price's division.
He is ordered to support Vicksburg.

30 Grant sets his army for Objective Vicksburg.

G.W. Morgan is replaced by McClernand who will lead XIII Corps.
Two engineer officers are sent to Lake Providence, La., to consider
   construction of a canal into the Tensas River and beyond.

February 1863

1 The Confederate packet *City of Vicksburg* shocks the Union navy by
   docking at Vicksburg in full view of the enemy.
Ellet intends to ram the steamer using his Ram *Queen of the West.*

2 The *U.S.S. Queen of the West* rams the steamer *City of Vicksburg.*
She passes Vicksburg's guns to go disrupt traffic near the Red River.
The recovered *City of Vicksburg's* engines are sent to Mobile, Ala.

Porter floats 20,000 bushels of coal by Vicksburg, unnoticed.
The Ram *Queen of the West* passes Grand Gulf without drawing fire.

3 Porter and Sherman both have elements staged at Helena, Ark.
Union engineers dig through the Mississippi River-Yazoo Pass levee.

The swift Confederate Ram *William H. Webb* is working the Red
   River.

4 Consensus is building for Johnston to replace Bragg.
Bragg himself is amenable to the proposition.

5 Grant orders McPherson to canal to the Red River via Lake
   Providence, La.

Grant inspects McPherson's troops at Lake Providence.

February 1863 (Cont.)

5 Sherman court-martials Thomas Knox of the *New York Herald*. Knox is the **first correspondent tried in a war zone**.

6 Vicksburg Inflation – multiply 1863 prices times 36 for 2023 dollars: Chicken, $1.50; flour per lb., 50¢; shoes are $18; boots are $50. That pair of boots in 2023 dollars – $1,800. The chicken – $54.

7 4,500 Union troops face the grueling Yazoo Pass expedition.

9 Isaac Brown to Pemberton: *"The Yazoo Pass levee has been cut."*

11 Col. Charles Ellet's rams are a threat to the *open* Confederate Vicksburg-Port Hudson river corridor.

12 The *Emancipation Proclamation* has some U.S. troops on edge. Many U.S. soldiers threaten desertion rather than to fight for *darkies*. Logan, fearing wholesale mutinies, encourages his troops. Grant orders a halt to enticing Negroes to come to the Army.

  Ellet's destructive Red River raid enters the Atchafalaya River. Lt. Cdr. Watson Smith leads U.S. gunboats into Yazoo Pass.

13 The *U.S.S. Queen of the West* is steaming up the Red to the Black River.
The ironclad *U.S.S. Indianola* runs by Vicksburg for the Red River. Its mission is to protect the *Queen of the West* and *DeSoto* from the *Webb*.
The *Indianola* is also to remove cotton from the Davis plantations.

  A Tennessee soldier:
"Vicksburg is the worst, the dirtiest place on earth."

14 Porter to Welles:
"We have cut off Confederate supplies and troops from Texas."

The powerful and highly prized *U.S.S. Indianola*.
(USNHHC)

February 1863 (Cont.)

14 U.S. vessels below Vicksburg are ordered to *"burn, sink, and destroy enemy vessels."*

An untrusted pilot grounds the *U.S.S. Queen of the West* at Fort DeRussy, La.

15 Sherman's 6,000 on steamers reach the Yazoo Pass breach.

On the Red River, the *DeSoto* loses its rudder and is burned.
The same untrusted pilot then grounds the *Era No. 5* and is jailed.

16 Ellet finally links with the *Indianola* 10 miles below Natchez, Miss.
Confederates have refloated the *U.S.S. Queen of the West*.
Porter's effort to close the Red River corridor is in jeopardy.

17 The *U.S.S. Indianola* and *Era No. 5* head south.
The *C.S.S. Ram Webb* appears but withdraws when fired on.
Ellet reaches the mouth of the Red River.

18 Grant to Halleck: *"The Canal work is progressing well."*

Union soldier pay is slow in coming.

The Yazoo Pass Expedition is below Helena preparing to launch.
Reports of a Union gunboat *above* Snyder's Bluff creates a stir.

Without a guide for the *U.S.S. Indianola*, Ellet takes the *Era No. 5* up the Red River.

19 A C.S. troop train sent to Vicksburg derails into the Chunky River.
Dozens are killed and dozens more drowned when the train is
submerged in the river.
A rescue is effected by the C.S. 1st Battalion of the Choctaw.

20 Richard Taylor offers Vicksburg token Trans-Mississippi Dept. help.
Taylor is Davis' former brother-in-law, now a major general.

21 Union pioneers clear the route into the Coldwater River.
Loring arrives at Greenwood to counter the Yazoo Pass Expedition.

The *U.S.S. Indianola* has blocked the Red for three days, enticing the
C.S.S. Webb to come out.
The *Indianola* steams for Vicksburg when the enemy fleet appears.

23 Spirits soar at Lake Providence when McPherson arrives.

24 The *C.S.S. Queen of the West*, *Webb*, and *Dr. Beatty* enter the
Mississippi.
The *Indianola* is damaged in battle and captured at New Carthage.
The *Dr. Beatty* tows her to nearby Palmyra Island for repairs. Porter
and Welles fear the Confederates will employ the *Indianola*.

Thirty Union war vessels and quartermaster boats enters Yazoo Pass.

February 1863 (Cont.)

25 Porter builds a 300-foot-hoax ironclad *Black Terror* at Vicksburg. The vessel, designed to reveal C.S. artillery locations, cost $8.63. The hoax disrupts the Confederate recovery of the *U.S.S. Indianola. The C.S.S. Queen of the West* must withdraw, warning her group to withdraw.

    John Logan puts his division on boats at Memphis.

26 The *Black Terror* comes to rest just miles from the *U.S.S. Indianola.* Confederates abandon the *Indianola* recovery and blow the ship.

27 Bill Porter's ironclad *U.S.S. Lafayette* is commissioned in Cairo. *Originally covered in rubber, it is later overlain with iron.*

The hoax *Black Terror* on its maiden and only voyage.
Sketch by Theodore R. Davis, Harper's Weekly, April 11, 1863.

March 1863

3 U.S. soldiers threaten executions if firing on U.S. transports continues.
C.S. soldiers threaten to retaliate.

4 C.S. soldiers complain that U.S. soldiers are trying to drive them crazy. *"They are beating their drums day and night."*

    U.S. soldiers also complain about their camp drums.
"They are burying our boys, one funeral procession after another."
The swamps at Young's Point are claiming nearly a score a day.

5 The Yazoo Pass Expedition reaches the Tallahatchie River.
McPherson hopes to take 30,000 down to Yazoo City via Yazoo Pass.

    Stevenson advises Pemberton that Grand Gulf must be protected.

March 1863 (Cont.)

5   Brig. Gen. John Bowen is endorsed by Stevenson to protect Grand Gulf.

The *Vicksburg Whig* ridicules the loss of the *Indianola* to the *Hoax*.

6   Grant to Halleck: *"Will have Vicksburg in a month or fail trying."*
Grant tells Halleck that the Desoto Point canal is nearly complete.
Porter falsely reports that Watson Smith has reached the Yazoo
     River.

Pemberton orders executions of deserters in various divisions.

7   The Mississippi River fails to scour the Desoto Point canal.
Reb batteries are prepared to fire on the canal's lower two thirds.

Kirby Smith assumes command of the Trans-Mississippi Dept.

9   Johnston replaces Bragg who is sent for reassignment.

Pemberton complains to Richmond about his lack of artillery.
Bowen marches 2,000 Missouri soldiers to Grand Gulf.

10   C.S. soldiers receive their allotted $11 a month pay in Vicksburg.

Loring completes *Fort Pemberton* on the river at Greenwood, Miss.

Grant invites Rep. Elihu Washburn to witness his operation.
Grant to Washburn: *"Yazoo Pass is going to be a perfect success."*
The Union fleet lands about 20 miles above Fort Pemberton.

Asst. War Secretary Charles Dana is dispatched to *report on Grant*.

11   Bowen is officially assigned the task of fortifying Grand Gulf.
Pemberton asks Davis for more heavy guns to match the Union fleet.

Bitter Loring and Tilghman disagree with Pemberton's strategies.

The Yazoo Pass fleet reaches the confluence of the Yalobusha and
     Tallahatchie rivers above Greenwood.
The *U.S.S. Chillicothe* scouts Loring's cotton-bale *Fort Pemberton*.
The channel is too narrow for U.S. gunboats to fight Fort Pemberton.
Union troops under Leonard Ross are repulsed there.

12   Bowen arrives at Grand Gulf, his first independent command.
Bowen, at Charles Hamilton's plantation, reviews the 1862 works.

Martin Green's brigade is on the Big Black River.
John Forney commands Price's old division.

Union soldiers are creating an artillery position near Fort Pemberton.

The gunboat *U.S.S. Tuscumbia* is commissioned at Cairo.

13   Union soldiers launch a third attack on Fort Pemberton.

March 1863 (Cont.)

13   Porter develops an operations plan for Steele Bayou above Vicksburg.

Farragut prepares to move north after the capture of the *U.S.S. Indianola.*

Banks will add land elements to distract Port Hudson, La., gunners.

14   Porter's Steele Bayou expedition for Rolling Fork, Miss., begins.
Porter invites Grant on the first leg of his Steele Bayou operation.
Grant worries that Porter's force will be trapped.

Bowen collects slaves to work on the Grand Gulf defensive network.

Farragut tries the guns at Port Hudson, losing the *U.S.S. Mississippi.*
The flash of the *Mississippi* explosion is seen in New Orleans.
Four sailors are awarded the Medal of Honor for saving the
   U.S.S. Richmond.

Banks, learning of Farragut's troubles, withdraws to Baton Rouge.

C.S. soldiers spend a precious $150 on costumes and sets for a play.
Their investment is $5,400 in 2023 dollars.

15   Barriers and artillery block five ironclads and four mortar scows near
   Rolling Fork, Miss.

McClernand sends a report that Grant was drunk at Belmont, Mo.
   It is ignored.

Wade's Artillery Battery will cover Thompson's Hill on the Big Black
   River and Grand Gulf's rear.
Big Black's Winkler's Bluff area and Bayou Pierre are blocked by trees
   felled by Confederates.

16   After four attacks on Fort Pemberton, the Union fleet withdraws.
Engineer James Wilson and Porter blame Lt. Cdr. Watson Smith for
   the failure.
Porter: *"Smith showed symptoms of an aberration of the mind."*

18   The levee cut at Lake Providence creates a six-foot channel.

Watson Smith's health fails and he is sent *dying* to Helena.
Yazoo Pass Expedition command passes to the *Chillicothe's*
   Lt. Cdr. James Foster.

The Steele Bayou Expedition berths at Hill's Plantation.
Sherman, aboard the tugboat *Fern,* meets with Porter.

Loring and Pemberton argue over reinforcements for Fort
   Pemberton.

19   5:00 a.m. – The Yazoo Pass Expedition departs Fort Pemberton.

March 1863 (Cont.)

19   Flood and fire from hill batteries end the DeSoto Point canal work.

The *U.S.S. Hartford* and *Albatross* threaten Bowen's artillery shipment.

Porter's flotilla is within sight of Rolling Fork, Miss.

Confederates fell trees to trap Porter on Black Bayou.

20   Bowen's heavy artillery is unloaded at Grand Gulf.

200 Waul's Texas Legion soldiers under Loring verify the Yazoo Pass Expedition's departure. They find 15 Union graves.

Thomas Weldon is building a blocking raft at Yazoo City for Liverpool Landing or another strategic point.

Sherman sets up a base camp near Porter's expedition.

21   Pemberton to Johnston, worried about cavalry: *"Have you separated Van Dorn from my command?!"*

22   Sherman drives Rebs from Porter's gunboats on Black Bayou.

Porter's expedition reaches Rolling Fork, headed to the Sunflower River.

Grant is one week from breaking his Young's Point camp. McPherson is ordered back to Young's Point, ending his canal work.

Fort Pemberton is secure with Waul's Legion and the 2ᵈ Texas. Waul: *"My other units can go chase Yankee boats on Steele Bayou."*

23   The reinforced *U.S.S. Chillicothe* withdraws after a torpedo explodes near Fort Pemberton.

Bill Porter's ironclad *U.S.S. Choctaw* is commissioned at St. Louis.

To Loring's surprise, Maj. Gen. Isaac Quinby's new U.S. task force arrives two miles above Fort Pemberton.

24   A tornado at Warrenton wrecks rebel trenches, killing dozens.

Bowen mounts his new artillery on newly arrived naval gun carriages.

Pemberton appeals to Simon Buckner in Mobile for cavalry. *He gets no help.*

With Porter away, Ellet agrees to send two rams to Farragut nearby. Farragut knows Ellet is exceeding his authority but accepts the help.

25   Col. John Ellet's *U.S.S Lancaster* is sunk running Vicksburg's guns. Ellet's flagship *U.S.S. Switzerland* survives and reaches Farragut. Porter *suspends* Charles Ellet of command over the incident.

March 1863 (Cont.)

25   Bowen obtains corn for his starving men; their meat arrives rancid.

Loring is reinforced at Fort Pemberton by John Moore's brigade.

26   The Union flotilla returns to Yazoo Pass, licking its wounds.

Porter to Welles: *"Get 150,000 sent men to Vicksburg via Grenada."*
Grant is not aware of the Navy communique about Army troops.

Adj. Gen. Lorenzo Thomas is ordered to organize contraband
regiments.

27   Grant is days from departing Young's Point.
He orders the Desoto Point canal works to be abandoned for good.
Grant to Halleck: *"Canal dead."*

The *U.S.S. Cincinnati* is sunk by Vicksburg's Wyman's Hill Battery.
Local businessman Antonio Genella had offered a $5,000 bounty
for any battery that could sink a Union ironclad.

Porter returns to base after *"an eleven-day excursion into futility"*
on Steele Bayou.
He labels the Yazoo delta swamps and bayous *"a green hell."*

Pemberton knows that dry roads mean Union *ground* operations.
Pemberton *again* requests cavalry but gets none.

Bowen reports his excellent Grand Gulf progress to Pemberton.
Bowen produces furnaces and a magazine from the old jail.
Old Grand Gulf iron remnants will be used as red-hot canister.
Bowen has designed a proposed rotating casemate tower with guns.

R.E. Lee to Davis: *"We have no supplies in the territory we occupy."*
Supplies from the Trans-Mississippi are no longer crossing the
Mississippi River.

28   Additional Fort Pemberton reinforcements, including Brig. Gen.
W.S. Featherston's brigade, are being mobilized.

29   McClernand scouts a route from Milliken's Bend to New Carthage, La.
Grant marches south. *"I will be a hero or be destroyed."*
McClernand and McPherson go south with Grant and Porter.
Grant departs without a siege train or mortars.

Sherman and Lt. Cdr. Kidder Randolph Breese are left behind to
serve as a Haynes Bluff diversion and to maintain supply roads.

Lincoln to a naval officer: *"They are doing nothing in Vicksburg."*

A Carter Stevenson force is sent toward Rolling Fork.

March 1863 (Cont.)

29 Grant has few military engineers and only two Corps of Engineers officers, Peter Hains and Frederick Prime.
His shortage will add 30 days to any siege requirements.

Sherman does not support Grant's Mississippi overland plan.
"The Rebs could not have maneuvered us into a worse situation if they tried two years to do so."

Vicksburg's Philip Sartorius is wounded reconnoitering Grant's army, the first Confederate overland campaign battle casualty.
He is also the first Jewish casualty.

30 Halleck to Grant: *"A.G. Thomas will inspect and arm black troops."*

Featherston's soldiers spread forward to engage Quinby's troops.

31 The 69th Indiana scouts, the *Argonauts*, create a New Carthage, La., land route.

The *U.S.S. Hartford, Albatross*, and *Switzerland* steam into the Red River about 40 miles below Natchez.

The Union Navy tests the batteries of Grand Gulf.
Bowen's alarm system fails; he is caught off guard.

Col. George Pride begins the Duckport Canal near Richmond, La.

April 1863

1 Maj. Gen. Dabney Maury arrives at Fort Pemberton on the *Magenta*.
Lt. Cdr. Isaac Brown protests his cottonclad being used as a transport.
Loring has 7,000 troops.

Biting *buffalo gnats* claim 24 mules at Fort Pemberton.

Grant, Porter, and Sherman reconnoiter Haynes Bluff for an assault.
To reduce bloodshed, Grant decides to attack Vicksburg from the east.

2 Davis threatens to shoot protestors in the *bread riots* in Richmond.

Halleck advises Grant that he is under close White House scrutiny.

Grant's troop transports are reported heading north at Greenville, Miss.
Pemberton thinks Grant is returning to Memphis or to Rosecrans.

McClernand is ordered to depart south to New Carthage, La.

Union engineers break the levee in hopes of flooding Fort Pemberton.
Dabney Maury probes Isaac Quinby's positions at Fort Pemberton.
Quinby is setting up a siege battery against the fort.

Steele launches the Greenville feint to cover Grant's intentions.

April 1863 (Cont.)

2   Pemberton to Davis: *"It is indispensable that I have more cavalry!"*
No help is forthcoming from any quarter.

3   The remainder of Quinby's 7ᵗʰ Division arrives at Fort Pemberton.

Col. Thomas Bennett's 69ᵗʰ Indiana reaches Smith's Plantation, La.

4   Southern farmers are ordered to grow food, less cotton and tobacco.
Challenges of distribution, inflation, and loss of territory are hurting.
Hiring a C.S. Quartermaster General is caught up in petty politics.

The last ironclad attack on Fort Pemberton ends the mission.
Steele is below Greenville to destroy supplies and divert attention.

Porter agrees to support Grant's move south, though still cautious.
Porter can't power upstream without facing an incredible barrage.
Once his ironclads are below Vicksburg, Grant must take the city.

Maury orders fortifications on the Heard Plantation four miles
   southwest of Greenwood in support of Fort Pemberton.
10:00 a.m. – Grant's order to end Quinby's expedition is posted.
Grant is moving south overland to Vicksburg.
The great U.S. buildup for a Fort Pemberton conflagration falls flat.

Pemberton blows off Grant's movements.
He offers to send reinforcements to Bragg.
Johnston cautions Pemberton about Grant's intentions and location.

Bowen, trying to interpret Union activity:
"No boats are crossing. This must be a Union raiding party."
Bowen asks permission to send troops across to aid Louisiana
   troopers.

5   Bowen sends the 2ᵈ and 3ᵈ Missouri across the river, half of his force.

6   Bowen's intelligence is being ignored by Pemberton and others.
Carter Stevenson: *"McClernand's movement south is a diversion."*

Lead Union elements arrive at New Carthage, La.
Grant: *"It is time to send the boats,"* i.e., run the Vicksburg batteries.

Charles Dana, the *mole*, arrives at Grant's headquarters at Milliken's
   Bend, as if Grant needed another challenge.

C.S. War Secretary Seddon, eyeing Pickett's foraging brigades.
*"Could reinforcements be safely sent to Vicksburg from this (Lee's)
   department?"*

7   Davis asks Pemberton to send reinforcements to Bragg.
Davis is receiving confusing messages about Grant's movements.

April 1863 (Cont.)

7   Pemberton to Johnston regarding the Yazoo Pass Expedition:
    "The enemy is definitely leaving the Tallahatchie River."

    U.S. soldiers study the wreck of their *Tishomingo* in Yazoo Pass.

    Pemberton agrees to Bowen's sortie into Louisiana to *interfere*.
    Bowen: *"15,000 of McClernand's XIII Corps are at Bayou Vidal!"*
    Pemberton continues to ignore Grant and Bowen.
    Carter Stevenson is watching Sherman north of the city.

    Union forces are defeated at the Charleston, S.C., Navy Yard.
    Davis requests 5,000 South Carolinians for Mississippi.

8   A reorganized Featherston brigade is reviewed at Fort Loring.
    Brig. Gen. S. D. Lee arrives at Deer Creek to counter Frederick
        Steele's diversion.

    Sherman asks Grant to consider something like Porter's *land plan*.

    Bowen asks if he should engage his whole force against McClernand.
    Pemberton deems Bowen's plan too risky and is noncommittal or
        ambiguous.
    Pemberton believes the Union movements are a feint.

9   Bowen to Pemberton:
    "This is an invasion force about to cross."
    Pemberton to Richmond: *"I much doubt it."*
    The future of the Confederacy is fading minute by minute.

    Lee suggests other strategic moves, not his troops, to help Vicksburg.
    Lee has a May 1 deadline to launch an offensive and needs his troops.
    *"Our system is always late in moving soldiers from one department
        to another and shifting troops will hurt foraging operations here."*
    He recommends that the Army of Northern Va. cross into Maryland
        to relieve pressure on Vicksburg.
    Sedden: *"Relying on our unreliable railroads would invite trouble."*
    Lee leaves the decision with Sedden who already agrees with Lee.

10 Johnston falls ill at Tullahoma, *"Not now able to serve in the field."*
    Bragg remains in command of the Army of Tennessee.

    Levee-cut flooding forces Loring away from Fort Pemberton briefly.

    Pemberton again pleads with Davis for cavalry.
    None is forthcoming.

    Lorenzo Thomas inspects troops at Lake Providence, arranging for
        black soldiers.
    Frederick Steele returns to Greenville.
    He will receive Grant's first freed black soldiers.

April 1863 (Cont.)

11   Welles to Porter: *"Occupy the river below to release Farragut."*
Grant agrees to meet an anxious Porter's timetable.
Porter will not abandon Grant.
McClernand expresses disdain at Navy involvement.
Porter: *"Davis slave Ben Montgomery is an ingenious mechanic."*

Pemberton: *"Frederick Steele's Deer Creek incursion is no threat."*

Porter to Welles: *"The Yazoo Pass Expedition has returned safely."*
He zings: *"The Army did not think itself strong enough for the task
and, while awaiting reinforcements, lost their chance."*
Confederates sank three of four C.S. vessels to block the Union path.

Bowen orders Cockrell to attack McClernand's rear.
Bowen's plan is to deny Grant a high-ground base at Hard Times, La.

12   Grant orders McClernand to take Grand Gulf *with all possible haste.*

13   The levee dividing the Mississippi from the Duckport Canal is cut.
The steamer *Victor* makes a trip through the canal before stages fall.

Pemberton agrees to send Rust, Buford and Tilghman to Bragg.
Johnston refuses to return Pemberton's cavalry for defensive troops.

14   Carter Stevenson assumes command of Vicksburg.

Pemberton is in Jackson, firing out troop movement orders.
Pemberton to Abe Buford: *"Leave Port Hudson. Go to Chattanooga."*
Pemberton to John Vaughn: *"Prepare to go back to Tennessee."*
Pemberton to Lloyd Tilghman: *"Move from Greenwood to Jackson."*
Pemberton to Johnston: *"Grant has ordered 200 wagons at Helena."*

Bowen to Pemberton: *"Grant can cross in my rear."*
Bowen's whole force is needed to protect Port Gibson and Grand Gulf.
In the chaos, the *Daily Whig* reports the threat to Vicksburg is over.
Citizens are exuberant and a ball is planned.

The last vessel from the Yazoo Pass mission enters the Mississippi.

Grant orders McClernand to Perkin's Plantation facing Davis Bend.

15   Cockrell strikes Union cavalry at Dunbar's but is pushed back.
Union casualties at Dunbar Plantation are two wounded.

McClernand orders soldiers to take 10 days rations.
No tents and minimum baggage are Grant's orders.
Yet, McClernand brings wife Minerva, servants, and her baggage.

Reports: 64 Union boats loaded with troops are headed *SOUTH!*
Bowen intel: *"They are gonna run the Vicksburg batteries!"*
Pemberton again doubts Bowen's reports and hesitates.

April 1863 (Cont.)

15   Pemberton to Stevenson, leading from the rear in Jackson:
"Expect an attack soon."

Dabney Maury is transferred to Tennessee, replaced by John Forney.

Running the Batteries at Vicksburg, April 16–17, 1863

16   A ball at Maj. William Watts' home *celebrates the Union departure.*

Army volunteers are required for dangerous Union steamer duty.
Porter organizing pilots: *"If fired on, rush to the Mississippi side.*
  Don't fire unless they use big guns. Use grape and shell to disturb
  Vicksburg's gunners."
Grant, Julia, Fred, and Ulys, Jr., will watch from the steamer
  Henry von Phul.

9:15 p.m. – In order, these ironclads move downstream:
  U.S.S. Benton, Lafayette, Louisville, Mound City, Pittsburg,
  Carondolet, and *Tuscumbia.*

Midnight – The signal gun at old Fort Nogales fires an alert.
Rebs torch barrels, buildings, and bonfires to light the river.

Porter's boats struggle to keep straight in the river current and
  smoke.
Union crews are close enough to the city to hear bricks falling.
The only Union vessel lost is the transport *Henry Clay.*

Porter realizes the river batteries are not such a threat.
River defenses have failed their primary mission when overwhelmed.

Pemberton decides not to send reinforcements to Bragg.

The Yazoo River raft at Snyder's Mill is swept away by high stages.

The 1st Mississippi Regiment, African Descent, is organized.

17   *Pemberton:*
"Now Grant's possibilities are endless and bewildering."
Grant is pushing Pemberton outside of his comfort zone and skill
  set.
Pemberton gets no Confederate help, only disdain from Johnston.
Confederate leadership is frozen at the helm.

Pemberton recalls Buford, who is already in Atlanta.
Bowen recalls Francis Cockrell from Louisiana.
Bowen is given an entire division with Forney's reassignment.

Grant suffers a painful ride to New Carthage due to piles or boils.

Grant discounts Warrenton as a landing site, a disastrous scenario.

April 1863 (Cont.)

17 Benjamin Grierson departs LaGrange, Tenn., with three regiments.
Grierson is Grant's next in a series of distractions and diversions.
His cavalry sweep will draw Pemberton's focus to east Mississippi.

Grant's team is opposed to his overall plan as too dangerous.
McClernand sides with Grant, interested in a chance for glory.
Sherman is openly very agitated with Grant and his plan.
McPherson, the boy general, is just excited to be in the action.

Pieces of a U.S. packet float by Ione, La., disheartening the troops.
They fear all their transports have been destroyed at Vicksburg.
The main transport fleet then appears, to great jubilation.

18 Grant is at Hard Times, La., to assault Grand Gulf.

Porter continues to support Grant's operation.
Welles is pressing Porter to move south to support Farragut.
Smaller transports are coming south to Grant via area bayous.

Pemberton makes his situation crystal clear to Kirby Smith:
"I cannot oppose Grant without you."
Help from the Trans-Mississippi Dept. is not forthcoming.

The lack of a combined Confederate Mississippi River command,
requested by Johnston, is a fatal flaw in Davis' Vicksburg plan.

19 Porter expresses disdain for Vicksburg's ineffective batteries.

Confederate scouts suggest an impending Mississippi River crossing.
5,000 Confederates are positioned at Warrenton just south of
Vicksburg.

Maury's transfer to Tennessee is to the great regret of his soldiers.

The 3ᵈ Mississippi Regiment-African Descent is mustered into
service.

20 Porter: *"Bowen is ramping up at Grand Gulf."*
Porter orders two gunboats downriver to destroy Bowen's flatboats.

Brig. Gen. Grierson captures Pontotoc, Miss.

Pemberton orders a supply depot at the Big Black River Bridge
(BBRB) near Bovina, Miss., 10 miles east of Vicksburg.
Green's Arkansans are ordered from BBRB to Grand Gulf to support
Bowen.

Pemberton to Johnston:
"I have no cavalry from Grand Gulf to Yazoo City." In other
words, *"I am blind for 70 miles around me."*

April 1863 (Cont.)

21   Pemberton asks Kirby Smith to disrupt Grant on the Louisiana side.
No help is forthcoming.

700 2^d Iowans detach from Grierson's Raid to decoy Confederates.
Grierson destroys tracks of the Mobile and Ohio RR.

22   Porter cancels a heavy probe due to Grand Gulf's strength.

Six transports with 600,000 XIII Corps rations run Vicksburg's guns.
Logan's soldiers man unprotected transports.
"Any man leaving his post will be shot."

Confederate river batteries report 1 killed and 2 wounded.
400 rounds sink the *Tigress,* Grant's Shiloh command boat.

Pemberton learns of Grierson's raid and reacts.
Infantry under Buford and Tilghman are sent to intercept cavalry.
Featherston moves from Greenwood to save Grenada from Grierson.
Stevenson moves his division to Warrenton.

Bowen orders the Big Black River levee cut to thwart a U.S. landing.
The Bowens meet exiled Missouri C.S. governor Thomas Reynolds.

Pemberton makes a second appeal for support from Kirby Smith.
Smith is new to the area and again offers no significant assistance.

23   The **first major U.S. Colored Troop action (Port Hudson)**
fails against the insurmountable Confederate fortifications.

Kirby Smith to Pemberton:
"Grant's probably going after the Mexican supply line."

Stevenson to Pemberton: *"Don't send my men on a goose chase."*
Pemberton agrees.

Only John Bowen seems to grasp Grant's intent.

24   Porter believes Grant should avoid powerful Grand Gulf.
Grant is not convinced about abandoning his Grand Gulf plan.
Grant needs *one division* on the Mississippi side.

Grierson cuts the Meridian telegraph and railroad at Newton, Miss.
He burns the depot.
Pemberton is, at last, aware of Grierson's location.

25   Charles Dana reports confusion in McClernand's Corps to Stanton.

Loring refuses to surrender to Grierson's squad at Enterprise, Miss.

26   Abel Streight's 1,500 *Lightning Mule Brigade* moves to cut the
Western Atlantic railroad.
They want to divert Forrest away from Grant's theater.

April 1863 (Cont.)

26 *Grant's diversions are dizzying in complexity and very successful.*

27 Grant *"asks"* Sherman to make a diversion at Haynes Bluff.
Sherman agrees even though the press may see his action as a defeat.
He scoffs at any press response. *"I prefer secesh to the press."*

Grierson's raiders reach Hazlehurst, Miss.
Pemberton sends seven precious companies of cavalry after Grierson.
Pemberton is also distracted by Sherman north of Vicksburg.

Bowen pleads with Pemberton, describing Grant's whole plan.
Bowen: *"Without cavalry, I can only wait to be attacked."*
Pemberton to Johnston:
"I am in desperate need of cavalry."
None is sent by a sulking Johnston who hated Davis' Vicksburg plan.

28 Pemberton is confused by a myriad of operations all around him.

Grierson cuts telegraph, destroys railroad, and moves on Hazlehurst.
Union spies telegraph Pemberton: *"Grierson is headed to Jackson."*
Wirt Adams turns Grierson at Union Church east of Fayette, Miss.

Stephen D. Lee's brigade departs the Greenville area.

Bowen protests being left blind without cavalry.
Bowen sees Grant's armada: *"Send me everything you have!"*

Pemberton to Stevenson: "Prepare 5,000 for Grand Gulf."
Stevenson balks, *doubts Bowen's judgement*, still fearful of Sherman.

By nightfall, 17,000 of XIII Corps are on transports.
They represent Hovey and Osterhaus' divisions.

Battle of Grand Gulf, Miss., April 29, 1863

29 Grant launches **modern history's largest amphibious operation**.

Sherman to wife Ellen: *"My opinion is this plan will fail, must fail."*
Sherman, Lt. Cdr. Breese, and Maj. Gen. Blair are at Chickasaw.

Stephen Hurlbut's raids hold Pemberton's Tallahatchie cavalry.
Pemberton responds to Hurlbut, further draining his cavalry.

7:15 a.m. – Porter's Mississippi Gunboat Squadron pushes off.
U.S. vessels engaged are the *U.S.S. Pittsburg* in the lead, while
the *Louisville, Carondelet, Mound City, Benton, Tuscumbia*,
and *Lafayette* complete the flotilla.
Grant is aboard the packet *Ivy*, assembling above Bowen's force.

8:15 a.m. – Porter begins a six-hour, intense bombardment.

April 1863 (Cont.)

29 Bowen has 4,000 troops at Fort Cobun and Fort Wade.

Bowen asks Vicksburg for brigades from Baldwin and Tracy.
The Confederate telegraph is down.
Pemberton gets no message from Bowen.
Stevenson's Grand Gulf reinforcements are frozen in confusion.

Sherman opens fire at Snyder's Mill and lands at Blake's Plantation.
22^d Louisiana gunners hit Breese's *U.S.S. Choctaw* 53 times.

Maj, Gen. John Forney hears both battles and senses a feint by
    Sherman north of the city.

Stevenson still believes that Sherman's threat is real.
Forney reports, *"Sherman is a demonstration!"*

Pemberton releases Edward Tracy and William Baldwin to rush
    30 miles through the Big Black swamp to Bowen's aide.

Fort Wade is silenced but not the much higher Fort Cobun.
Col. William Wade, Bowen's artillery chief, is killed by a shell to the
    head.
The *U.S.S. Benton* is disabled briefly by fire below Fort Cobun.
Bowen orders his men not to target Porter who is inspecting damage.

Porter advises Grant that he cannot silence Fort Cobun.
1:15 p.m. – Porter suspends action.
XIII Corps exits the leaky barges they have be in all morning

Casualties:
U.S., 18 K, 57 W, including RAdm. Porter who is wounded slightly.
C.S., 3 K, 19 W, including Col. William Wade, KIA.

Silent guns at Grand Gulf signal Sherman to prepare to disengage.
Confederates at Haynes Bluff report 3 killed and 18 wounded.

2:30 p.m. – Porter's flotilla arrives at Hard Times, La.
XIII Corps is making a long march south to Disharoon's Plantation.
U.S. vessels run Grand Gulf at sunset to blind Reb gunners.

8:00 p.m. – Sherman is ready to move south to Grant.

Loring, in Jackson, is recommending an offensive strike.
Pemberton ignores Loring who he believes is *stepping out of rank*.

Pemberton recommends Bowen for major general.

Brig. Gen. Lloyd Tilghman arrives at BBRB at Bovina.

Bowen knows he is unable to scout 50 miles of river with infantry.

April 1863 (Cont.)

30 Longstreet has his eye on Vicksburg and *dear friend* Grant.
"Honor, interest, duty, and humanity call us to that service."

Grant still wants Grand Gulf as a Union supply depot.
There are no Confederates at Bayou Pierre just below Grand Gulf.
Noon – Grant lands two jubilant divisions at Bruinsburg unopposed.

Grant has very limited ammunition.
He will risk committing his whole present strength, two Corps.
He officially orders Sherman south via Navy semaphore.

Reports: *"Yank boats have been crossing all day below Grand Gulf."*

Bowen: *"I will fight at Port Gibson with or without reinforcements."*
Martin Green has a brigade at Port Gibson to find and block Grant.
Green's Arkansans are dispersed down the five incoming roads.

Pemberton moves his headquarters from Jackson to Vicksburg.
Grierson has wreaked havoc and left Pemberton blind.

Stevenson is dug in at Warrenton along Redbone Road.
Loring is preparing to come to Bowen's aid.
Baldwin and Tracy are quickly moving from Warrenton to Port
  Gibson.

**At this critical juncture, Vicksburg has sent two exhausted
brigades to Bowen to help face two Union Corps.**

McClernand's troops stop at *Windsor* mansion, intent on camping.
Plantation widow Catherine Daniell is a *vicious secesh* host.
A slave advises them of Confederates just down Rodney Road.
McClernand's staff fails to bring rations, delaying his movement.

McClernand orders pickets down the Rodney Road *until engaged.*
Grant has left son Fred asleep on the boat for safe keeping.

12:00 a.m. – Green assures evacuating Rodney Road residents that
  Yanks cannot possibly arrive before morning.
As he is talking, Union troops open fire on them at the Shaifer House.

3:00 a.m. – Skirmishing ends in the Shaifer House area.

May 1863

GRANT ESTABLISHES A FOOTHOLD

The Battle of Port Gibson, Miss., May 1, 1863

1 The transports *Moderator* and *Horizon* collide in night operations.
The *Moderator* is lost with an Ohio artillery battery and horses.
Grant stops night ferry operations due to safety concerns.

Grand Gulf-Port Gibson Theater

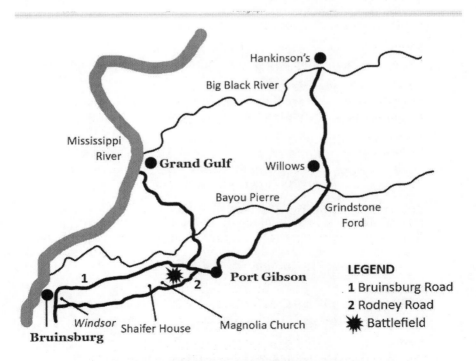

Battle of Port Gibson and Aftermath

May 1863 (Cont.)

1   Bowen leaves Col. Francis Cockrell in command at Grand Gulf and
    rushes to the Rodney Road.
    Bowen is badly outnumbered but can use terrain to his advantage.
    Union forces are jammed up by terrain and narrow roads.

A prisoner tells Bowen that 20,000 are coming down Rodney Road.
He doubts the report.
Pemberton: *"You'd better whip them before Loring arrives."*

The battle resumes around Magnolia Church at dawn.
Tracy arrives and is sent down the Bruinsburg Road.
He faces Maj. Gen. Peter Osterhaus division.
Tracy is killed, shot through the neck while giving commands.
Isham Garrott assumes command of Tracy's brigade.

Baldwin's brigade arrives completely exhausted and must recover.
They face Eugene Carr, the Pea Ridge Medal of Honor recipient.
2ᵈ Lt. William Titus Rigby is with the 24ᵗʰ Iowa, the Red Oak Boys.

Loring at Jackson is told to *proceed at once.* Loring replies, *"Where?"*
Tilghman at Edwards also receives confusing commands.
Vital time is lost on poor communications, a Pemberton trait.

Pemberton's angry responses build enmity among his staff.
Loring has Pemberton's animosity for overstepping his bounds.

By afternoon, Bowen's brave band is being overwhelmed.
Bowen executes a brave right-flank assault to save his army.
His ammunition exhausted, he advises Pemberton he is withdrawing.

Pemberton to Richmond:
  *"A furious battle has been going on since daylight just below Port
  Gibson. Enemy's movement threatens Jackson and, if successful,
  cuts off Vicksburg and Port Hudson from the east."*

Fred Grant sneaks into the battle aftermath, following burial and
    medical details before linking up with Dad at Grand Gulf.
  "Here were scenes so terrible that I became faint," he remembered,
  *"and making my way to a tree, sat down, the most woebegone
  twelve-year-old lad in America."*

Casualties:
U.S., 131 K, 719 W, 25 C/M
C.S., 60 K, 340 W, 387 C/M. Brig. Gen. Edward Tracy, KIA.

Bowen retreats across Bayou Pierre.
Loring is reported coming with two brigades – in actuality, two
    regiments.
Bowen believes he can hold all Bayou Pierre crossings – with Loring.

May 1863 (Cont.)

1 Loring arrives too late and leads the retreat to Hankinson's Ferry.
He persuades Pemberton to deploy John Gregg to Jackson.
Gregg must execute a forced 150-mile march from Port Hudson.

Grant moves toward Hankinson's Ferry.
He reaches McClernand and Governor Yates politicking with XIII
   Corps troops west of Hankinson's Ferry on Ingleside Ferry Road.
Grant chastises McClernand to resume pursuit of the enemy.

Johnston: *"Strike Grant, even if it means abandoning Vicksburg!"*
Davis: *"Hold Vicksburg at all costs!"*
Pemberton is caught between two competing bosses and strategies.

Pemberton, now in Vicksburg, again begs Johnston for cavalry.
Pemberton to Davis: *"Bowen is in retreat at Port Gibson."*
Johnston to Pemberton: *"Unite your whole force to defeat Grant."*

Pemberton's north Mississippi outposts are reporting a flurry of
   activity.
Pemberton is painfully feeling the loss of Van Dorn's cavalry.

The C.S. Congress authorizes execution of U.S.C.T. white officers.

Lee routs Joe Hooker and his Union force at Chancellorsville, Va.

The ruins of Windsor mansion where Grant's army landed at Bruinsburg, 1863.
The mansion, spared by Union forces, burned February 17, 1890.
From the 2014 photograph by Janie Fortenberry, Photography with a Southern Accent.

May 1863 (Cont.)

2   Grierson's raiders triumphantly arrive in Baton Rouge, La.

The 13th U.S. Infantry is on the *Thomas E. Tutt* bound for Milliken's
   Bend.
Union vessels in front of Snyder's Mill have departed.

Grant, at Grindstone Ford on Bayou Pierre, threatens Bowen's force.
Bowen requests a burial and medical truce.
Grant senses a *stall tactic to gain reinforcements* and refuses.
McPherson is flustered when USMA classmate Bowen says his 4,500
   soldiers held McClernand's Corps all day.

A second U.S. bridge on North Fork Bayou Pierre is being built.
A single Union soldier is wounded at South Fork Bayou Pierre.
Loring assumes command and orders a Bayou Pierre retreat.

Pemberton orders Grant Gulf, about to be cutoff, abandoned.
Pemberton's confidence is badly shaken.
He advises the state archives to evacuate Jackson.
Pemberton to Davis:
"Concentrating on this side of the Big Black River."

W.S. Featherston leaves Grenada to rejoin Pemberton's main body.

3   Forrest captures Streight's *Lightning Mule Brigade* at Rome, Ga.
The diversion to busy Forrest has succeeded.

Carter Stevenson is still in defensive works at Warrenton.
Confederates fire the magazine at Grand Gulf and retreat.
Grant hears the explosion and knows that Grand Gulf is his to use.

Bowen's troops push north toward the Big Black River.
Loring's delaying action at Kennison Creek saves Grand Gulf's men.
Loring stages opposite of Grant along the Big Black River.
Loring outnumbers a scattered U.S. force 18:11 but does not attack.

McPherson engages a feisty plantation mistress at Ingraham's.
She demands respect as the **sister of Maj. Gen. George Meade**.
Union Gen. Meade will win the Battle of Gettysburg in two months.
Mrs. Elizabeth Ingraham has two sons in *the Confederate army*.

Loring to Pemberton: **"Grant has a foothold."**

Pemberton has lost contact with Loring: *"Where is Loring?"*
Loring is not responding to Pemberton's messages.

Logan sends out foraging parties from Port Gibson.
A Union soldier is killed at North Fork, Bayou Pierre.

May 1863 (Cont.)

3   Porter occupies Grand Gulf, establishing a huge supply depot.
Porter then heads south, following Welles' orders to support
   Farragut.
He leaves Grant with three ironclads.

Grant arrives at Grand Gulf for a bath and change of clothes.
He loses his false teeth in his discarded soaking water.

4   Grant is focused on dividing Pemberton's forces and uniting his own.
He is concerned about Bowen's whereabouts.
Grant: *"Pemberton would evacuate by river without a railroad."*

Union engineers stop work on the Duckport canal.

Grant: *"How much worse will Vicksburg (terrain) be?"*

Buford moves to the BBRB near Bovina to link with Loring.
Bowen sets up camp on Clear Creek near Bovina.

Union boats at Vicksburg still represent an assault threat.
A Union tug with two barges is sunk by water batteries.

Davis faces a month-long bed stay due to stress and overwork.
His malaria and facial neuralgia threaten his good eye.

Illinois troops recognize Missouri prisoners as relatives and friends.

5   Loring sends a cavalry probe to Big Sand Creek near Rocky Springs.
Pemberton, confused, digs in from Warrenton to Bovina.

McPherson's XVII Corps rejoins the Army of the Tennessee.
McPherson reconnoiters to Warrenton and nearby Redbone Road.
Stevenson, spotting McPherson, reports a Redbone Road attack.
McPherson to Grant: *"The Rebs are dug in, not counterattacking."*

Grant is ready to seize the initiative.

Grant camps at Hankinson's Ferry.
He decides not to attack Vicksburg through the Big Black swamps.
Grant refocuses on the Southern RR from Clinton to Edwards.

6   When fired on, Union forces land and burn Greenville to the ground.

7   Maj. Gen. Earl Van Dorn is killed over adultery in Spring Hill, Tenn.

Only now, six days later, does Johnston learn of the Port Gibson loss.

Miss. Gov. John Pettus *will raise hell* if Vicksburg is abandoned.
Pemberton remembers Governor Pickens anger regarding Charleston.

Pemberton's garrison troops are *unfit for campaigns.*
Nonetheless, defeating Grant will require *open-field battle.*

Vital Crossings on the Big Black River

May 1863 (Cont.)

6 Pemberton pleads to Richmond for reinforcements.
   "The stake is a great one. I can see nothing so important."

Longstreet and Seddon are in a Vicksburg consultation.
Davis: *"You may expect whatever is in my power to do."*
Beauregard's contribution of 5,000 troops boards trains.

Sherman moves to Hard Times, La.
James Tuttle's rowdies burn mansions facing Lake St. Joseph, La.

Loring disobeys Pemberton, blocks Fisher's and Hall's ferries instead.
A frustrated Pemberton to Loring: *"Do whatever you think best."*

Wirt Adams' cavalry strikes a Union supply train on the Ingleside-
   Karnac Ferry Road a few miles from Grand Gulf.

Grant awaits Sherman at Hankinson's Ferry with Tuttle and Steele.
Frank Blair departs Milliken Bend.
Sherman crosses at Grand Gulf and proceeds to link with Grant.
McPherson returns to Hankinson's Ferry after his reconnaissance.

Pemberton divides his forces.
Forney and Smith are in Vicksburg.

May 1863 (Cont.)

7   Grant: *"Pemberton may evacuate south if Warrenton Road is open."*
Grant hopes Pemberton *will* evacuate.
Pemberton, after all, had considered evacuating Charleston, the
  Citadel of Secession.

Carter Stevenson and William Loring are at the BBRB near Bovina.
John Bowen is mirroring Grant's eastward movements.

Johnston orders Pemberton to *"Abandon Vicksburg."*
Davis to Pemberton: *"Hold Vicksburg at all costs."*
Davis overrules Pemberton, *"Do not abandon Port Hudson."*
Abandoning Port Hudson would have released Banks to join Grant.
Banks would have assumed command of Vicksburg operations.

The Warriors' Trail
May 7 to 14, 1863

May 1863 (Cont.)

8   The editors of the Jackson *Mississippian* express to Davis, in a
  private letter, *no confidence* in Pemberton's capacity or loyalty.
"Send us Beauregard, D.H. Hill, or Longstreet and confidence will
  be restored and all will fight to the death for Mississippi."

Grant moves to Rocky Springs, Miss., a small cotton community.
Grant envisions three parallel, self-supporting columns moving east.

Half of the Army (McClernand) is directed to Edwards.
Sherman will march to Bolton; McPherson will go to Clinton.
Grant, as a rule, usually accompanies Sherman.
He keeps the young McPherson farthest from the largest threats.

The Big Black River will screen Grant's flank and movements.

May 1863 (Cont.)

8   Sherman is moving east from Grand Gulf to Hankinson's Ferry.
McClernand is near Rocky Springs. *"I can't move without rations."*
Union supply trains arrive that evening.

Johnston calls Pemberton's placement of troops *judicious*.
Gregg's 3,000 exhausted Port Hudson soldiers reach Jackson.

9   Seddon tells Lee that he wants Pickett sent to Vicksburg.
Longstreet proposes to Lee his troop movement plan for Vicksburg.

Grant finds many subsistence farmers to be *pro-union*.
Their communities have New York names, e.g., Utica and Cayuga.

Grant organizes his army at Rocky Springs.
He reviews XIII Corps at Big Sand Creek with Governor Yates.

200 motley supply *vehicles* supply the Army from Grand Gulf.
Sherman expresses concern about the supply line.

Grant to Julia:
"Two days must bring the fight to settle Vicksburg's fate."

Davis to Johnston: *"Get to Mississippi and take charge."*
Vicksburg and the war hinge on Johnston trapping Grant.

Pemberton again asks the Trans-Mississippi for support and cavalry.
His widespread requests for C.S.A. support are falling on deaf ears.
*He is holding Vicksburg at "all costs" yet no one is willing to help
    pay for the Confederacy's most important asset.*

10   Grant is in the driver's seat.
Pemberton is in a defensive posture.

Longstreet wants to attack Rosecrans to draw Grant north.
Lee: *"The distance and the uncertainty of the employment are
    unfavorable. But, if necessary, order Pickett at once. It becomes
    a question between Virginia or Mississippi. Troops would be
    greatly endangered by the climate which will force the enemy to
    retire in June."*

A shortage of resources has put Davis in a no-win situation.
Lee is giving the idea of supporting Vicksburg serious consideration.
But Lee has also lost Stonewall Jackson, dying this day in Virginia.

Banks advises Grant that he is unable to withdraw from Port Hudson.
Grant decides to go without Banks, a turning point.
Grant's is a career choice, the Vicksburg victor gets a third star.
Banks is Grant's senior; a joint operation favors Banks.
Grant is already at Cayuga, Miss., days from pivoting north to the RR.

May 1863 (Cont.)

10   Grant is determined to fight quickly *before his rations fail.*
Sherman commends Col. William S. Hillyer as *transportation czar.*
Hillyer is a member of Grant's original staff in the early Illinois days.

McPherson is moving toward Utica.
Sherman reaches Big Sand Creek.
McClernand is ordered to move slowly, probing toward Edwards.
The three prongs move in unison, all foraging on fresh ground.

A single barn is found storing seven tons of bacon.
Seven tons of bacon is 6 oz. of bacon for 37,000 soldiers.
A U.S. *marching* soldier is authorized daily *(U.S. 1861 Army Regulations):*
    "A 'short' ration': 1 lb. of hardtack, 3/4 lb. of salt pork or
    1/4 lb. of fresh meat, 1 oz. of coffee, 3 oz. of sugar and salt."

John Gregg begins a forced march from Jackson to Raymond.
Wirt Adams' cavalry is vaguely ordered to Raymond.
Pemberton's *poorly worded message* holds Adams' force at Edwards.

Bowen suggests that he advance to Edwards; Pemberton agrees.
Bowen goes to Mt. Moriah south of Edwards and digs in with Loring.

Pemberton intends to give battle at Edwards Station.
He is expecting Bowen's Big Black River bridgehead to be complete.
Bowen fully expects a *wary* Pemberton to *retreat* if attacked in force.

Water is extremely short due to a major seasonal drought.
Rising dust clouds are an indicator of army movements and strength.

Thirteen Union casualties are reported at Pinhook Plantation, La.

11   Halleck to Banks:
"Unite with Grant. Attack Vicksburg and Port Hudson as one Army."

Grant, at Cayuga, learns of the Union defeat at Chancellorsville.
"My President can't stand another loss." Grant is determined.

Grant is on the eastern approaches to the Big Black River.
Sherman is in advance of the column at Auburn, Miss.
McClernand reaches Five Mile Creek west of Rocky Springs.
Grant to McPherson: *"Move to Raymond."*
McPherson advances out of Utica under drum and bugle silence.

Grant to Halleck: *"You may not hear from me for several days."*
Grant has dropped his lines of communications to Grand Gulf.

States Rights Gist and William Walker bring 10,000 into Mississippi.
These are Beauregard's contribution to Vicksburg.

Pemberton assumes direct command of the Army of Vicksburg.

May 1863 (Cont.)

11   Pemberton believes that Grant's movement toward Jackson is a feint.
"He will hit us at the Big Black River."
Scouts report that Grant has moved through Cayuga and Utica.
Pemberton to Gregg near Raymond: *"Hit Grant's flank."*

Gregg gets to Raymond in the afternoon, not expecting a big force.
Pemberton to Walker: *"Move to Raymond to help Gregg."*
Wirt Adams' cavalry is at Edwards, not at Raymond as planned.
Adams had been told to scout and harass Grant in a *garbled message*.

Johnston to Pemberton: *"Withdraw to Jackson."*

R.E. Lee restates his opposition to moving his troops to Vicksburg.

Bowen completes a bridgehead on the *east* bank of the Big Black.
His soldiers will surprisingly have their backs to the river.

Loring moves from Lanier Farm to the nearby Big Black River.
Stevenson moves east from Warrenton.

12   Pemberton moves his headquarters to Bovina.
Johnston urges Pemberton to strike Grant's rear.
Pemberton says that he will attack Grant if he moves on Jackson.
Pemberton tells his Vicksburg troops, *"Our hour of trial has come."*
He is organizing for a defense at Edwards and the Big Black River.

Sherman is about to cross Fourteen Mile Creek headed to Bolton.
The *Flying Dutchman's* battery drives Adams away at the bridge.
A U.S. soldier finds his C.S. brother dying after the skirmish.

Grant and Sherman move toward Dillon's Plantation.
Grant is concerned by news of enemy forces to his right.

Banks advises Grant that he cannot join him at present.

Grant has been in Mississippi 12 days.
The Confederacy nor Pemberton know Grant's intent.

Battle of Raymond, Miss., May 12, 1863

McPherson turns onto Telegraph Road south of Raymond.

Three McClernand divisions are at Whitaker's Ford below Edwards.
Bowen opens fire on McClernand at Mt. Moriah.
Grant orders a risky McClernand withdrawal from Mt. Moriah.

10:00 a.m. – Logan's Division hits skirmishers south of Raymond.
McPherson is confused by Gregg's vicious attacks against a Corps.
Gregg, in heroic action, believes he is facing a Union brigade.
Hiram Granbury and his 7th Texas hold up in Fourteen Mile Creek.
The dry bed makes a perfect sunken trench firing across flat ground.

May 1863 (Cont.)

12   Col. Randal W. McGavock, 10th Tennessee, launches a flanking attack.
McGavock, former mayor of Nashville, is killed leading his regiment.

1:30 p.m. – Logan is reinforced by five brigades and a strong
line of artillery including Samuel DeGolyer's 8th Michigan battery.

4:00 p.m. – Gregg realizes that he is engaging a Union *Corps*.
Lt. Col. Thomas Beaumont, 50th Tennessee quickly, wisely retires.
Gregg retires toward Jackson pressured by Logan's artillery.

Walker links with Gregg the night after the battle, too late to help.
Gregg to Pemberton: *"I have been fighting the enemy all day."*

McPherson is too scattered in the smoke and dust to pursue.
His 20th Ohio enjoys a town feast prepared for *Confederate victors*.

Casualties:
U.S., 68 K, 341 W, 37 C/M
C.S., 72 K, 252 W, 190 C/M

McPherson doubles the enemy estimate when he briefs Grant.
Grant knows by the sounds of battle that the *Boy General* is wrong.
In his style, he doesn't embarrass McPherson over the count error.

Pemberton to Bowen: *"Wait at the Big Black River for an attack."*
Pemberton has forces under Forney and M.L. Smith in Vicksburg.

Grant ponders: *"To push Johnston away or turn on Pemberton?"*
Grant is happier now, knowing the challenges that face him.
Grant advises Washington of his intent to attack Jackson.
Grant spends the night at *Waverly* on the Raymond-Clinton Road.

JACKSON, MISS. – GRANT'S PIVOT AND TURNING POINT

13   Banks to Grant: *"I may be able to join you in 10 or 12 days."*

McPherson: *"Enemy reinforcements are moving to Jackson."*
McPherson turns toward Clinton.
Sherman moves into Raymond with Grant.

The Clinton RR and telegraph are cut by McPherson's troops.
McClernand positions his force between Raymond and Bolton.
Hovey establishes his force west of Raymond to check Pemberton.

Johnston arrives in Jackson as Grant prepares to sack the Capital.
His orders: *"Assume command of operations to save Vicksburg."*
Johnston to Pemberton: *"March to Clinton and link with me."*
Pemberton is indecisive.

Hugh Ewing is guarding Union supply wagons from Grand Gulf.
They mainly carry medical supplies and ammunition.

May 1863 (Cont.)

13 Johnston to War Secretary Seddon from Jackson: *"I am too late."*
Severed Confederate communications are too poor for a campaign.
Johnston does not want to be part of a Vicksburg failure.
Johnston to Pemberton:
"Come up on Sherman's rear. I will cooperate."

A Union spy brings Grant a Johnston message detailing C.S. actions.
McClernand is known to be on Pemberton's flank.

Davis and Lee confer.
Davis is still visibly ill, not recovered.
This is an early discussion of the Maryland-Pennsylvania Campaign.

More Union casualties are reported around Fourteen Mile Creek.

Halleck believes that Benjamin Grierson, safe in Baton Rouge, has
    been captured.

Longstreet, still seeking a solution for Vicksburg:
"Swap Bragg two divisions for two divisions for Vicksburg."
Lee believes Vicksburg can be helped by invading Pennsylvania.
Lee: *"My men will be wasted on Pemberton's passivity."*

Pemberton: *"What if I go to Johnston and Grant bypasses me?"*
Pemberton has too many options and too many unknowns.

Loring reports many sources say that Grant is moving on Jackson.
Pemberton misses an opportunity to fall on an isolated McClernand.

The U.S.S. Neosho, an ironclad river monitor, is commissioned at
    Cairo.
The vessel is an Eads design and construction, with Porter's input.

The Fall of Jackson, Miss., May 14, 1863

14 Grant to Halleck: *"I will attack the state capital today."*
Sherman and McPherson's two Corps hit two Confederate brigades.

Grant: *"Let's sweep these rebels aside."*
Grant's confidence is growing and showing.

9:00 a.m.– C.S. artillery fires on McPherson at O.P. Wright's farm.
11:00 a.m. – Union soldiers fighting hand-to-hand push C.S. forces
    back into the Jackson works.
Sherman faces artillery north of Lynch Creek.
2:00 p.m. – Sherman's forces are halted by canister fire.

Johnston evacuates Jackson.
Gregg is left behind for a brief delaying action.

May 1863 (Cont.)

14   After a delay, Sherman sends a regiment to the right and finds the city
essentially unprotected.
Capt. L.B. Martin of the 4th Minnesota raises the 59th Indiana flag
over Jackson.

"Red Jack" John McGuiggan is released from prison by Union
troops in Jackson where he was serving 20 years for forging
slave passes in Vicksburg.

Casualties:
U.S., 300: 42 K, 251 W, 7 C/M
C.S., est. 845 KWM

Grant cannot expend combat troops on occupation forces.
Sherman remains in Jackson to destroy facilities and military assets.
Grant's troops at Bolton will prevent a Johnston-Pemberton link up.

Johnston moves north to Canton to build his *Army of Relief*.
Johnston has 31,000 but he considers his army too weak to help.
He tells Pemberton that he is *willing to cooperate*.

Confederate reinforcements enroute are told to stop and stand by.
Samuel Maxey, enroute from Port Hudson, stops at Brookhaven.
Gist from South Carolina holds up at Forest.
Bragg's other contributions stop at Meridian.

Pemberton receives Johnston's message to attack Clinton.
Pemberton responds:
"I only have 16,000 but will comply. Vicksburg is vulnerable."
Pemberton has left a sizeable force behind to guard Big Black ferries.

Pemberton holds a Council of War at Edwards.
Loring: *"Attack Grant's supply train from Grand Gulf."*
Most of Pemberton's officers vote to link up with Johnston.

Pemberton has few cavalry to see for him.
Pemberton wants to retreat to BBRB, as Bowen predicted he would.

Loring's proposal is selected by Pemberton.
Pemberton to Johnston:
"I will cut Grant's communications and supply lines at Dillon's."
Pemberton cannot know that Grant's reduced U.S. supply train has
already passed Dillon's Farm.

15   Lee comes to Richmond to discuss *Vicksburg options*.
Davis is still ill with sore throat and neuralgia threatening blindness.
He rouses from a two-week sickbed to attend the meetings.
Davis is essentially an ineffective leader himself.

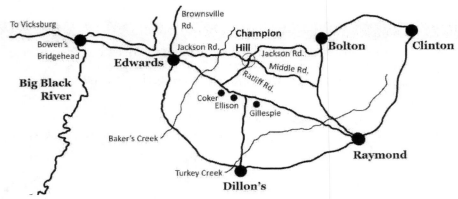

The Champion Hill Battle Theater

May 1863 (Cont.)

15 Grant's army is concentrated on a seven-mile front.
McPherson stops three miles east of Bolton.
Grant himself is speeding to Clinton after McPherson's urgent call.
McPherson fears having McClernand in command in a major battle.

Sherman is ravaging Jackson.
McPherson asks McClernand's Carr and Hovey to move to Bolton.
Grant gets intel from railroad workers that Pemberton is at Edwards.

Pemberton has *failed to order rations* from Vicksburg.
After rising at dawn, soldiers must wait seven hours for rations.

His scouts find the Baker's Creek Bridge ahead washed out.
Pemberton's Army is again stalled for long, hot hours at Edwards.
Pemberton departs Edwards very late in the day headed to Dillon's.
His weary troops should be bivouacking, not marching.

Loring resents his Commander. It is Loring's nature and pattern.

Johnston revokes Pemberton's Dillon cutoff plan as *impracticable*.
8:00 p.m. – Grant has 32,000 fed, camped, and resting at Bolton.
10:00 p.m. – Loring's men are arriving exhausted at the *Crossroads*.
Bowen sees many Union campfires in the distance.
He sets his army for battle before sending them to sleep on their
weapons for a few hours.

An angry Johnston to Pemberton: *"Move to Clinton!"*
Johnston is marching north of Jackson at Tougaloo, away from
Pemberton.

Calls are heard for Longstreet or Beauregard to replace Pemberton.
Fifteen days in, Davis is finally made aware of *Vicksburg's dilemma.*
Lee's Maryland movement *in response to Vicksburg* is approved.
Davis agrees to reinforce Pemberton from *other sources.*

May 1863 (Cont.)

15 Davis believes Lee's threat to the U.S. Capital will pull Grant north.
If Grant is assigned to Maryland, the Vicksburg operation will likely
fall apart without his skills and leadership.

Reaching Dillon's, Pemberton finds no sign of Grant's supply train.
He headquarters at the Ellison's home.

16 3:00 a.m. – Stevenson's exhausted soldiers begin to collapse on the
roadside as the column arrives at the *Crossroads*.
6:00 a.m. – The 46th Mississippi, the column's rear guard, reaches the
Crossroads having not slept.

Loring and staff are saying ill-natured things about Pemberton.
Pemberton removes Tilghman from command for insubordination.
Loring threatens to resign if Tilghman is not restored. He is.
Loring: ***"I would lose a battle to get rid of John Pemberton."***
Pemberton is fighting for the C.S.A.'s life with a mutinous Loring.

Pemberton, at last, decides to obey Johnston and move to him.
Pemberton receives another order reiterating Johnston's directive.

McClernand is camped between Raymond and Bolton.
McPherson is satisfied that Grant is in command of the field.

Sherman begins moving west under orders to come quickly.
Grant has 37,000; Pemberton has 23,000.
Johnston has 31,000 committed to him at Canton, Miss.
Forney and Smith's divisions remain in the works at Vicksburg.

McClernand is ordered *not to fight unless victory is certain.*
Grant has his political general on a tight leash.
McClernand is in a pout, Grant's version of Pemberton's Loring.

Pemberton prepares to reverse his army in place for Clinton.
6:00 a.m. – The 46th Mississippi must reverse the supply train after
no sleep.
The narrow road must be widened in spots to turn wagons around.
The Confederates are out of time and valuable stamina.
The ammunition wagons are sent away with the other wagons.

Pemberton's army departs with Stevenson's division now in the lead.
Stevenson is on the Jackson Road paralleling Champion Hill.
Bowen and Loring are trailing on Ratliff Road.

Emma Harrison Balfour makes the first entry in her *Siege diary.*

The Battle of Champion Hill, Miss., May 16, 1863

16 Stevenson sees McPherson's Corps about to top Champion Hill.
He urgently throws his exhausted troops into a battle line.

May 1863 (Cont.)

16   McPherson, Carr, and Hovey hit Stevenson caught in the open alone.
Hovey strikes Stevenson at the murderous peak, the *Hill of Death*.
They are both being beyond decimated.

Bowen and Loring keep watch on an *immobile* McClernand on
    Middle Road and A.J. *Whiskey* Smith on the road from Raymond.

Pemberton repeatedly calls for Loring and Bowen to counterattack.
Bowen and Loring: *"His orders are laughable."*
Bowen reconsiders. The fate of the Confederacy may be at risk.

Bowen launches a furious counterattack at the *Crossroads*.
Francis Cockrell leads the Missourians, a magnolia bloom in one
    hand, a sword in the other.
The reins of Cockrell's horse are in his teeth, *such are the
    Missourians.*

The Union army is manhandled by Bowen's division.
Grant almost loses his nerve as Bowen bulges his center.
Bowen's troops can see Grant's supply train 600 yards away.
Col. George Boomer throws his soldiers into a maelstrom of lead and
    iron, sealing a crucial gap to help regain Union momentum.

McClernand, on the exposed Confederate flank, holds his position.
Capable of finishing the battle with his Corps remnants, *McClernand
    sits, awaiting a direct order to attack.*
Grant messengers cannot find McClernand in the broken country.
Grant: *"Several of my divisions have vanished."*

McClernand:
"I have been told not to attack unless a win is certain."
McClernand is withholding the rest of the strongest division with the
    Confederate right flank *in the air.*

Bowen is repulsed by a fresh Union division and DeGolyer's guns.
Bowen and Pemberton call Loring to come forward. *He sits.*
Loring: *"The enemy is in my front"* (not advancing).

Without their ammo wagons, the Confederates are running out.
Grant senses the Rebs are running out and orders a final push.

After four Loring refusals, Pemberton mounts to go find Loring.
Loring, at last, makes an independent, meaningless hint of an attack.

Pemberton's army goes into a running retreat over Baker's Creek.
Loring is ordered to conduct a rear-guard action.
Lloyd Tilghman jokes about a near-miss from the Chicago Mercantile
    Battery at the Coker House.
Their next round hits him in the chest and also kills his horse.

May 1863 (Cont.)

16 A single officer of a Confederate battery is seen working his piece alone, despite many pleas to join in the retreat.

Loring, seeing fires at Edwards, decides to move to Johnston.
In the swamps, Loring loses 10 artillery pieces and all of his wagons.
Half of Loring's strength straggles enroute to Jackson.
His division is virtually destroyed after only a minor skirmish.

McPherson remains behind to police the battlefield.

The 46th Mississippi escapes with the supply train up the Brownsville Road, crossing at Bridgeport on a rickety pontoon.

Sherman also Army pontoons the Big Black River at Bridgeport.
He is in a race to cut off Pemberton's main body, to no avail.

Grant frowns at McClernand's actions that day but *bides his time.*

Pemberton will not see Loring again in the field.
Pemberton's men are rushing back to Vicksburg, *cursing his name.*

Alvin Hovey cries in his tent that night over the loss of his division.

Champion Hill:
The most decisive Vicksburg Campaign battle.

Casualties:
U.S., 410 K, 1,844 W, 187 C/M
C.S., 381 K, 1,018 W, 2,441 C/M

The Battle of Big Black River Bridge, May 17, 1863

17 Bowen has three brigades at the BBRB to await Loring.
Johnston marches 15 miles toward Edwards on the Brownsville Road.

Grant is anxious to reconnect with a Yazoo River supply depot.
His soldiers are almost depleted of rations.

Brig. Gen. William Dwight brings a Banks order to link up.
Grant wads up Banks' order and disposes of it.
"He would not have sent this if he knew where I was right now."

Eugene Carr and Peter Osterhaus reach the rebel bridgehead.
In the process, soldiers find a book lost by an evacuating Joe Davis.

Grant tells XIII Corps not to attack or press the Confederates.
Sherman is attempting to encircle and capture Pemberton's army.

Michael Lawler's men find an old river slough that flanks the Rebs.
Lawler surprises Bowen's left flank, forcing a quick retreat.
The battle is over in a matter of minutes.
Their backs to the river, many Confederates drown in their escape.

May 1863 (Cont.)

17   Other Rebs escape over the BBRB and four steamers used as bridges.
The steamers are the Dot, Charm, Bufort, and Paul B. Jones, Mark
* Twain's first boat.*
18 pieces of Confederate artillery and 1,751 soldiers are lost.

Fred Grant, observing at a distance, is hit in the leg by a spent bullet.
To his attending colonel, *"Don't tell mom. She will call me home."*
His leg will become infected. Briefly, his leg and life are in danger.

Chief Engineer Samuel Lockett burns everything spanning the river.
Bowen's artillery west on high ground halts the Union advance.

Davis does not approve of a Pemberton escape plan into the Delta.
Pemberton will look to Davis and Johnston to break a siege.

72 pieces of captured Reb artillery will be used against Vicksburg.
A very dejected Pemberton is enroute to Vicksburg.
"On the same date my career started years ago, it ends in disgrace."

Casualties:
U.S., 276
C.S., 1,751, mostly captured.

Grant Begins Tightening the Trap

17   Grant: *"Bridge the Big Black River in three places."*
XVII and XIII Corps build bridges with cotton bales and scraps.
Grant rides to Bridgeport to inspect Sherman's Army pontoon bridge.

Pemberton's 10,000 cannot protect the crossings and must retreat.
"The Army is too weak. Evacuation from Vicksburg is impossible."
Pemberton retires to strengthen defenses and morale in Vicksburg.

M.L. Smith and Forney still have two fresh divisions at Vicksburg.

Johnston: *"Leave Vicksburg. It can't be held without Haynes Bluff."*
Haynes Bluff is the future site of Grant's hypercritical supply depot.

Loring reaches Crystal Springs, Miss., 45 miles southeast of Jackson.

18   **Confederates evacuate Haynes Bluff.**
Grant arrives with Tuttle and links with Sherman at Haynes Bluff.

Grant and Sherman visit Chickasaw Bayou, briefly under fire.

Seeing Porter's fleet, Sherman has an epiphany and credits Grant.
"This is a campaign. It is a success if we never take the town."
*Grant's campaign is the **most brilliant in American history**.*
He has written new concepts in modern warfare.
He is executing at the genius level.

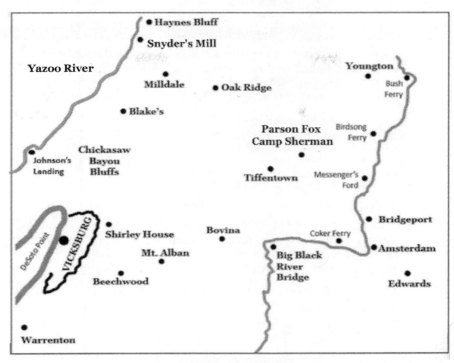

The Vicksburg Theater

May 1863 (Cont.)

18 A quick U.S. victory would free up troops to face Bragg.

Halleck receives Grant's week-old *out of communications* message. In the meantime, Grant is at the gates of Vicksburg.

Lawler remains behind to guard the Big Black River Bridge.

The 3ᵈ Louisiana moves into the Jackson Road redan at Vicksburg.

Vicksburg is a *mad house, buildings being burned and torn down.* Union troops shoot a Reb attempting to burn the Shirley House.

Johnston to Pemberton:
"If invested, you must ultimately surrender."
Pemberton improves troop morale by guaranteeing to hold the city.

Sherman arrives at the Stockade Redan on Graveyard Road. McClernand is at Beechwood and Baldwin Ferry Road. McPherson is on the Jackson Road before the 3ᵈ Louisiana Redan.

Grant leaves southern routes open for a Pemberton escape. He prefers to catch the Army of Vicksburg out *in the open.*

May 1863 (Cont.)

18   The Confederate forts on Graveyard Road are virtually unmanned.
Sherman and Grant, unaware, are discussing strategy in full view.
They miss an opportunity to take Vicksburg *in two hours*.
Francis Shoup rushes C.S. soldiers to man the Stockade Redan.

5:00 p.m. – The Waterhouse Battery fires on the Stockade Redan.
Pemberton's Council of War hears the opening U.S. artillery.

Lockett's lines built by 6,000 soldiers and 5,000 slaves are ready.
His eastern defenses are nine miles of rifle pits and nine forts.
Lockett combines heavy abatis and clearings to create *a killing field*.
The winding ridges around Vicksburg provide Lockett triangular fire.

His 30,000 P53 Enfield Rifles can hit a man at 500 yards and more.
The Union 1861 Springfield can hit a man at 200 to 300 yards.
The terrain represents a *10-times Confederate force multiplier*.
Grant will attack with near equal numbers with lesser rifles.

Grant orders a *reconnoiter in force*, feeling his way into Vicksburg.
"No better time to attack than when they are demoralized."
After the December massacre at Chickasaw Bayou, Sherman balks.
Grant does not know that he is facing two fresh, angry divisions.

Sherman's force is virtually starving and exhausted after operations
    in Jackson, 50-miles of heated march, river pontoon operations,
    and skirmishing in Warren County.
They must mountain-climb 10-story jungle bluffs just to get online.

Officers threaten to shoot or bayonet fearful advancers.
"Do not shoot your rifle until you reach the Confederate works."
Awaiting them, the worst iron and lead curtain of their war to date.

Sherman and McPherson will attack the northern half of the lines.
McClernand is still coming forward near Beechwood.

Sherman refuses to *use up his Corps on this hill*.
Frank Blair's single division gets the nod to attack a human *buzz saw*.

Union soldiers want a quick victory before the summer's furnace.
Grant is facing career, military, political, and Army health issues.

19   Union cavalry destroys the abandoned works at Haynes Bluff.
The Navy takes the credit and is rebuffed.
Union soldiers under Hovey loot and ransack Bovina farms and homes.

Johnston to Port Hudson: *"Evacuate. Come to Jackson."*
Davis to Port Hudson: *"Disregard Johnston. Hold at all costs." Davis has
overruled Johnston again.*

Loring reaches Johnston in Jackson with dramatic battle tales.

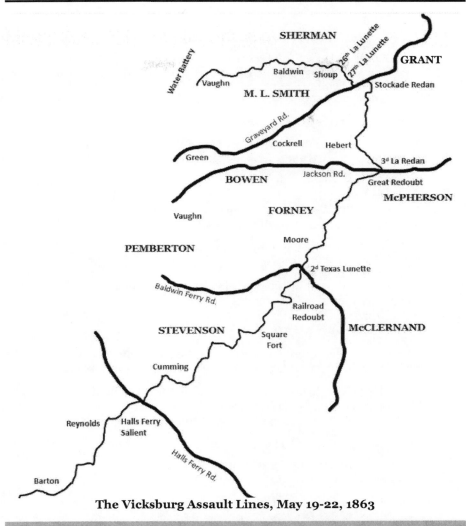

The Vicksburg Assault Lines, May 19-22, 1863

May 1863 (Cont.)

19 All available food caches have been moved into Vicksburg. Huge stockpiles had to be abandoned due to a lack of wagons. Pemberton fears his Army will evaporate if the city is evacuated. Stevenson and Bowen miraculously rebuild Vicksburg morale.

A huge Union supply landing is rising at Johnson's Plantation. Frederick Steele opens a land route to the river and Union supplies. Union soldiers are already setting up camps around Vicksburg.

Lt. Cdr. John Walker destroys the Yazoo City Navy Yard and ironclads *C.S.S. Mobile, Republic,* and the 300-foot unfinished *"monster."*

THE DEFENSE OF VICKSBURG
The First Assault of Vicksburg, May 19, 1863

May 1863 (Cont.)

19 2:00 p.m. – Sherman and McPherson will cooperate in soaring heat.

Francis Cockrell's Missourians man the 27th Louisiana Lunette.

The Stockade Redan is topped with an 8-foot poplar-log wall and is
   supported by two wing forts, Green's Redan and the 27th Lunette.

In the Union advance, three of four Union bullet carriers are killed.
One regimental flag is hit 58 times, the intensity of fire horrid.
E. Crawford Washington, George's great nephew, is killed in action.
Maj. Arza Goodspeed, leading the 4th West Virginia, is killed.

At least three soldiers in McPherson's 95th Illinois are women.
Priv. *Albert D. J. Cashier* is Jennie Hodgers from Ireland.

Orion P. Howe, age 14, succeeds in a suicide mission to Sherman,
   crawling wounded in both legs.
Fred Grant reports his Dad's eyes filled with tears when he
   witnessed Howe's brave act.

Union casualties approach 1,000, 10 times the Confederates losses.
The Union artillery batteries fire 9,598 rounds in support.

Grant leaves his dead and severely wounded on the field.
To him, requesting a burial truce signals *admission of defeat.*
Cries from the ramparts will haunt Union comrades for days.

Sherman: *"McPherson is a noble fellow; McClernand, a dirty dog."*

20 Grant's inefficiency of the 19th surprises Pemberton.
Pemberton: *"An Army will be needed to save Vicksburg and quick."*

Johnston meets with Lt. Col. Arthur Fremantle, Britain's emissary.

Grant is distracted by Joe Johnston's buildup in his rear.
Johnston is on Grant's mind and in his rear.
Grant begins a second road for supplies to his troops.

Ambulatory wounded sneak away from the Stockade Redan by dawn.
Officers and troops want to *go again* to get this over soon.

Grant's staff agrees on a larger, better coordinated May 22d assault.
Jacob Lauman arrives with 12 XVI Corps regiments and five batteries.

Grant to Porter:
"Bring every gunboat and mortar to bear on Vicksburg."
 Porter's mortar assault begins, the first of 7,000 mortar balls fired.
A 13-inch, 200-lb. mortar round creates an elephant-sized hole.

May 1863 (Cont.)

21   Banks has 40,000 to take Port Hudson and then bring to Vicksburg.

New Union supply roads finally bring troops a *good, square meal*.

Sherman declares that he is finished sending soldiers up the hills.
He decides to use a 150-man suicidal *storming party*.
It is deemed the *Forlorn Hope Brigade*, single men only.
He receives many more volunteers than needed.

U.S. troops begin to construct fortifications.
In loess soil, 100 soldiers can dig a 100-yd., 8x8-ft. trench in one day.

Grant must move a million pounds of war material per day.
His soldiers will need 37,000 gallons of fresh water delivered daily.
An estimated 700 wagons will be moving through the ravines daily.
Miles of two-laned, corduroy roads over extreme terrain are needed.

Grant brings 220 artillery pieces to Vicksburg; the Navy adds 180.
Grant has 160 steamboats and 60 Navy war vessels.
An estimated 23,000 horses will power his Army and require fodder.
Grant's equine count *equals Vicksburg's 2023 population*.

His is the **largest amphibious operation in modern history**.

Bowen complains of *"excessive exploitation"* of his troops in reserve.

C.S. scouts: *"Grant is not digging in. Another attack is coming."*
Grant plans an assault on his entire three-mile, three-Corps front.

U.S. troops host 3ᵈ La.'s "Shanghai" Masterson for dinner and drinks.

A first in world military history, U.S. watches are synchronized.
An *attack* signal cannon cannot be heard during a bombardment.

Pemberton sends Johnston four messages describing events.
Loring's force is now part of Johnston's Army of Relief (AOR).

The Second Assault of Vicksburg, May 22, 1863

22   6:00 a.m. – A four-hour Union barrage of the Vicksburg lines begins.
10:00 a.m. – A three-mile general assault is launched by XV, XVII,
    and XIII Corps from the 26th Louisiana Lunette to Square Fort.

49,000 Union soldiers engage 29,000 behind heavily fortified
    heights.
Sherman declares the heights to be worse than Crimea's *Sevastopol*.
Undermanned, under-gunned soldiers face impenetrable ramparts.
Union soldiers attack over wounded and rotting dead from May 19th.

The Forlorn Hope Brigade attacks the Stockade Redan in the *Beaten
    Zone*, maneuvering around untold obstacles and dead.

Confederate artillerists fire into a Union assault column at the Stockade Redan.
Diorama from the Missouri State Museum in Jefferson, Mo.

May 1863 (Cont.)

22   The *Forlorn Hope Brigade's* following units, the 30ᵗʰ Ohio, and 37ᵗʰ
Ohio, are not given the orders to advance, dooming the action.
Sherman is livid that the attack order was not given.
Of 150 *storming party* volunteers, 78 survive *in some piece or part.*

McPherson attacks the Great Redoubt with ladders that are eight feet
long; the Confederate trench is disastrously 16 feet deep.
The 81ˢᵗ Illinois' Edwin Loosely is one caught in the trench:
*"Two ranks of soldiers within ten yards of me were shot. I was just
waiting for my bullet. Enough lay around me to fill my hat."*

Heavy obstacles strip away Union regiments' ability to stay cohesive.
Grant's *coordinated* attack melts into piecemeal attacks hours apart.
30,000 Enfields scan Lockett's *killing field* for scattered attackers.
Regimental colors change bearers by the minute, torn to shreds.

Midafternoon, McClernand urges Grant to resume the attack.
He claims to control the Railroad Redoubt and Square Fort.
Grant, on Mt. Ararat in the center of the line, claims that he can see
that McClernand is not in control of the facts or the forts.
Sherman reminds Grant that McClernand is a *"**good soldier**."*
"McClernand is the only officer to always meet your intent."
Grant begrudgingly orders a second full-frontal assault.

Ewing, Giles Smith, Kirby Smith, and Tuttle attack with Thomas
Ransom.
Giles Smith digs in 75 yards from the enemy, refusing to leave.

Carr, A.J. Smith, Benton, and Burbridge attack the 2ᵈ Texas Lunette.

May 1863 (Cont.)

22   Michael Lawler and William Landram assault the Railroad Redoubt.

The 30ᵗʰ and 46ᵗʰ Alabama are defending the Railroad Redoubt.
The 20ᵗʰ Alabama is at the Square Fort.

After two suicidal assaults, Sgt. Thomas Higgins, 99ᵗʰ Illinois, is alone
   climbing the 2ᵈ Texas Lunette, where Union bodies are stacked up
   10 feet deep at the foot of the Lunette.
The Rebs stop shooting and cheer the flagbearer into the fort.

The Chicago Mercantile Battery is on the Lunette, firing into
   artillery embrasures.

George Boomer dies in the ravine, preparing a third hopeless charge.
Holden Putnam assumes Boomer's command and calls it *suicidal*.

Sherman recalls his units: *"This is not warfare. This is murder."*

C.S. Brig. Gen. William Baldwin is severely wounded near the 26ᵗʰ La.
   Lunette.

5:30 p.m. – The 20ᵗʰ Alabama's Col. Edmund Pettus sees a breach.
He leads 30 of Waul's Texas Legion to occupy the Railroad Redoubt.
Waul's men name Pettus an *honorary Texan, his life's highest honor*.

The 21ˢᵗ Iowans invest 85 percent casualties on the fort and fail.

Grant suffers 3,000 additional casualties on the 22ᵈ.
"This was an unbelievable, miraculous Confederate recovery."
He blames *"enemy resistance and poorly coordinated, simultaneous
   attacks"* for his defeat on the 22ᵈ.

Grant again leaves his dead and seriously wounded on the ramparts.
The carnage joins those left behind on the 19ᵗʰ.
Union soldiers are tortured by the scent and screams of their losses.
One soldier pleads for someone to save them from attacking hogs.

Sherman to Blair: "Hold your ground and begin Siege operations."

Pemberton's 7.44-in. *Widow Blakely* gun bursts while in action and is
   sawed off.

Pemberton reports receiving 38,000 percussion caps for 18,000
   effectives, **barely 2 caps per soldier**.

Grant appreciates his shortage of military engineers:
His soldiers use textbooks from West Point and *Western innovation*.

Pioneers open a road from the Yazoo River to the rear of the Army.

Nathaniel Banks lays siege to Port Hudson La.

May 1863 (Cont.)

The Siege of Vicksburg, May 25 – July 4, 1863

23   Grant, McPherson, and A.J. Smith discuss siege works.
G.O. 140: Vicksburg siege operations will begin May 25th.
Grant's plan: Artillery domination, saps and parallels, and mines.

Capt. Frederick Prime, chief engineer, Army of the Tennessee, begins
    earthworks.
Work begins on Ewing's approach facing the Stockade Redan.

Grant ignores McClernand's request for a medical and burial truce.
Both sides are repulsed by the stench and groaning wounded.

Union troops rest *"after the fatigue of yesterday."*

Vicksburg's forage shortage gives priority to artillery and ambulance
    horses.

Davis to Johnston:
"Do not expect a lot from us. Do something now!"
Bragg cannot support without jeopardizing his Tennessee position.
Davis had said earlier that he would give up middle Tennessee to save
    Vicksburg.
Davis asks Governor Pettus to mobilize his militia for Johnston.

Grant's hungry army, 23 days on quarter rations, gets a good meal.

24   Pemberton to Johnston: *"Enemy repulsed suffering heavy losses."*

Loring has 4,862 troops after losing 2,000 after Champion Hill.
Pemberton and Johnston's combined strength: 52,000.
Grant is outnumbered at 49,000.

25   Grant grossly oversimplifies his plan: *"We will out-camp the enemy."*
The most extensive siege operation in U.S. history begins.

Grant's timetable is hypercritical.
Political pressure on Grant and his President is extreme.
A third star hangs in the tedious balance for Grant.
The subtropical environment is melting his Northern army.
"Disease drips from the trees in the evening dew."
The Mississippi Gunboat Squadron is *on loan.*
His IX Corps soldiers coming south are *on loan.*
The Army of the Tennessee's strength is needed elsewhere.

Northwest states may elect to secede to restore vital Mississippi River
    access as a *Northwest Confederacy.*

Copperheads (peace activists) at home are melting the Union will to
    fight the war.
U.S. soldiers in the field generally despise the Copperheads.

May 1863 (Cont.)

25 *If Grant does not take Vicksburg in time for Sherman to take Atlanta in 1864, McClellan, the peace candidate, will sign a peace treaty with the South as soon as he is inaugurated.*

Pemberton moves his headquarters to the John Willis home on Crawford Street.

Sherman: *"We have perfect communications with our supplies."*

Killed and severely wounded Union soldiers remain morbidly exposed between the sweltering lines, some for seven days.
The stench is so bad that both armies want to surrender.
Confederates complain, *"Are you trying to stink us out?"*
Pemberton: *"In the name of humanity, call a burial truce. We'll help your bury your dead."*

During a two-hour burial truce, enemies play cards and trade.
Rebs pilfer Union bodies.
Sherman hosts Lockett, in his tent to prevent *snooping*. They joke.
Decaying remains are lightly buried between the lines, 10 stories tall, three miles long.

Banks requests troops from Grant after severe losses at Port Hudson.

Johnston to Pemberton:
"I will move to you as soon as Bragg's division arrives."

Capt. Samuel DeGolyer is mortally wounded while reading a newspaper near his shelter.

26 Lincoln:
"Grant's campaign is the most brilliant in the world."

Work begins on Logan's Approach toward the 3^d Louisiana Redan.

Grant fears Johnston will destroy his supply depot at Haynes Bluff.

27 Grant is feeling *hunted* by Johnston, instead of being *the hunter*.
He destroys Way's Bluff Bridge on the Big Black to stall Johnston.

Several ladies are killed by mortar shells.

Capt. William Parks conceals his Wyman's Hill guns from Porter.

A.P. Hill is rumored to be in Jackson and Canton with 45,000.

Sherman asks Porter to help destroy river batteries on his right.
The hidden Wyman's Hill Battery sinks the *U.S.S. Cincinnati* and 40 sailors are killed in the action.
Like her durable sisters, the *Cincinnati* will be put back into service.

Porter and Selfridge thank the Army with a battery of naval guns.

The *U.S.S. Cincinnati* on the Mississippi River.
(USNHHC)

May 1863 (Cont.)

28   Grant sends a force under Blair into the Mechanicsburg Corridor.
Lincoln to Rosecrans: *"Keep Bragg busy."*

Bowen complains his troops are in trenches left squalid by others.

The 3ᵈ Louisiana with new Enfield rifles surprise U.S. snipers.

8,000 rifle caps arrive from Johnston, the first courier in 10 days.

29   Peter Osterhaus at BBRB reports much enemy activity.
Grant realizes the potential for a trap and orders Blair to return.

Ellet's Mississippi Marine Brigade (MMB) arrives above Vicksburg.

Johnston: *"I am too weak to save Vicksburg. We must cooperate."*

A very heavy U.S. bombardment kills many Vicksburg soldiers and
some citizens.

30   Work begins on John Thayer's Approach toward the 26th Louisiana
Lunette.
Francis Shoup responds with a timber stockade atop the Lunette.
Buckland's Approach begins north of the Stockade Redan.
Giles Smith's Approach begins in front of Green's Redan.

The 10ᵗʰ Illinois cavalry and 1ˢᵗ Miss. African-Descent have an
altercation.

McClernand pens a Congratulatory Order No. 72 to his troops that
will be picked up by the press.

Union sharpshooters have killed all of the field officers in the 27ᵗʰ
Louisiana Lunette.

Bowen sends his Missourians to burn the sunken *U.S.S. Cincinnati*.

May 1863 (Cont.)

30 Vicksburg's soldier rations are cut in half.
Rebs experiment with distasteful pea bread, *Cush Cush*.

31 Johnston to Davis: *"Grant is at Vicksburg and likely entrenched."*
Davis to Lee:
*"I made a serious mistake giving Johnston the Vicksburg relief
    command."*

The MMR is firing 300 Rodman rifled rounds per day into the city.

A seven-day Union bombardment begins.
The Union mortar fleet finally hits their favorite, the Court House.

June 1863

1 John Breckinridge arrives in Jackson with his 5,200 from Tennessee.
W.H.T. Walker is on Johnston's right with 13,500 at Yazoo City.
Loring is on Johnston's left with 11,000.
Nathan Evans' brigade arrives from South Carolina.
Johnson's strength is 28,000.

Alfred Cumming attacks Lauman's Halls Ferry Road Approach.

A Union mortar shell sets a Vicksburg city block on fire.

2 Grant sends a larger expedition up the Mechanicsburg Corridor.

Work begins on Carr's Approach at the Railroad Redoubt.
Hickenlooper reduces his sap crew from 150 to 100.
Lauman retakes rifle pits in front of his Approach.

Sherman implores Grant to mix veterans with green regiments.

Pemberton issues tobacco to improve morale.

The experiment of *pea bread* ends.
Peas are now half the Confederate ration.
Black-eyed peas are considered cow food.

3 Grant to Halleck:
"Five days more and our guns will be on their parapets."

Nathan Kimball's provisional division, 12 U.S. regiments, arrives.
Kimball is assigned to man a Mechanicsburg base in development.

Pemberton to Johnston: *"Have not heard from you since May 25th."*
William H. Jackson's 3,000 cavalry arrive at Canton after 350 miles.

4 U.S. field reports: *"20,000 entrenched at Yazoo City with 25 guns."*

The 12th Michigan stops at Satartia to join Kimball's expedition.

Seddon to Johnston: *"Attack Grant now! I will be responsible."*

June 1863 (Cont.)

4 Johnston's combined force is 62,000.

Six U.S. casualties, including 1 killed, are reported at Mechanicsburg.

5 Kirby Smith to the Missouri Confederate governor: *"Occupy Helena."*

Pemberton seizes surplus provisions to feed soldiers and civilians.
Richard Taylor wants Milliken's Bend as a food base for Vicksburg.
He considers catapulting food across the river.

A court-martial is convened over the U.S. black/white soldier
    altercation to assign blame or vindicate the unjustly blamed.

Hickenlooper's Battery sharpshooters protect Logan's sappers.
Most of Pemberton's guns have been disabled or withdrawn.
Union artillerists claim to be able to hit the muzzle of a C.S. cannon.

Milliken's Bend is a training ground for newly recruited freed slaves.
Col. Hermann Lieb commands.

6 Kirby Smith at last launches a Trans-Mississippi offensive.
Richard Taylor is directed to Young's Point and Milliken's Bend.
He detaches the 13th Louisiana Cavalry Battalion.

Maj. Gen. John Walker engages with 5,000.
Henry McCulloch's brigade is directed to Milliken's Bend.
James Hawes is directed to Young's Point.
A Confederate brigade is held in reserve.
C.S. cavalry is sent to Lake Providence.

Lieb's 9th Louisiana U.S.C.T. and 10th Illinois cavalry, their feud
    subsided, engage C.S. troops at Tallulah, La.
Lieb requests reinforcements.

Grant surveys the Mechanicsburg Corridor with Charles Dana on the
    steamer *Diligent.*
Kimball's force begins a tortuous hot march back to Haynes Bluff.

U.S. sharpshooters are preventing Vicksburg from firing its big guns.

Battle of Milliken's Bend, La., June 7, 1863

7 1,500 Texans attack 1,100 Union forces at Milliken's Bend.
Vicksburg hears cannon of another Confederate force to the west.
U.S.C.T., barely trained, fight viciously, some using guns as clubs.

Confederates briefly take Milliken's Bend, screaming *"no mercy."*

The gunboats *U.S.S. Choctaw* and *Lexington* and the 23d Iowa help
    push back C.S. troops.
McCulloch withdraws to Oak Grove plantation.

June 1863 (Cont.)

7   James Hawes returns from Milliken's Bend without firing a shot:
"The challenge was too big."

Casualties:
U.S., 652 K, 285 W, 266 C/M
C.S., 185

The 9th Louisiana U.S.C.T. loses *68%* of its strength.
Many of the black Union troops captured are returned to slavery.
Reported execution of black troops is denied.

Richard Taylor moves to Alexandria to focus on New Orleans and
the Red River. ***Vicksburg is no longer his focus.***

Johnston: *"I am about ready to move to Vicksburg."*
Pemberton: *"I am ready to cooperate; subsistence down to 20
days."*

Six U.S. mortars bombard day and night from DeSoto Point.
Heavy siege guns are reported moving into Grant's lines.
Two 11-inch guns arrive from the gunboats courtesy of the Navy.

Grant's Mechanicsburg Expedition hurries back to Haynes Bluff.
Dozens of 12th Michigan soldiers suffer from sunstroke.
Soldiers threaten to hang the march's leader for torturing them.

Grant seriously doubts that 70,000 enemy troops are north and east.

Night truces are occurring sporadically along the Vicksburg lines.
A high degree of fraternization and personal truces are occurring.

8   Logan's sappers push to within 75 yards of the 3d Louisiana Redan.
Andrew Hickenlooper is working around the clock, his health at risk.

A Union line soldier usually fires 50 to 150 rounds per day.

Grant is eager to get more black regiments.
Sherman does not trust them to perform yet.

9   A Union soldier is wounded at Bayou Baxter, La.

The *body snatchers* – sharpshooters – are the biggest fear.
Some carry days of rations, but often can't find enough targets.
They can hit a four-inch target at 200 yards with open sights.
Some use 38-lb. Whitworth rifles capable of killing a mile away.

Indiana Lt. Henry *Coonskin* Foster's 40-foot sniper tower is
reported on John Logan's Approach.

10   Logan's Approach at 433 yards is the longest of the 13 Approaches.

Lt. Henry "Coonskin" Foster's tower above John Logan's Approach.
From a photograph by Armistead & Taylor at the Chicago History Museum, ICHi-068339.

June 1863 (Cont.)

10 Grant: *"The first soldier under a fort can set off the charge."*
His offer sets off a competition to complete an underground gallery.

McClernand's *Congratulatory Order* is in the St. Louis newspaper.

11 C.S. and U.S.N. Masons bury *U.S.S. Albatross* Lt. Cmdr. John Hart.
He is given a service at Grace Episcopal Church, St. Francisville, La.
He is buried in the Masonic section of the church cemetery.
The chronically despondent Hart committed suicide at Port Hudson.

Work begins on A. J. Smith's Approach at the 2^d Texas Lunette.

Hickenlooper installs two 9-inch guns south of the Shirley House.

Maj. Gen. Jay Herron's division arrives with eight regiments and
   three batteries.
Herron's division completes the investment of Vicksburg.

A Union assault on the northern lines is repulsed before sunset.

The MMB is declared a *"contingent of the Army, not the Navy."*

Johnston moves to Vernon, Miss., near the Big Black above Flora.
He tells Walker that preparations *are nearly complete.*

12 Pemberton to Johnston: *"Have received no word since May 25th."*

W. Sooy Smith arrives with 14 XVI Corps regiments and four
   batteries.

Sherman sees McClernand's Congratulatory Order in the *Memphis
   Bulletin.*
Grant's staff would love nothing more than to see McClernand sent
   packing.

June 1863 (Cont.)

12   A Union soldier is wounded at Birdsong Ferry.

A.J. Smith's Approach can support artillery and soldiers two abreast.

"A man can't raise his head without being targeted by six guns."

13   "Capt. Sanders" arrives from Johnston two weeks late.
He brings 200,000 precious percussion caps.

C.S. rations – 13 oz. of meal drops to 7.4 oz. of meal and 6 oz. of peas.
Confederates are butchering cattle nearest death.
Soldiers are refusing *"blue beef"* that makes glue, not gravy.

Hickenlooper is within 40 yards of the 3^d Louisiana Redan.
His project is without military precedent.

Union musketry sounds like *nine miles of logging axes chopping.*

14   Two IX Corps divisions arrive under Maj. Gen. John Parke.

The MMB with Brig. Gen. Joseph Mower has three wounded at
     Richmond, La.

Johnston admits to not being sufficiently forced to raise the Siege.

U.S. batteries complain about delays caused by a lack of engineers.
The *Engineers' War without engineers* is taking a month longer.

"At 10 a.m. daily, we loose the dogs of war on the Rebs for an hour."

15   Confederates have lost collective superiority at 62,000.
Grant has been reinforced with 21,000, bringing his total to 77,000.

Grant assigns the Army of Maneuver (34,000) to Sherman.
Sherman uses the reinforcements to start Grant's rear *Exterior
     Lines* designed to protect him from Joe Johnston.
Stronger than Vicksburg, the line runs from Snyder's Mill to
     Tiffentown.
Cadwallader Washburn is ordered to *"fortify the area from attack."*

Grant to his father: *"I have the enemy closely hemmed all around."*

Seddon to Johnston: *"IX Corps has been sent downriver to Grant."*

Johnston: *"I consider saving Vicksburg hopeless."*
Davis is furious.

Seddon to Johnson: *"Attack!"*
Johnston to Seddon: *"I am too weak."*
Theophilus Holmes to Sterling Price: *"Prepare to attack Helena."*

Pemberton to Johnston: *"In pretty good spirits here, but weak."*

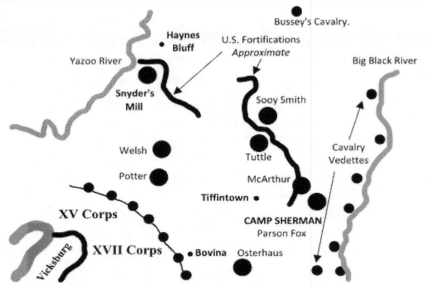

Grant's Exterior Lines and the Army of Maneuver

June 1863 (Cont.)

15 Grant is managing a Siege, an offensive war, and a defensive war.

Thomas Ransom's Approach against the 37th Mississippi begins.

Capt. John Wesley Powell, 2d Illinois Light Artillery, heroically advances cannon across the worst of terrain to fire at point-blank range down the Confederate lines.

An assault on the 27th Louisiana Lunette fails.

Work begins on Herron's Approach near Stout's Bayou.

A soldier: *"McPherson seems interested only in his ease/comfort."*

James Watts, 97th Indiana, Snyder's Bluff:
"We are all sunburnt and have the marks of hardships written on our general appearance."

16 Grant asks Porter for incendiary materials to burn Vicksburg.

Osterhaus' artillery pieces fire their 100 allotted rounds every day.

Daily Citizen editor J. M. Swords is using wallpaper as print stock.

500 caves have been dug for citizens in and around Vicksburg.

Lee's belief that Grant would leave Vicksburg during the heat of June is being disproved.

17 Brig. Gen. Isham Garrott is killed by a sniper at the Square Fort.

June 1863 (Cont.)

17 200,000 percussion caps arrive in Vicksburg over several days.

Sherman shows Grant McClernand's *Congratulatory Order*.
Sherman is so angry that he is speechless for minutes.

McClernand's line is weaker than the others; no guns are planted.

Hickenlooper is building platforms for two 30-pdr. Parrott rifles.
A 30-pdr. Parrott can hit a four-foot target at 2.5 miles.
It can penetrate 14 feet of earth.

18 McClernand pleads that he thought Grant saw a copy of his order.
James H. Wilson gladly gives McClernand his *marching orders*.
E.O.C. Ord replaces McClernand.

19 Ellet orders work on a casemate fort on the point opposite Vicksburg.

Carr's Approach has rifle pits 60 yards from the Railroad Redoubt.

Rats are selling in Vicksburg for $3.50 each, $125 in 2023 dollars.
Chickens bring $150 and molasses cost $200 in 2023 dollars.
Salt and sugar are used as currency.

20 West Virginia is admitted to the Union with 48 Virginia counties.

Grant requests mortars. *His order will not be filled.*
Sherman declares his Exterior Lines *impregnable*.

Grand Gulf appears evacuated.

Grant sees blue and gray soldiers playing checkers, a regular affair.
He tells his soldiers to share his next assault plans with the Rebs.
Rebs are too sick to fight or run.

Johnston to Pemberton: *"Suggest a breakout plan."*
Pemberton has 23,000 fit for duty; 5,700 in hospitals.
C.S. morale is hit by exposure, starvation, and no mail from home.
They are recognizing that their country has abandoned them.

Food stores contain about three weeks of supplies.
The Confederate supply of corn meal is exhausted.

An all-gun Army bombardment falls along the Siege lines.
Very little Vicksburg return fire is noticed.
Sherman: *"20,000 cannon balls fired into the city but no breach."*

Porter: *"Two MMB 10-pdr. Parrotts are much annoying Vicksburg."*

21 Messages from Johnston, the first since May 25th, arrive.
Pemberton: *"Attack the BBRB. I will escape to Hankinson's Ferry."*
Johnston to Pemberton: *"Build skiffs. Escape across the river."*

June 1863 (Cont.)

21   Grant tells his pickets to spread the word about the big upcoming July 6th Union assault.
"Give Pemberton a chance to consider."

22   Sherman's Army of Maneuver, 25,000, moves to Birdsong Ferry.
The two armies fight at Hill's Plantation near the ferry.

Casualties:
U.S., 8 K, 16 W, 23 M
C.S., 5 K, 16 W, 1 M

Texas regiments inflict many U.S. casualties at Vicksburg, lifting their morale.

Buckland's Approach is halted. He is ordered to the Exterior Lines.

After digging 1,500 feet in 30 days, Hickenlooper reaches the 3[d] Louisiana Redan with Logan's Approach.

23   9:00 a.m. – Soldiers begin mining under the 3[d] Louisiana Redan.
U.S. Illinois lead miners complete the cavernous galleries under the fort.

Approaches move forward near the Square Fort.
Work finally begins on Hovey's Approach in front of the Square Fort.
Hains is making good progress without McClernand's meddling.

Ellet's casemate is complete in four days, covered with railroad iron.
A 20-pdr. Parrott gun emplaced within Ellet's casemate opens fire.
The Confederates respond by firing 17 rounds from five guns.

Grant is miffed: *"The MMB is not subject to my orders."*

Union lines, in places, are within a few feet of the enemy.
"We can tap our bayonets against the enemy's bayonets."
The investment line around Vicksburg is impenetrable.

Johnston and Pemberton exchange final communications.
Pemberton suggests leaving the city to Grant and escaping.
"I will strain every nerve to hold out 15 days longer."

John Bowen is notified that he is officially a major general.
Margaret Lord sews Bowen's gold wreath on his collar.

Sherman arrives at Birdsong Ferry with Tuttle and John McArthur.

Enemies call *"blackberry truces"* to harvest leaves, roots, and fruit to help with diarrhea.

Soldiers agree to scattered battlefield oaths:
"Don't shoot at us and we won't shoot at y'all."

The Battle of Grant's First Crater, June 25, 1863
From a sketch by A.E. Mathews, 31ˢᵗ Ohio Volunteer Regiment, Missouri Historical Society.

June 1863 (Cont.)

24 Vicksburg troops, on quarter rations, must sleep on their weapons.
Lockett has a secondary line behind the 3ᵈ Louisiana Redan as a
backup.

McPherson plans the June 25ᵗʰ attack on the 3ᵈ Louisiana Redan.
It will be 102° *in the shade.*
Logan's sweltering troops are prostrate, close in, with fixed bayonets.

25 Hickenlooper is ready to detonate his 3ᵈ Louisiana Redan mine.
Grant issues a simple order: *"Let's blow it and see what happens."*
Hickenlooper must estimate the powder needed for rare *loess soil.*

10 pioneers under Hickenlooper will enter the crater to clear debris.
Coonskin Foster and 100 picked sharpshooters are 25 yards away.
The 20ᵗʰ Illinois has the suicide mission to install crater head logs.
Col. William Strong, 12ᵗʰ Wisconsin, helps Hickenlooper light the
fuse.

3:30 p.m. – The explosion blows a 40-foot-wide, 20-foot-deep
crater.
It is the **first successfully detonated mine in the Civil War.**

A 15-minute Union bombardment follows.
The incomplete breach becomes *a hell within a 500-foot radius.*
The crater can only contain 60-80 soldiers at a time.

The battle is known as *Slaughter Pen, Death Hole,* and *Fort Hell.*
An unprecedented 26 hours of bloodletting is hand-to-hand.

June 1863 (Cont.)

25 Logan recalls his soldiers from the 3ᵈ Louisiana Redan crater.
"My bravest men are being butchered in that hole."

6ᵗʰ C.S. Missouri Col. Eugene Irwin, grandson of Henry Clay, is killed.

Lt. Col. Samuel Naismith, 25th Wisconsin, begins a Greenville
incursion with an MMB detachment on the steamer *John Rains*.

Wirt Adams' cavalry seeks potential C.S. Big Black crossings.

Sherman requests that Seneca tribe member Ely Parker be assigned
to his staff.
Capt. Parker, a civil engineer, is permanently added to Grant's staff.

26 The Stockade Redan detonates two countermines to thwart Ewing.

Flag Officer Andrew Foote dies in New York of *Bright's Disease*.
He had been seeking treatment for his Fort Donelson wound.

27 Sherman to wife Ellen:
*"No parallel to the enmity of Southern women. I begged and
implored the South not to take this path. They will cave in in a
week."*

Douglas the Camel, the 43ᵈ Mississippi mascot, is killed by a
sharpshooter.
Brig. Gen. Martin Green, peeping at a U.S. approach, is killed.

Capt. Cyrus Comstock replaces an ill Prime as U.S. chief engineer.

Engineers will place a second mine under the 3ᵈ Louisiana Redan.
Stewart Tresilian fills in for a deathly overworked Hickenlooper.

Ellet's artillery is interfering with Vicksburg's foundry and shop work.

Johnston: *"Trans-Mississippi troops, mismanaged, have retreated."*

28 Johnston is confirmed to be approaching from a Brownsville route.
Grant is satisfied that he has a grasp of the Johnston threat.

Pemberton is surprised at the small size of Johnston's Relief Army.

Buckland's Approach is resumed by Joseph Lightburn's brigade.
Ransom's Approach is abandoned due to extreme terrain issues.

U.S. soldiers are tossing lit cannonballs; Rebs use hand grenades.

Pemberton receives a letter signed *"Many Soldiers"* asking for food
or surrender to preclude a mutiny.

Col. Leon Marks, 27ᵗʰ Louisiana, is mortally wounded by an exploding
shell while having his meal.

June 1863 (Cont.)

29   Hickenlooper is critically ill from sleep deprivation and nervous
strain.

Lake Providence reports 144 U.S. missing, 1 killed, and 3 wounded.
Union casualties on DeSoto Peninsula are 1 wounded.

U.S. soldiers are using *sweet-gum mortars*, the first in the Civil War.
Others are using improvised springboard hand-grenade launchers.
An improvised C.S. incendiary bullet is burning U.S. cotton
structures.

A sweet gum mortar on a stand at the Missouri State Museum.
From the Museum Muse, Winter/Spring 2014.

Sharpshooters are claiming 10 percent of Pemberton's force.
*"My friend said he wanted just wanted a quick peek at the Rebs.
When he showed only his eyes, he was shot in the forehead."*

30   The *American Freedman's Inquiry Commission* issues a report,
"A Social Reconstruction of the Southern States."
It offers a Bureau of Emancipation, black equality, and property.

Grant supports a reconciliatory mood toward citizens and soldiers.

C.S. daily rations are a handful of peas and rice, @ 200 calories.
The *"dead wagon"* retrieves about 100 C.S. corpses per day.
They are being buried in Cedar Hill Cemetery behind the north lines.

At Goodrich's Landing, La., south of Lake Providence, the MMB loses
120; Capt. Wright is killed.

Work begins on Slack's Approach fronting the 23ᵈ Alabama.

Grant has 220 artillery pieces engaged at Vicksburg in 89 batteries.

June 1863 (Cont.)

30   A bullet smashes *Coonskin* Foster's mirror after he had fired 100
rounds.

July 1863

1   Davis is rethinking his decision not to send troops to Vicksburg.

Vicksburg soldier water rations are down to a quarter cup per day.

Lt. Col. John Reese, 31st Illinois, dies of 43d Mississippi sharpshooter
wounds when he was chosen as revenge for *Douglas the Camel*.

A second mine is detonated to demonstrate on Logan's Approach.
100 Confederates litter the explosion field.

A Confederate slave, Abraham, is blown into the U.S. trenches.
He says that he that he had flown *about three miles*.
A nickel is charged to view *the first person ever to fly to freedom*.
He joins the Army as Maj. Gen. McPherson's kitchen team.

Based on the two previous detonations, the correct charge size for
future detonations is refined.
Hickenlooper, now fully conscious, is visited by Grant.

Three Union soldiers are wounded at Edwards Station.

Brig. Gen. William Orme puts more faith in starving out the
Confederates, than in assaults.

Johnston's Army of Relief is suffering greatly from straggling.
Wirt Adams' Big Black probe is attacked near Hankinson's Ferry.

Pemberton is working out of a *rust-encrusted dugout* in a hillside.
He queries his division commanders: surrender or breakout?

U.S. sniper Peter Knapp shoots C.S. sniper Willis Meadows in the
eye through a small hole in a piece of boilerplate.
Meadows miraculously survives.

Maj. Gen. John Reynolds, exchanged earlier for Brig. Gen. Lloyd
Tilghman, is killed in the first day of fighting at Gettysburg.

2   Wirt Adams' cavalry is driven away from Hankinson's Ferry.

U.S. sympathizers are helping Grant and confusing Confederates.

Capt. Comstock issues guidelines for the proposed July 6th attack.
More than half of Grant's army is within pistol shot of the enemy.

Widened approaches will handle artillery and soldiers four abreast.

The Mississippi Marine Brigade crosses Big Black River.

July 1863 (Cont.)

2   Green's Redan attacks Giles Smith with grenades and countermines.
A countermine is fired on Carr's Approach.
A defective shell destroys two U.S. sweet-gum mortars.

100-pdr. Parrott rifles, accurate to five miles, open fire on the city.

Bowen, exhausted, dying, writes a Pemberton surrender position.

Engineer Andrew Hickenlooper returns to duty.

Union soldiers are boasting they will soon dine in Vicksburg.
The Daily Citizen prints its final Siege edition, chiding U.S. troops,
   "You must first catch the rabbit before you can eat it."

3   Union approaches at the Square Fort are within 10 yards of the works.
Thayer's sappers dig the gallery under the 26ᵗʰ Louisiana Lunette.
Grant will blow *"whatever mines are available"* on July 6ᵗʰ.

Mule meat in Vicksburg is $1 a pound ($36 in 2023 dollars).

C.S. scouts report potential southern Big Black crossings unguarded.
Grant prefers to let Pemberton escape and capture him later.

3:00 p.m. – At the *exact hour* of the Confederate defeat at
   Gettysburg, Grant and Pemberton began the interview to discuss the
   surrender of Vicksburg.

The Army of Relief sits motionless at the Big Black River.
Johnston's War Council: *"Move through Edwards to Hankinson's."*
Johnston, hearing no Vicksburg artillery, ends his relief mission.

4   5:00 a.m. – A 34-gun Union salute for July 4ᵗʰ honors *all 34 states*.
"Vicksburg is Silent."

Grant orders respect to be shown to the Defenders of Vicksburg.
"They are our brothers, as misguided as they may be."
Grant initially wants to send Confederates north to prisoner camps.
Paroling 29,491 reduces U.S. logistics, supplies, labor ... and time.
Union parole camps are in Enterprise, Miss., and Demopolis, Ala.

10:00 a.m. – Rebel columns parade out of their trenches.
They stack arms, flags, and equipment and march back into the city.
Cheers of tribute from Union counterparts ring out along the lines.

Grant sends a message to all commanders: *"Go in."*
The 4ᵗʰ Minnesota is the first regiment to enter Vicksburg.
Grant to Herron: *"Watch the southern exits for trouble."*

E.O.C. Ord is ordered to join Sherman's Jackson expeditionary force.

July 1863 (Cont.)

4 Union forces capture 142 pieces of artillery and vast military stores.
The Confederacy loses 11% of its artillery at Vicksburg.

U.S. troops trade lesser rifles for 50,000 C.S. Enfields.
Vicksburg Enfields rearm two Union armies with superior firepower.

Kirby Smith agrees to take Helena with Holmes' 8,000 men.
Smith suffers heavy losses at Helena, *the last hope for Vicksburg*.
The loss opens Arkansas and Little Rock to a Union offensive.

Col. Marcus Spiegel, 120th Ohio:
"Grant is the greatest chieftain of the age.
  The boys all love him."

U.S. soldiers reprint the *Daily Citizen: "Grant has caught the rabbit."*

Siege Casualties:
U.S. soldiers on gunboats, 6 K, 26 W
U.S., 94 K, 425 W, and 119 C/M
C.S., 875 K, 2,169 W, and 158 C/M
Union sharpshooters account for extreme Confederate losses.

Five Confederate general officers die during the Campaign and
  Siege: Tracy, Green, Bowen, Garrott, and Tilghman.
The highest-ranking Union officer killed: Col. George B. Boomer.

Lincoln:
"Grant is my man, and I am his, for the rest of the war."

Porter's rear admiral rank is made permanent.

5 Grant establishes his headquarters in Vicksburg's Lum House.

Bowen is violently ill from dysentery, possibly from eating green corn.

Logan's troops occupy the Confederate lines.

Porter lands his fleet at the Vicksburg city front.
Grant and Porter share Catawba wine in a congratulatory gesture.
Grant's Galena lead miners, the 45th Illinois, are given provost duty.

McPherson is assigned to parole 29,491 prisoners.

U.S. soldiers give Vicksburg defenders five days of rations and
  supplies.
Enemies socialize as though they *"have been at peace 47 days."*
Others defiantly declare: *"We didn't talk to them people."*

Confederates tell Lauman's Division:
"Grant has the best Army in the World."
"We don't mind losing to Grant, just the Army of the Potomac."

July 1863 (Cont.)

6   Joe Johnston withdraws to Jackson.

Capt. John M. Wilson begins a smaller Vicksburg fortification line.
The new fortifications ring is called *"Fort Grant."*

William Sherman begins his eastward campaign.
He crosses the Big Black River in force in three places.

Bowen refuses the best Federal medical care at Vicksburg.
Mary Bowen comes from her Edward Siege refuge to care for John.
She has been with him the entire Campaign, their children at home.
Bowen is taken to an ambulance away from the *"hated enemy and
   defeat."*

7   Lincoln receives Porter's message of Vicksburg's surrender.

Pemberton's Army is being paroled. 709 prefer prison camps.

Looting in Vicksburg is met with a bayonet.

Texas, the Confederacy's main source of beef, is now cut off.
Key sources of corn, hogs, salt, sugar, rice, molasses, lead, horses and
   men are also lost, along with the port at Matamoras, Mexico.

Sherman moves toward Jackson unopposed; he begins *Total War*.
Poisoned water sources are complicating Sherman's scorching route.
Sherman's soldiers and animals are suffering in the hot march.
Grant is instructing Sherman not to push too hard in the heat.
Sherman: *"It is cruel to march soldiers in this heat."*

Louisiana soldiers leave as *citizens* rather than as soldiers.
Many cross the river in pirogues.

8   Capt. Patrick White, Chicago Mercantile Battery, hero at the 2ᵈ Texas
   Lunette, is ill on Sherman's march to Jackson.

Nathaniel Banks advises Franklin Gardner, C.S. commander at Port
   Hudson, that Vicksburg has fallen.

9   Johnston has restored his fortifications at Jackson.

The Mississippi Marine Brigade reaches Clinton.

Port Hudson, Pemberton's southernmost fort, surrenders to Banks.

Trans-Mississippi messages take two weeks to reach Richmond, Va.
Isolated, the Trans-Mississippi Dept. becomes independent *Kirby*
   Smith's personal *Smith-dom.*

10   Sherman reaches Jackson and decides to lay siege to the city.
Ambulances are transporting 3,200 sick from Jackson to Vicksburg.

July 1863 (Cont.)

10 The Eads ironclad monitor *U.S.S. Osage* is commissioned at Cairo.

Matilda Champion to husband Sid:
"Almost everyone is leaving for Georgia."

11 6:00 a.m. – John Bowen's ambulance departs from Vicksburg.
The Army of Vicksburg begins its departure for the parole camps.
3,600 sick and wounded remain in hospitals.
Vicksburg Confederate soldiers are furloughed as they heal.
C.S. medical attendants encourage them to return to the Army.

Halleck to Grant: *"U.S. Colored Troops should occupy Vicksburg."*

11:30 a.m. – The last able Confederate soldier departs Vicksburg.
Pemberton to Davis: *"Many desertions; I have no armed guards."*
Parolees sleep on the east side of the Big Black after a 14-mile march.

Pemberton receives Johnston's message that he will attack on July 7.

An unsupported 2ᵈ Michigan attack on Loring's Jackson position
   fails.

The Siege of Jackson, Miss., July 12, 1863

12 The ambulance containing Bowen departs Edwards for Raymond on
   the Mt. Moriah Road, site of Bowen's earlier earthworks.

Sherman fires 3,000 rounds into Jackson.
He outnumbers Johnston 2 to 1.

Maj. Gen. Jacob Lauman leads a desperate charge on Sherman's
   right in which his units are decimated.
Ord removes Lauman from command for this ill-conceived action.
Sherman's assault fails.
Col. William Witherspoon's father dies in the barrage as a volunteer.

The *U.S.S. Baron DeKalb* is moving upriver near Satartia.

Bowen's ambulance must stop at the Walton house six miles beyond
   Edwards near a Baker's Creek crossing.

Most of Vicksburg's remaining parolees camp at Raymond.
Carter Stevenson departs Vicksburg.

13   **Lincoln to Grant:**
            "You were right and I was wrong."

Maj. Gen. John Stevens Bowen dies of dysentery.
Bowen is buried in the garden of the Walton home (Valley Farms).

Bowen is officially exchanged for Chancellorsville prisoners.

July 1863 (Cont.)

13 The Vicksburg parolee column avoids Jackson.
Parolees cross the Pearl River, headed to Brandon.
Johnston's outposts make connection with the parolees.

Parolees are straggling hourly, despite Pemberton's pleas.
Sick soldiers, facing a powerful foe and abandoned by their country,
 are *finished with the war*.
Only about 5,000 of Pemberton's force will reenter the war.

The Yazoo River is mined with much improved mines.
Isaac Brown places the last two mines in the river himself.

The U.S.S. Baron DeKalb is sunk by a Fretwell-Hunley mine at
 Yazoo City.
She is blown to smithereens by her crew.

Sherman is lobbying for a Red River-Texas Campaign.

Lincoln wants Louisiana and Texas represented in 1864 elections.

14 Union batteries at Jackson fire every five minutes, day and night.

Only 1,600 Missouri Confederates are willing to fight as ordered.

15 Johnston orders Brig. Gen. James Chalmers to take Yazoo City.

Davis essentially accuses Johnston of *dereliction of duty*.
Johnston is relieved of his theatre of command.

16 The packet *Imperial* safely travels from St. Louis to New Orleans.
Lincoln:
**"Once again, the Father of Waters flows unvexed to the
 sea."**

Sherman tightens his grip on Jackson.
Johnston orders a retreat.

Vicksburg's generals are exchanged for Chancellorsville prisoners.

17 Davis is more bitter toward Johnston after Vicksburg's fall.
He blames a lack of resources and *"a general who would not fight."*

Johnston evacuates Jackson and escapes across the Pearl River.
Parke's IX Corps elements enter Jackson.
Sherman's forces are too exhausted to follow Johnston.

Grant advises Sherman to give up marching to trap Johnston.
Sherman burns Jackson again, creating *Chimneyville*.

19 Sherman takes Brandon.

Most Vicksburg citizens are living *"on the bounty of the fort."*

July 1863 (Cont.)

19	Arkansas complains about being isolated, devastated, and forgotten.
20	W.S. Featherston's brigade reaches Forest, Miss.
	Union soldiers are setting charges under Yazoo City fortifications.
21	Parolee remnants reach the Enterprise, Miss., exchange camp.
22	Burned and sunken packets litter the Yazoo and Tallahatchie rivers.
23	Sherman departs Jackson for Vicksburg after feeding the citizens.
	Pemberton gives parolees a 30-day furlough over Davis' objection.
24	Pemberton reaches Demopolis, Ala., the other exchange camp.
25	The 13th Infantry is Sherman's guard at Parson Fox's (*Camp Sherman*) on Woodburne Plantation near Birdsong Ferry.
26	Davis' constituents are suggesting the use of slaves as soldiers. *"Better to use them for defense than to have them used against us."*
27	Sherman reaches his Camp Sherman headquarters.
28	The battle for the Yazoo River is declared over.
30	Lincoln's *Order of Retaliation* provides the same punishment for C.S. troops that they use against U.S. soldiers, black or white. Exchanges are stopped. Prisoner camps grow, creating living hell for prisoners of both sides.

August 1863

1	Fearing an epidemic, throngs of freedmen are moved to the disease-ridden Louisiana mudflats across from Vicksburg.
6	Lloyd Tilghman, Jr., falls from his horse and dies in Selma, Ala. His father's assistant, Lloyd Jr., helped move his dad's body on May 16.
7	Capt. Samuel DeGolyer dies of his May 25th wound in Hudson, Mich.
8	Johnston responds to Davis' accusations with anger. A *paper war* between Johnston and Davis begins. Pemberton and Johnston are pointing fingers at each other. Davis takes attacks on Pemberton personally against his staff's advice.
9	Lincoln supports Grant's recruitment of and use of black troops. *"100,000 should be raised so white troops can fight elsewhere."*
10	Lincoln and Frederick Douglass discuss recruiting additional black troops.

August 1863

12   Johnston only commands the troops that were with him at Jackson.

14   Brig. Gen. Thomas Welsh dies in Cincinnati of malaria after Jackson. He had commanded the 1st Division of Parke's IX Union Corps.

Davis is warned, *"Protecting Pemberton will destroy you."*

15   Maj. Gen. Frederick Steele is camped on the Big Black at Bovina.

19   Pemberton receives Johnston's delayed message to *work a surrender*.

26   The Chicago Mercantile Battery leaves Vicksburg on the steamer *Atlantic* headed south to New Orleans.

30   Soldiers comparing memories determine that the single Confederate officer seen firing his gun alone at the Champion Hill retreat was killed in action manning his piece.

U.S.C.T. soldiers from a *Library of Congress image*.

U.S. Naval Memorial featuring Foote, Davis, Porter and Farragut.
(GJMC)

PART VI
Vicksburg's Peacemakers Conclude the Matter

On the Warrior's Trail with
the Triumvirate forged at Vicksburg
September 1863-December 1865

The Rodney, Miss., Presbyterian Church where *U.S.S. Rattler* sailors were captured. *(ALB)*

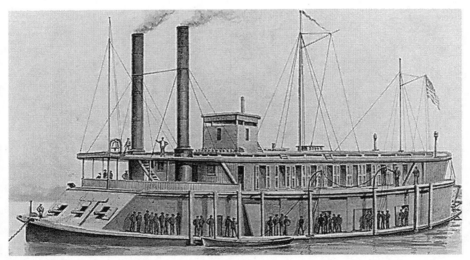

The *U.S.S. Rattler and crew, many of whom were captured in the church service.* *(USNHHC)*

PART VI
Vicksburg's Peacemakers Conclude the Matter

September 1863

4   Nathaniel Banks holds a grand review for Grant in New Orleans. Grant is severely injured when his nervous horse falls with him.

7   Joe Johnston sends his idle 9,000 troops from Mississippi to Bragg. Lee prepares to send Longstreet with two divisions to Bragg.

10 Little Rock, Ark., falls, sending its Confederate government into exile.

13 Halleck directs Grant and available troops to Chattanooga, Tenn.

15 Confederate scouts briefly capture many of the *U.S.S. Rattler's* crew attending church services at Rodney, Miss.
*Acting Capt. Walter Fentress is the **only U.S. Navy officer ever captured by Confederate cavalry**.*

18 Longstreet's forces begin to arrive in Tennessee to support Bragg.

Bragg's 62,000 hit disorganized U.S. forces south of Chattanooga.

21 C.S. Brig. Gen. Benjamin Hardin Helm, Lincoln's brother-in-law, is killed at Chickamauga, Ga., leading the 1st Kentucky Brigade, the *Orphan Brigade*.
His widow is the former Emilie Todd.
Lincoln seeks Emilie's forgiveness for Helm's death.

22 Kirby Smith orders Vicksburg parolees in his area reorganized.

23 Col. Leon Marks, 27th Louisiana, dies in Shreveport from wounds.

27 Sherman and the 13th U.S. Infantry depart Vicksburg aboard the steamer *Atlantic*.
His family entourage includes son Willie, ill with diarrhea.
Sherman had convinced Ellen to let the boy join him at Camp Sherman on the Big Black River where it was *"free of fever."*

The War Department gives the Army jurisdiction over the Mississippi Marine Brigade.

The Steamship *Atlantic*, often used by the 13th U.S. Infantry.
By Samuel Ward Stanton, American Steam Vessels.

September 1863 (Cont.)

30 The Shermans and surgeons are desperately caring for Willie.
The *Atlantic* is a slow-moving boat.
The surgeon of the 55th Illinois is personally attending Willie.

October 1863

1 Johnston's hatred of Davis is at a boiling point.

2 10:30 p.m. – The Sherman family finally arrives in Memphis.

3 5:00 p.m. – Willie Sherman dies in Memphis of typhoid fever.

4 A 13th U.S. Infantry funeral procession carries their beloved mascot
Sgt. Willie to the waterfront.
The family boards the *Grey Eagle* for passage to Cairo, Ill.
Sherman remains in Memphis.

Sherman to Grant: *"I cannot but must and will compose myself."*

6 Sherman:
"All the ambition I ever had was based on the future of that child."

10 Ten generals sign a petition to Davis for Braxton Bragg's removal.

Sherman in grief to Ellen: *"Why was I not killed at Vicksburg?"*

11 A devastated Sherman departs Memphis by special train for
Corinth, Miss.
Brig. Gen. James Chalmers attacks Sherman's train and garrison
at Collierville, Tenn.

13 Davis is personally seeking a Corps position for Pemberton.
He drops the idea when a *mutiny of the Army* is threatened.

14 Grant passes Memphis by boat enroute to Cairo.

Logan breaks camp at Vicksburg to move toward Canton, Miss.

16 Grant meets with Secretary of War William Stanton in Indiana.
He is given command of the Military Division of the Mississippi.

October 1863 (Cont.)

16 Sherman assumes command of the Army of the Tennessee.
Grant assigns the Army of the Cumberland to George Thomas.

17 McPherson's diversion to Canton, Miss., helps relieve pressure on
George Thomas at Chattanooga, Tenn.

19 Grant to Thomas: *"Hold Chattanooga at all costs."*

20 Still on crutches, Grant is assisted onto the train to Chattanooga.

22 Grant is strapped to his horse, riding over the most terrible roads.

23 Grant arrives at Thomas' headquarters at Chattanooga in pain.

26 Grant makes a brazen move to break the siege on his forces.
Grant's move is every bit *as bold as running the Vicksburg batteries*.

27 The *Cracker Line* to Union forces near Chattanooga is finally open.

Grant orders the use of contrabands as noncombatants.
They will be paid, then clothed and cared for out of their pay.

The Battle of Wauhatchie, Tenn., October 28, 1864

28 Maj. Gen. Hooker protects the Union supply line at Brown's Ferry.

Grant is fighting Julia's *cousin*, his own *best man*, James Longstreet.

Runaway Union mules sound like a mad Union charge.
Longstreet's soldiers retreat away from the noise of the mules.
The mules are recommended for brevet promotion *to horses*.

November 1863

14 Sherman arrives ahead of his army to a *beaming, jovial* Grant.

19 Sherman's leading divisions arrive in Chattanooga.

20 Vicksburg's parolees in Louisiana are to report to Alexandria, La.

23 George Thomas' Corps pushes 634 Confederates off of Orchard
Knob.
The victory proves that Braxton Bragg still has a viable fighting
force.
The hill will serve as Grant's Missionary Ridge observation post.

The Battle of Lookout Mountain, Ga., November 24, 1863

24 Maj. Gen. Carter Stevenson is defeated by Maj. Gen. Joe Hooker.
The victory sets Hooker on Stevenson's left flank for the next day.

The Battle of Missionary Ridge, Tenn., November 25, 1863

25 The usually calm Grant is nervous.
Arthur McArthur, bearing the 24th Wisconsin banner, calls
"On Wisconsin!"
Grant wins the impromptu 50-minute assault.

November 1863 (Cont.)

25   Col. Holden Putnam, 93rd Illinois, is killed on Missionary Ridge.
Holden replaced Col. George Boomer killed in the assault May 22.
Confederates lose 40 precious artillery pieces captured.

Casualties:
U.S., 753 K, 4,722 W, 349 C/M
C.S., 361 K, 2,160 W, 4,146 C/M

27   Davis asks Congress to increase slave personnel to release whites for
other duties.

Sherman must march in haste 85 miles to Knoxville, Tenn., to save
Maj. Gen. Ambrose Burnside who is besieged.

29   Burnside pushes Longstreet back at Knoxville.

December 1863

1   Davis temporarily replaces Braxton Bragg with William Hardee.

7   Davis is trying to convince Robert E. Lee to go South.
Lee will, if ordered.
Lee convinces him to restore Johnston to command over Beauregard.

8   Lincoln publishes his *Proclamation of Amnesty and Reconstruction.*
Its pardons and land restoration omits the highest Confederate
officials.
It allows new state governments where 10% of voters sign oaths of
allegiance.
Readmitted states could develop freedmen plans that respect their
freedoms.

Davis' response to the Proclamation is publicly defiant.

16   Davis to Johnston: *"Assume command of the Army of Tennessee."*

22   Brig. Gen. Sul Ross departs the Big Black River to deliver rifles to
Kirby Smith and the Trans-Mississippi Dept.

25   Sherman, home for Christmas, is amazed at Grant's popularity.

Congress passes Joint Resolutions for Vicksburg and Chattanooga.
A 1-lb. gold medal is authorized for Grant *in the name of the people of
the United States.*

31   Under orders from Sherman, the Lum House is destroyed.
Grant had promised the Lum family when he departed Vicksburg that
it would be spared.

January 1864

16   C.S. Maj. Gen. Patrick Cleburne supports the idea of slave soldiers.
He is condemned by Tennessee Gov. Isham Harris.

January 1864 (Cont.)

17   Sherman to McPherson: *"Control the Mississippi River raiders."*

Fred Grant is stricken with typhoid fever, Willie Sherman's killer.

19   Sherman shares his idea of destroying railroads with RAdm. Porter. His focus is Mississippi's Meridian-to-Jackson RR.

21   McPherson orders Yazoo River ferries destroyed to block guerillas.

28   Sherman arrives in Vicksburg to meet with McPherson.

30   U.S. troops are picked to busy Sul Ross' Yazoo River cavalry raiders. They may take cotton as prizes and burn anything not wanted.

31   Sherman's Meridian Campaign prevents him from joining the Red River Campaign led by Nathaniel Banks.

February 1864

1   The Confederate Army has no bayonets.
In winter, only one-third of the shoes needed are available.
Artillery horses are too feeble to move a battery.
There is insufficient food for man or beast.
Johnston believes that starting an offensive is impractical.

Brig. Gen. William Sooy Smith and 7,000 cavalry are ordered by Sherman to depart Memphis to link up with him at Meridian on February 10th.
Smith is to destroy Forrest's cavalry, maintain communications with Middle Tennessee, and add troops to the Atlanta Campaign.
Nathaniel Banks will stage boats near Mobile, Ala., to occupy area Confederate forces.

2   The U.S. Yazoo Expedition moves up the Yazoo River, with the 3[d] U.S.C.T. Cavalry, 11th Illinois, and 8th Louisiana-African Descent.
Its goal – to distract Forrest from Sherman's Georgia supply line.
The *U.S.S. Mamora* accompanies the expedition.

3   Sherman's Meridian Expedition and *Mississippi Pacification* begins. He departs Vicksburg with four divisions (20,000 soldiers).

Sul Ross' cavalry fires on the Yazoo Expedition at Liverpool Landing. Two Ross regiments entrench while two go to the Yazoo City road.

4   The Yazoo Expedition is again under heavy fire from Sul Ross. The vessels struggle forward as Ross folds in behind them.

5   Realizing the city is heavily armed, the Yazoo Expedition pulls back.

6   The Yazoo Expedition backs away and requests the *U.S.S. Louisville*.

7   Capt. James Owen's 1,600 U.S. troops disembark and move on Ross.

Ross, realizing Owen is a feint, departs, taking his units to the east.

Yazoo City

Liverpool
Landing

Satartia

Yazoo River

Mechanicsburg●

Mississippi
River

Haynes Bluff

Big Black River

Vicksburg

The
**Mechanicsburg
Corridor**

February 1864 (Cont.)

8 U.S. Brig. Gen. John McArthur is ordered to Yazoo City.

Yazoo City is captured by the Yazoo Expedition.

10 *Grant recalls to Julia his broken-down condition three years earlier.*
Now, he has 700 times the soldiers and will *decide the national fate.*

Lt. Gen. Leonidas Polk alerts Richmond of Sherman's movement,
possibly against Mobile.
Davis asks Johnston for reinforcements for Polk.
Johnston replies that he cannot weaken his position to help.

11 Sooy Smith inexplicably delays **10 days** to begin his march to link
up with Sherman.

14 Polk believes Sherman's objective is Mobile.
He evacuates Meridian without a fight, moving to Demopolis, Ala.
Sherman's forces reach Meridian.
He gives his soldiers an unmistakably clear order.
"Wipe Meridian off the map."

February 1864 (Cont.)

14 The Yazoo Expedition reaches Greenwood, serving as a diversion for Sherman's Meridian Campaign.

Sherman: *"Poor secesh horses make 40-50 miles day; our costly fat ones only make 10 miles a day."*

16 The Yazoo Expedition departs Grenada, having successfully drawn Forrest away.
Sooy Smith and his 7,000 enter New Albany, Miss., behind schedule.

17 Davis *orders* Johnston to send three divisions to attack Sherman.
An angry Davis blasts the missed opportunity to destroy Sherman.

18 Sooy Smith pushes Rebs at West Point, 90 miles north of Meridian.

19 The Yazoo Expedition departs Yazoo City with 2,000 cotton bales.

C.S. Brig. Gen. William Baldwin dies after a fall from his horse in Alabama.

McClernand returns to XIII Corps under Banks' Gulf Department.

20 Sherman, worried about Sooy Smith's whereabouts, departs Meridian for Vicksburg.
He reportedly said, *"Meridian with its depots, storehouses, arsenal, hospitals, offices, hotels, and cantonments no longer exists."*

This burning of Meridian was practice for his *March to the Sea*.
Sooy Smith hears of Sherman's move west and turns back toward Okolona, Miss., encountering enemy outposts.

21 Forrest stops Sooy Smith at Ellis Bridge near West Point.
Smith turns back to Tennessee.

22 Forrest's 2,500 defeat Smith's 7,000 at Okolona.
Sherman's right flank is eliminated by Forrest's much smaller band.

Forrest's younger brother, Col. Jeffrey Forrest, is killed at Okolona.
Forrest is devastated, attacks like a demon, and is victorious.

26 Congress restores the historic rank of lieutenant general for Grant.
Only George Washington had held the rank previously.

Sooy Smith is criticized for jeopardizing Sherman's Meridian effort.

28 The Yazoo Expedition arrives in Yazoo City.

Ross with his Texas cavalry has returned and reinforced Yazoo City.
Ross engages Yazoo Expedition pickets.
He begins a five-day standoff against Col. James H. Coates.
Coates calls for reinforcements.
Ross strengthens his defenses.

March 1864

2   Grant learns of Sherman's Meridian Campaign success.

Sherman meets with Banks in New Orleans to discuss Red River.
Banks pulls rank and a miffed Sherman decides not to go.
Sherman will loan 10,000 soldiers to Banks' effort.

Porter agrees to send *every vessel in his fleet* with Banks.
He will go personally.
Lt. Cdr. James Owen is transferred to the Red River Campaign.
Yazoo ships are entrusted to the *U.S.S. Petrel*'s acting master
    Thomas McElroy.

Brig. Gen. Robert Richardson brings Tennessee cavalry to Ross' aid.

3   McPherson departs Vicksburg to replace Sherman.

Grant receives his lieutenant general rank.
To Sherman:
"To you and McPherson I am indebted above all others."
Sherman to Grant:
"Your chief characteristic is your faith in success."

5   Richardson and Ross attack the Yazoo Expedition in a brutal fight.
The furious fight is street-to-street, house to house.
The Union's captured cotton and other stolen goods are burned.
Confederates withdraw as ammunition dwindles and negotiations
    fail.

6   Sherman's Meridian Expedition ends.
5,000 freed negroes follow Sherman back to Vicksburg.
Federals can move at will throughout the entire state of Mississippi.

The Yazoo Expedition returns to Vicksburg.

8   Grant and son Fred arrive in Washington, D.C.

Two sailors are killed in the sinking of the timberclad *U.S.S.
    Conestoga* when it collides with the *U.S.S. General Price near
    Bayou Pierre, Miss.*
The *Conestoga* is commanded by Thomas O. Selfridge, Jr., the
    commander of the *U.S.S. Cairo* torpedoed in 1862.

9   By Grant's promotion to lieutenant general, he outranks Halleck.
Halleck is made Grant's *chief of staff.*

Grant intends to consolidate many independent armies into just two.
Sherman will resume command of the Army of the Tennessee.
Sherman will attack Johnson's Army of Tennessee.
Grant, headquartered with the Army of the Potomac, will attack
    Robert E. Lee and his Army of Northern Virginia.

March 1864 (Cont.)

10 Porter departs Vicksburg for the Red River with Sherman's troops. Sherman asks Grant to man Haynes Bluff to protect the Mississippi.

11 Davis does not blame Pemberton for the fall of Vicksburg. **Both Lee and Davis blame Johnston** and a lack of resources.

Sherman's soldiers are at the mouth of the Red River in Louisiana. Lt. Cdr. Seth Phelps grounds the lead *U.S.S. Eastport* on a sandbar.

15 *The U.S.S. Osage (below)*, Thomas Selfridge's new command, peacefully captures Alexandria, La.

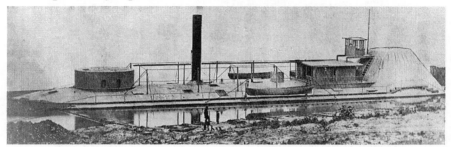

U.S.S. Osage on the Western waters.
(USNHHC)

March 1864 (Cont.)

16 Porter's fleet is docked at Alexandria, La., his crews enjoying the town.

17 Grant meets Sherman to transition Western and Deep South duties. *Enlightened Warfare* is born after wrecking Jackson and Meridian.

19 Receiving no offers as a general, John Pemberton resigns his rank.

20 **A closely guarded meeting is held in Parlor A of the Burnet House in Cincinnati, Ohio.** Grant and Sherman detail the final strategies of the war for the Virginia and Georgia campaigns.

24 Porter requests adjudication of 2,129 cotton bales from Alexandria. In 2023 dollars, Porter claims $65 million.

John McArthur is serving as Vicksburg commandant.

31 Sul Ross' Texas cavalry brigade is sent to Alabama.

April 1864

6 Banks makes a mistake in moving his Army away from Porter's gunboats.

April 1864 (Cont.)

8   Porter's fleet arrives at Coushatta, La.

Banks is defeated at the Battle of Mansfield, La.

Two brigades of U.S.C.T. are stationed at Vicksburg, half the garrison.

Large C.S. arsenals have been established from Richmond to Selma.
Josiah Gorgas, C.S. Ordnance, is boasting of the ordnance recovery.
"We now make ordnance and guns sufficient for our army."
Head of Confederate arsenals is James Burton, formerly of the
   Harper's Ferry Arsenal and developer of the .577 *Burton bullet.*

9   Grant to George Meade:
"Lee's Army is your objective point. Where he goes, you go."

10   RAdm. Porter is blocked by the sunken Reb steamer *New Falls City*.
He learns of Banks' defeat.
Porter and Kilby Smith agree to return to Grand Ecore, La.

12   Black soldiers are massacred at Fort Pillow, Tenn.

Porter's *U.S.S. Lexington* and transport *Rob Roy* collide at
   Coushatta Chute, La.

13   Porter's fleet reaches the safety of Grand Ecore.

14   A nervous Kilby Smith, fearing a trap, abandons the struggling
   steamers *John Warner* and *Fort Hindman*.

15   The steamer *Fort Hindman* frees the *John Warner* of its entrapment.
Both vessels arrive safely at Grand Ecore.

16   Porter's fleet steams three miles downstream, led by the *U.S.S.*
   Eastport.
The *Eastport* strikes a Singer torpedo and blocks the fleet.

17   John McArthur calls in Col. Hiram Schofield to capture Yazoo City.

19   Pemberton solves his dilemma by taking a lieutenant colonel's rank.
The decision returns Pemberton to Virginia closer to wife Pattie.

Maj. Gen. Henry W. Slocum is now fortress Vicksburg commandant.
McPherson asks Schofield to harass Grenada once Yazoo City is secure.

20   Union troops land and occupy the Liverpool heights near Satartia.
Wirt Adams' cavalry, unsure of the enemy, withdraws to Yazoo City.

21   The *U.S.S. Eastport* is refloated and the fleet continues downstream.

Coordinated Navy and Army units land at Yazoo City.
Schofield calls for occupying Yazoo City, if not too strong.
The *U.S.S. Petrel* is shelled by the Arkansas *Monticello Battery*.

April 1864 (Cont.)

22 Wirt Adams, by a surprise surge attack, captures the *U.S.S. Petrel*.
He is joined by Col. John Griffith's Arkansas regiments.
13 Union officers and 40 crewmen escape to the *U.S.S. Prairie Bird*.

23 Two Miss. Marine Brigade boats return Schofield to Haynes Bluff.
The loss of the favorite *U.S.S. Petrel* galls the Western naval group.
Wirt Adams continues to guard his part of the Yazoo theater.

26 At Montgomery, La., the *U.S.S. Eastport* is hopelessly stuck by snags.
Fearing the *Eastport* will block the fleet, Porter orders it destroyed.

McArthur sends troops to push west to busy Wirt Adams and others.

The *Champion No. 3* is sunk near Cane River with 100 freed blacks
below her decks.
The *Cricket*, with Porter onboard, is hit 38 times, losing half her crew.

29 Falling river levels threaten to trap Porter's fleet.
Banks engages engineer Lt. Col. Joseph Bailey to raise river levels.
Bailey begins a dam to raise river levels to float Porter's helpless fleet.

30 Joseph Evan Davis, aged 5, dies of an accidental fall in Richmond.

May 1864

1 William D. *"Dirty Bill"* Porter dies of heart disease in New York City.
His brother is fighting to save his many crews on the Red River.

The Red River fleet approaches Alexandria, its largest ship lost.
The *Gross Tete Flying Artillery (GTFA)* sinks Porter's *Emma*.

4 The GTFA attacks the steamer *City Belle*, carrying the 120th Ohio.
The entire regiment is killed, wounded, or captured.
120th Ohio Col. Marcus Spiegel dies; his brother Joe is captured.
Col. Spiegel and the 120th Ohio faced the Alabamians at Vicksburg.

The steamers *John Warner*, *Signal*, and *Covington* leave Alexandria.
20 miles south, the crews take small-arms fire while eating dinner.

Porter's fleet before the City of Alexandria, La.
Sketch from Frank Leslie's Illustrated Newspaper, April 30, 1864.

May 1864 (Cont.)

4 John McArthur sends a very large expedition to occupy Yazoo City. In lieu of Navy elements, he sends the Mississippi Marine Brigade.

5 Grant and Lee tangle at the Wilderness.
His first action with Lee has Grant *quite agitated* that night.

Confederate artillery units form *ship-hunting teams* to prey on Porter's unprotected fleet.
The 56th Ohio is on the *John Warner*, headed home on furlough.
She is attacked and the regiment is decimated at Dunn's Bayou.
The 56th Ohio begs the steamer *Covington* not to burn the *Warner*.
The *John Warner* has 125 dead and dying on its deck.

The *Signal* surrenders and the *Covington* is eventually burned.
The three vessels and 300 soldiers and sailors lost exceed losses experienced at Grand Ecore.

6 Grant is surprisingly calm and ready for renewed battle with Lee.

Grant refuses to let journalists send out their stories.

7 Grant orders his Army *south after Lee*, to the elation of his soldiers who expected the traditional retreat.

Sherman:
"Turning south was the greatest act of Grant's life."

Ellet skirmishes with Wirt Adams, capturing supplies and two troops.

8 Lee and Grant tangle at Spotsylvania Courthouse.

In Baltimore, Lincoln is nominated for a second term.

9 **Porter, shaken by low stages, considers destroying his fleet.**
Several vessels pass through Bailey's Dam chute.
Bailey plans wing dams to raise the stage above the main dam.

Pemberton's resignation as lieutenant general is accepted.

Banks must manage more soldiers as John McClernand has arrived.

10 Banks to Porter: *"You must move when the wing dams are ready."*

11 Lee's cavalry legend J.E.B. Stuart is killed at Yellow Tavern, Va.
Longstreet is seriously wounded.

When Bailey's wing dams are not successful, a bracket dam works.

12 John McArthur destroys Moore's Ferry on the Big Black River.

John Pemberton reverts to lieutenant colonel of artillery.

May 1864 (Cont.)

13 Adams hits McArthur at Luce's Plantation five miles from Benton.
McArthur's cavalry destroys the Vaughn station, trestles, and rails.

14 The ram *U.S.S. Switzerland* drops anchor in Yazoo City.

U.S.S. Ram Switzerland
(USNHHC)

May 1864 (Cont.)

15 Porter's fleet is, at last, in the safe, open waters of the Mississippi.
The Red River is crammed with the carnage of his Red River effort.

16 Two 11th Illinois soldiers are found hanged at Yazoo City.

17 Arsonists burn Yazoo City, despite efforts by all sides to save it.

18 Grant fails at Petersburg.
In the two weeks since the Battle of the Wilderness, Grant has lost
10% of his army.

Schofield's expedition returns to Vicksburg as planned.
Wirt Adams continues coexistence with Union forces in his area.

John H. Bobb is shot to death by U.S.C.T. occupation soldiers.

20 Porter, in G.O. 199, divides the Mississippi into 10 naval districts.

June 1864

1 The *Vicksburg Daily Herald* opens for business.
It uses J.M. Swords' old *Daily Citizen* equipment.

3 At Cold Harbor, Grant loses 7,000 in 30 minutes.
Mary Lincoln frequently refers to Grant as "the butcher."

6 Maj. Gen. Joe Mower loses 3 killed, 16 wounded at Ditch Bayou, Ark.,
near Lake Village.

June 1864 (Cont.)

18 At Natchez, Col. B.G. Farrar orders churches to pray for Lincoln.
His former classmate, Natchez bishop William Elder, wins on appeal.

The *U.S.S. Essex* is awarded $25,000 by Congress for its role in
destroying the *C.S.S. Arkansas*.
In truth, the Arkansas crew destroyed their own vessel.
The late Bill Porter is included in the award.

July 1864

2 The *Vicksburg Daily Herald* is run by Union veteran Ira A. Batterton.
He complains about no celebratory plans for Vicksburg's July 4th.

4 7:00 a.m. – The packet *Diligent* carries a Unionist crowd to Davis
Bend for an impromptu celebration.
Unionists and freedmen celebrate the 4th on the Davis plantation.

3:00 p.m. – A Surrender Interview Site Memorial is installed at the
Great Redoubt, the first on the battlefield.

**The Battle of Coleman's Plantation near Rodney, Miss., is
likely the first between white and black Mississippi
soldiers.**
"The negro troops contested obstinately every inch of ground."

5 The *Daily Herald* publishes no issue out of respect for the July 4th.

6 The *Daily Herald*: *"The 4th celebration was the state's biggest ever."*

7 Georgia's embittered governor and Davis argue over troop placement.
*"40 to 50 Georgia regiments defend Richmond while Atlanta is in
danger."*

11 Union forces headed to Tupelo from Memphis are routed by Forrest.
The action occurs 15 miles north of Tupelo at *Brice's Crossroads*.
Union casualties are 2,200.
Forrest suffers less than 500.

12 Davis to Lee: *"Johnston has failed. He will abandon Atlanta."*
Davis stumbles through the political risks of a Johnston firing.
He considers Beauregard but their ill will exceeds that of Johnston.

15 *Daily Herald* publisher Ira Batterton dies in a shooting accident.
J.M. Swords, former *Daily Citizen* publisher, assumes management
of the *Daily Herald*.

16 Davis gives Johnston one last chance.
Johnston plans to use state militia to hold Sherman while he *moves*.

17 Johnston is relieved of command of the Army of Tennessee.

The Cabinet unanimously supports John Bell Hood.

July 1864 (Cont.)

17   Davis and Benjamin meet with two U.S peace envoys in Richmond.
Davis explodes on hearing *amnesty*. *"Amnesty is for criminals."*
"You may free every slave, but we will govern ourselves."

Lincoln:
"This issue can only be tried by war and decided by victory."

18   Horace Greeley's meeting with C.S. peace emissaries is for naught.
Lincoln's future as a presidential candidate is waning.

22   McPherson is killed at Atlanta, the highest-ranking Union casualty.
Sherman and Grant show immense grief at McPherson's death.
Sherman: *"McPherson was the man destined to finish the war.*
"I thought the press or battle would claim Grant and I."

Maj. Gen. W.H.T. Walker dies at Atlanta, shot by Union pickets.

30   Grant is bogged down at Petersburg, Va.
The *Battle of the Crater* ends in *stupendous failure,* says Grant.

August 1864

10   Grant to Halleck: *"We need to get 10,000 troops to Sherman."*

12   Sherman is promoted to major general of the Regulars.

Natchez Bishop William Elder is ordered released from jail.
Brig. Gen. Mason Brayman arrested him over the *Lincoln prayer*
refusal.

13   Grant to Halleck:
"Send whatever John Pope can spare to relieve Sherman."

15   George McClellan, peace candidate, wants a treaty with the South.
Lincoln is emotionally packing his bags, anticipating certain defeat.

23   Lincoln commits his Cabinet to winning the war before the new
president takes office.

30   The Northern will to fight is diminishing daily.

September 1864

1   Hood begins the evacuation of Atlanta.

2   **Sherman's Army captures Atlanta.**
Lincoln's presidency is redeemed.
The Confederacy has lost its *perceived* momentum.

3   Sherman to Lincoln: *"Atlanta is ours and fairly won."*

Grant brags on Sherman:
**"The most gigantic undertaking of any general in this
war."**

September 1864 (Cont.)

20   Sherman proposes his *March to the Sea.*

Davis makes a rally rail trip through the Deep South.
He must deal with Hood issues and build a post-Atlanta strategy.
"If I had just half of AWOL Tennesseans, I could destroy Sherman."

21   Georgia's governor Brown and C.S. Vice President Stephens believe
that northern *Copperheads* hold the key to victory.

There is skirmishing for five days at Deer Creek north of Vicksburg.

22   Porter gets his desired post, the North Atlantic Blocking Squadron.
Its former commander, his adopted brother David Farragut, is ailing.
Porter takes many of his favorite captains with him.
RAdm. Samuel Phillips Lee assumes command of the Mississippi
Gunboat Squadron.

23   Davis has reassigned Richard Taylor who is feuding with Kirby Smith.

29   Brig. Gen. John Eaton *elopes north* with Alice Eugenia Shirley,
daughter of James and Adeline Quincy Shirley of Vicksburg.

October 1864

7   Brig. Gen. John Gregg, hero of Raymond, dies leading a
counterattack at the Battle of Darbytown and New Market Roads.

Davis to Congress:
*"Fund the purchase of 40,000 slaves for noncombat roles. They will
be freed after faithful service.*
"They may be armed if all hangs in the balance."

8   Sherman to Grant from Atlanta: *"I intend to make Georgia howl."*

13   Lincoln worries that a Sherman misstep might *destroy his army.*

26   Skirmishing occurs on Steele Bayou north of Vicksburg.

Grant and Sherman are maintaining equal pressure on Lee's ends.
If one weakens, Lee will turn and defeat the other.

27   Seth L. Phelps, left behind by Porter for losing the *Eastport,* resigns.
He was one of the original architects of the *brown-water navy.*
He becomes a coaling station manager in Acapulco, Mexico.

29   Brig. Gen. Thomas Ransom dies of dysentery in Rome, Ga.
Sherman is completely distraught over Ransom's death.

November 1864

1   Brig. Gen. George McKee commands Vicksburg's *Enrolled Militia.*
He was with the 11th Illinois at Vicksburg.

8   With winds of the fall of Atlanta propelling him, Lincoln is reelected
President with 212 of 233 electoral votes.

November 1864 (Cont.)

8 There is discussion of enlisting slaves as Confederate soldiers.

Richmond Examiner:
"A slave fit to be a soldier is not fit to be a slave.
  That would surrender the strength and power of our position."

15 Sherman begins his *March to the Sea* through Georgia.

22 Skirmishing occurs at Rolling Fork, Miss.

The Battle of Franklin, Tenn., November 30, 1864

30 Vicksburg veterans among the Franklin dead include:
Brig. Gen. Hiram Granbury, 7th Texas, a hero of the Battle of
  Raymond.
Brig. Gen. States Rights Gist, Johnston's Army of Relief (AOR).
Brig. Gen. John Adams, AOR.
Col. William W. Witherspoon, 36th Mississippi, the Great Redoubt.

McClernand resigns after a minor role in the Red River Campaign.

December 1864

2 Skirmishing is reported at Yazoo City.

9 Scores of contraband blacks die in the *Ebenezer Creek Massacre*
  when Union soldiers withdraw their pontoons behind them.
Many former slaves panic and drown trying to cross the creek alone.

11 Grant demands that George Thomas end Hood's northern threat.

15 Thomas defeats Hood at Nashville.

For 30 days, Union staff have had no news of Sherman's location.
Grant to Lincoln: *"He will show up on salt water someplace."*

18 Sherman still opposes recruiting black troops.

21 Sherman's army captures Savannah, Ga.
Sherman presents the city and its booty to Lincoln for Christmas.

24 Sherman declares South Carolina *deserving of the damage to come.*
"The whole army is burning with an insatiable desire to wreak
  vengeance upon South Carolina. I almost tremble at her fate."

27 There is a lack of ships in Sherman's theater of operations.
To reach Virginia, he must march through the Carolinas.

January 1865

1 Sherman begins his South Carolina Campaign.

Skirmishing is heard at Goode's Landing and Mechanicsburg, Miss.

2 Sherman to wife Ellen:
"Grant is almost childlike in his love for me."

January 1865 (Cont.)

12 Davis and old friend U.S. Maj. Gen. Frank Blair meet to seek common peace terms.
Blair suggests a truce and an alliance to fight France in Mexico.
Blair sees it as a move to reunion.
Davis wants an inter-nation agreement.
Lincoln wants to keep peace talks alive.

Sherman and Stanton discuss emancipation with Savannah, Ga., black leaders.
Sherman seeks a solution for the thousands of contraband following him.

Stanton must decide the future for Southern plantations for Lincoln.
Special Order No. 15 will redistribute South Carolina farmland to freedmen.
The Order is more Stanton's effort than Sherman's.
Sherman is also punishing rice planters for starting the war.

13 Davis orders the planting of subterranean landmines on roads.
Sherman orders prisoners to unearth them and defuse them.

John Bell Hood resigns.

15 Sherman: *"Stanton has left and is cured of that Negroe nonsense."*

16 The C.S. Senate approves Lee as General-in-Chief of all Confederate armies.

Sherman orders 400,000 acres redistributed to former slaves.
40,000 freedmen are resettled.

19 Sherman to brother John regarding a bill in Congress to promote him to lieutenant general:
"Squash any effort to promote me over Grant. He deserves what he has earned. I do not need more rank."

February 1865

1 Sherman begins operations in South Carolina.

3 Peace talks are held on the *River Queen* in Hampton Roads, Va.
Lincoln's meeting with peace emissaries reveals the impasse.

Davis, irritating his own emissaries, shapes the report to encourage citizens to *continue the fight*.

Grant creates the Military Division of Missouri to consolidate armies in the West.

Blair and Logan face Lafayette McLaws at Rivers' Bridge, S.C.
There are 124 Union casualties versus 97 Confederate.

February 1865 (Cont.)

6   Congress passes the 13th Amendment abolishing slavery.

Seddon is replaced by John Breckinridge as C.S. Secretary of War.

Davis rises from his sick bed to give inspiring victory speeches.
C.S. Vice President Alexander Stephens:
"Davis' forecast of military victory is the emanation of a demented brain."

10   Davis' request to Congress to convert slaves into soldiers fails.

11   Louisiana planter Duncan Kenner is sent on a secret mission.
Davis offers emancipation in return for French C.S.A. recognition.
Louis Napoleon gives Kenner the cold shoulder.

14   Great Britain's Lord Palmerston:
"England cannot recognize a nonexistent country."

15   Sherman's army is on the outskirts of Columbia, S.C.
The 1860 Secession Convention was held at the First Baptist Church in Columbia.

16   Grant has Lee in a vice-like grip.

17   Sherman captures Columbia, the capital of South Carolina.

18   Sherman captures Charleston, S.C., cutting its communication lines.

Davis is being pressured to restore Johnston to face Sherman.
Davis writes a long memorandum regarding Johnston's unsuitability.

Lee:
"The Negro, under proper circumstances, will make efficient soldiers."

21   Davis:
"We must employ every able-bodied man regardless of color. We are reduced to whether the Negro will fight for or against us."

22   Davis drops the Johnston memorandum and restores him to command.

Johnston has 20,000; Sherman has 60,000.
Lee has 60,000; Grant has 125,000.

Troops of African Descent: 180,000.
There are many more black U.S. troops in the field than C.S. soldiers.

Confederates total 126,000 fit for duty of 359,000.
Union forces: 621,000 fit for duty of 955,000.

23   Sherman's army is moving through swamps *10 miles a day.*

February 1865 (Cont.)

23 Johnston is awestruck with Sherman's operations:
"Not since the legions of Julius Caesar has such an army been seen."

March 1865

1 Lee reluctantly accepts the position of General-in-Chief.

3 The new *Freedman's Bureau to* help freedmen adjust to freedom is called the *Bureau of Refugees, Freedmen, and Abandoned Land.*

Many are hired as field hands with negotiated $15-a-month pay.
Others open shops or are contracted to repair war damage.

4 Lincoln is inaugurated. ***"With malice toward none."***

13 Led by Lee, Davis signs the act to create black soldiers.
A familiar chorus is heard: *"Fight for the Confederacy and you will be freed with the rights of freedmen."*

16 An expanse of land from the Big Black River Bridge to Four-Mile Trestle is proposed for Union and Confederate prisoner exchange.
The three-mile-wide band on the railroad is the *Aubrey Territory.*

The Confederate exchange headquarters is *Camp Townsend.*
The Union exchange headquarters is *Camp Fisk, named* for Col. Archie Fisk of the 23^d Ohio.

22 Sherman's men consider themselves an **irresistible force**.

23 Sherman to Grant: *"I might run up and see you for a day or two."*

24 *Sherman to Grant: "In one more move, we can checkmate Lee."*

27 Lincoln, Grant, Porter, and Sherman meet at City Point, Va.
They are planning the war's final phases and the first phases of peace.

Lincoln: *"But what is next?*
"Davis ought to clear out and escape the country."
Confederates who lay down arms can become citizens again.
Confederate governments would function until replaced.

Porter: *"Lincoln wants peace on almost any terms."*

29 A mine sinks the ironclad monitor *U.S.S. Osage, Thomas Selfridge's former command,* at Spanish Fort, Ala.

April 1865

1 Davis compares himself to great generals in history who overcame what appeared to be certain defeat

The ***Battle of Five Forks*** allows Grant to outmaneuver Lee.

2 Lee notifies Davis that Grant has breached the Petersburg line.
Jefferson Davis evacuates Richmond in advance of the Union army.

Vicksburg's titans meet to conclude the war and begin reconciliation.
"The Peacemakers" by G.P.A. Healy from the White House Collection.

April 1865 (Cont.)

2 Davis and the Cabinet are on the last train leaving Richmond.
Lee makes a daring effort to escape to North Carolina and Johnston.

The 1st Division, U.S.C.T., from Vicksburg assaults Fort Blakely, Ala.
Fort Blakely is the last major battle of the Civil War.

There is no time to recruit and deploy Confederate black soldiers.

3 Resident Minerva Cook is murdered by soldiers of the 52d U.S.C.T.

4 A Davis proclamation urges Southerners to continue the struggle.

Lincoln departs City Point for Richmond on the *U.S.S. Malvern*.
He is accompanied by RAdm. Porter.

5 Union prisoners at Camp Fisk are catching riverboats home.
Freedmen huts are crowding Vicksburg.

6 Lee loses 1/4th of his troops at Sailor's Creek near Farmville, Va.

9 Lee recognizes that Grant has blocked him from escape.
1:30 p.m. – Lee and Grant meet to discuss surrender.
Lee surrenders to Grant at the McLean House, Appomattox, Va.
Surrender documents are drafted by Seneca Col. Ely Parker.
Grant shows the same form of leniency that he showed at Vicksburg.

Fort Blakely, Ala., marks a victory for the 1st Division, U.S.C.T.

11 Lincoln makes his last speech on the challenges of Reconstruction.

13 Grant returns from Appomattox to City Point, Va.

Capt. James Mason Cass and the steamer *Sultana* depart St. Louis.

April 1865 (Cont.)

14   Johnston requests a cessation of operations from Sherman.

Julia has convinced Grant to pass on a Ford's Theater date with the Lincolns, opting to visit family instead.

15   Lincoln dies of a Ford's Theater assassin's bullet in Washington, D.C.

Andrew Johnson is sworn in as the 17th U.S. President.
A Southerner who never attended a day of school is now President.

16   The *Sultana's* Capt. Mason gathers Cairo newspapers about Lincoln.
He knows Southern telegraph is incapable of spreading the news.

17   Sherman and Johnston are scheduled to meet today.
Davis will only allow Johnston to surrender *his* army.
Johnston:
"It would be the greatest of human crimes to continue this war."

Sherman stops Union soldiers from destroying Raleigh, N.C.

19   Lt. Gen. Simon Buckner assumes Trans-Mississippi command.

20   Porter's luxury flagship, the *U.S.S. Benton,* is decommissioned at Mound City, Ill.

21   Sherman's proposed lenient Johnston surrender terms create an uproar.
U.S. Attorney General James Speed declares William Sherman *a traitor.*
"Sherman might march his victorious legions to take over Washington."

Grant is told to resume hostilities and take over Sherman's operation.

The steamer *Sultana* departs New Orleans.

22   Halleck suspects that Davis has large quantities of Confederate gold.
Sherman may have been bribed for an easy peace or a Davis escape.
New York Times: *"Halleck says Sherman may have a screw loose."*

The *U.S.S. Benton* accidentally burns three miles above Cairo, Ill.
The symbol of Porter's Mississippi Gunboat Squadron is no more.

Gen. Kirby Smith assumes Trans-Mississippi Department command.

23   The C.S. Ram *William H. Webb* breaks through the Union blockade.
Out into the Mississippi, she races for the Gulf of Mexico.
Jefferson Davis and John Wilkes Booth are rumored to be onboard.

Grant meets Sherman in Raleigh, N.C., attempting to contain the political and military damage surrounding his friend Sherman.
He orders hostilities if Johnston does not sign Appomattox terms.

Jubilant soldiers recently freed from prison aboard the *S.S. Sultana* at Helena, Ark. *From a carte de visite, April 26, 1865, the day before she was destroyed.*

April 1865 (Cont.)

24 The *Sultana* docks in Vicksburg for former prisoners returning home. *Sultana's* boiler is repaired but engineers recommend that she remain in Vicksburg pending stronger repairs. Crooked quartermaster Reuben Hatch is making a deal with Mason.

Hatch has been restored multiple times by Lincoln as a favor to a relative, despite repetitive unethical activity. Rather than 376 soldiers, the Sultana is crammed with 2,176 to maximize profits, each bringing $10 per passenger.

The *New York Times* publishes many stories ridiculing Sherman.

The trapped C.S. Ram *Webb* is destroyed by her crew at Algiers, La.

25 Sherman and Johnston agree on Appomattox terms. Sherman offers 10 days rations and horses and mules for farming.

26 Grant endorses Sherman's surrender document.

Johnston surrenders at Bentonville, N.C. The surrender is most expansive of the war: 89,270 in four states.

Davis is bitter that Johnston would surrender without a fight. *"It was unparalleled, without good reason or authority."*

27 Morbidly overloaded, the *Sultana* explodes at Marion, Ark., killing over 1,800, mostly prisoners who had suffered horribly in camps. **It is America's worst maritime disaster, worse than the R.M.S. Titanic.** The *U.S.S. Tyler* is pressed into rescue service with local volunteers.

The guilty parties, Hatch and Mason, die in the accident.

April 1865 (Cont.)

27 Col. Frederick Speed is dismissed from service over the disaster.
JAG Joseph Holt, a Vicksburg native, overturns Speed's dismissal.

28 Sherman writes an anguished letter to Grant about press coverage.

29 Sherman sends his letter to John Rawlins for Secretary Stanton.
*"I want it published. The South is broken and **deserves our pity**."*
He casts doubt on Davis hauling 15 wagons of gold.

May 1865

2 The Confederate Cabinet disbands at Burt House, Abbeville, S.C.

The press prints Halleck's letter asking officers to *disobey Sherman*.

3 Davis hopes to reach Texas and Kirby Smith's remaining forces.
The Confederate government is officially *out of business*.

Senior C.S. field officers must now clean up the administrative
residue of war.

4 Mississippi's war ends when Richard Taylor surrenders the
Departments in Alabama, Mississippi, and East Louisiana to
Maj. Gen. Edward Canby at Citronelle, Ala.

6 Sherman's G.O. 69 releases the Army of the Tennessee from service.
He reminds the country of his service and the debt owed them.
He intends the order as direct shot at Halleck.

Gov. Charles Clark calls for a special session of the Mississippi
legislature.

9 Halleck raises the white flag and apologizes to Sherman.
Grant to Sherman:
"We need to get on with our duties. Stop feuding."

The trial of the Lincoln conspirators begins in Washington, D.C.
Vicksburg's Maj. Gen. John Hartranft is assigned provost marshal.
He is also commanding officer of the Old Capitol Prison.
Hartranft is in the center on the Pennsylvania Memorial (*below*).

(GJMC)

May 1865 (Cont.)

10   Davis and his entourage are captured at Irwinville, Ga.

Confederate forces in the West under Kirby Smith surrender.

Sherman refuses Halleck's friendship and apology.
He writes to Grant to check on the *status of their relationship.*
Sherman's 55,000 march into Richmond and *ignore Halleck.*
A Sherman soldier *spits on the boots of Halleck's guard.*

12   The Battle of Palmito Ranch, Tex., is the **last battle of the war.**
34th Indiana Priv. John Williams is the last fatality.
The 34th Indiana fought with McClernand at Vicksburg.
Priv. Williams joined the regiment after Vicksburg.

17   Grant:
"Indians may need more protection from whites, than us from them."

18   Grant is called to the Joint Committee for the Conduct of the War.
Grant and Andrew Johnson have a heated argument about Lee.
Grant: *"While Lee honors his parole, I'll never consent to his arrest."*

The Mississippi legislature votes for a state convention on July 3.

19   Sherman arrives in Washington.
To Rawlins: *"Though in disgrace, I am untamed and unconquered."*

20   Rumors:
"Sherman's army wants to punish and remove Stanton and others."
Johnston heartily welcomes Sherman and blames Stanton.

21   Mourning wreaths and victory banners mix in Washington, D.C.

22   Jefferson Davis is incarcerated at Fort Monroe, Va.

Brig. Gen. Embury Osband arrests Mississippi governor Clark and
takes control of state records.
Mississippi is without civil government of any kind.

23   A two-day Grand Review begins in Washington, D.C.
None of the 180,000 U.S.C.T. troops appear in the parade.

26   52d U.S.C.T. troops convicted of murdering Minerva Cook are hanged
in Vicksburg.

Simon Buckner surrenders the Army of the West in New Orleans.

28   The Confederate raider *C.S.S. Shenandoah* continues the war, sinking
the whaling bark *Abigail* from New Bedford, Mass., in the Russian
Sea of Okhotsk.

29   Andrew Johnston grants amnesty to former Confederates who
will demonstrate loyalty to the United States.

June 1865

2 Smith issues Trans-Mississippi surrender orders in Galveston, Tex.

3 The previously feared *C.S.S. Missouri* surrenders at Shreveport, La.

8 Shreveport surrenders to the U.S. Navy.

The Mississippi Gunboat Squadron's mission is complete.

13 Andrew Johnson names William Sharkey as Mississippi's provisional governor.

20 The *U.S.S. Carondelet* is decommissioned at Mound City, Ill.

23 Brig. Gen. Stand Watie disbands the Confederate 1st Cherokee Rifles.

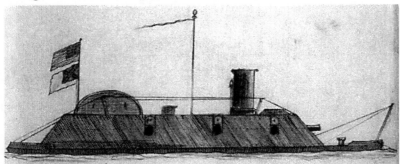

The Confederate Ram *Missouri* surrendered at Shreveport, June 3, 1865.
Sketch by Ensign David Stauffer.

July 1865

1 Municipal government in Vicksburg begins to be re-established.

Governor Sharkey calls for an August 7th election of state convention delegates.

2 The timberclad *U.S.S. Lexington* is decommissioned at Mound City.

7 Maj. Gen. Hartranft directs the execution of the Lincoln conspirators. During her imprisonment, Hartranft takes good care of Mary Surratt. **She is the first woman executed by the U.S. Government.**

17 Capt. William Titus Rigby musters out of the 24th Iowa.

20 The ironclad *U.S.S. Essex* is decommissioned at Mound City.

22 The ironclad *U.S.S.* Choctaw is decommissioned at New Orleans.

23 The monitor *U.S.S. Neosho* is decommissioned at Mound City.
The ironclad *U.S.S. Lafayette* is decommissioned at New Orleans.

Iron from Eads' five remaining City Class ironclads is sold for scrap. The remains of the vessels are sold as *warehouse barges*.

July 1865 (Cont.)

23 New York legal scholar John Codman Curd complains:
"The defeated people of state's rights still stalk national politics."

August 1865

1 **Mississippi is considered lawless country.**

2 The *U.S.S. Mound City* is decommissioned near Vicksburg, her final service guarding Baldwin's Ferry on the Big Black River.

4 The *U.S.S. Cincinnati* is decommissioned at Algiers, La.

11 The *U.S.S. Oneida* is decommissioned at New York City.

14 Mississippi holds the first state convention of Reconstruction.

15 Andrew Johnson congratulates Sharkey on assembling a state convention.
He calls for the following:
Abolish slavery in the Mississippi Constitution.
Ratify the 13th Amendment which abolishes slavery nationally.
Extend the vote to any who can read the Constitution in English and who owns $250 in property and pays taxes on that property.

The Vicksburg freedman population is down from 13,000 to 405.

16 A Vicksburg $10 monthly street-vendor tax is hurting residents whose earnings are often about $10 per month.

17 **The timberclad *U.S.S. Tyler* is auctioned at Mound City.**
As the steamer *A.O. Tyler*, it was fired on at Vicksburg on January 13, 1861, one of the first shots fired in anger, *three months before the attack on Fort Sumter*.

22 The Mississippi Convention revokes the state's Secession Ordinance.

24 Johnson congratulates Mississippi on its *exemplary* convention.
Many issues regarding black rights are passed on to the legislature.
The ratification of the 13th Amendment is rejected by the body.

September 1865

1 William Averts and John Clifford, Davis' prosecutors, meet in New York.
After that first meeting, they let the case fall by the wayside.

18 T.J. Randolph, long-time businessman and Vicksburg tax collector, is mayor of Vicksburg.

October 1865

26 *Italy's Giuseppe Garibaldi appeals for Jefferson Davis' release.*
His visit with Johnson puts the Davis case on the international stage.

30 Black leaders in Mississippi defend their reputation and demand legal equality.

November 1865

6   The *C.S.S. Shenandoah* surrenders to *H.M.S. Donegal* in Mersey
Bay near Liverpool, England.
The Confederate flag is lowered for the very last time,
under the watch of a Royal Navy detachment and the crew.

9   The remnants of the *U.S.S. Mound City* are auctioned at Mound City.

14 Indiana is willing to try Davis to get a *proper jury and justice.*

Johnson: *"Jurisdiction is one of the problems much in our way."*

29 The remnants of *U.S.S. Tuscumbia* are sold at Mound City.

December 1865

1   Chicago Tribune: *"The North will turn Mississippi into a frogpond
before allowing their discriminatory laws to stand, where the
bones of our soldiers lie and our flag flies."*

3   A Freedman's Savings Bank branch in Vicksburg is the **state's first**.

21 The Senate grills Johnson on the delay in the Davis trial.
The nation is divided at high levels over leniency or death.

24 The Ku Klux Klan is formed in Pulaski, Tenn.

The 5th U.S.C.T. Heavy Artillery at Vicksburg circa April 1864. Note the terrain.
*Library of Congress image courtesy of the Vicksburg Foundation for Historic Preservation
(VFHP).*

PART VII
Quieting the Echoes of Union Souls

*Forsaken Union dead are
returned to their Sacred Bluffs
1866 to 1930*

The Indian Mound on the Vicksburg National Cemetery circa 1906.
Library of Congress image from the Detroit Publishing Co.

The memorial to the John Trindle family
interred at VNC.
Photos by and courtesy of Natalie Maynor.

PART VII
Quieting the Echoes of Union Souls

1865

Dec 26 Captain E.B. Whitman, Department of the Tennessee, is given the special national duty of inspecting battlegrounds, cemeteries, and locations in the former Confederacy where Union dead are interred in the field.
He is the Superintendent of National Cemeteries.

1866

Feb 28 Col. James F. Rushing makes a depressing battlefield survey:
*"I regret to say that I found very little had been done here in the way of looking after our dead. Their condition is **more deplorable than any post I have visited** while inspector.*
Burials are scattered about or are in mass trenches.
Animals of all kind attack shallow, unmarked graves.

8,000 estimated dead are on the Vicksburg side. Another 2,000 are estimated on the Louisiana side, and 5,000 at other nearby battlefields.

"Is this not wrong, hideous?
These men died for the Union."

Rushing recommends that 5,000 idle troops at Vicksburg be tasked to locate the graves and that a cemetery be developed.

Mar 8 Rushing complains that Milliken's Bend burials are going to be buried in distant New Orleans, far from where they fell.
He insists they should remain locally.

Apr 10 Col. Gilbert Parker:
"Purchase 75 to 100 acres near the Surrender Interview Site Monument for the purpose."

1866 (Cont.)

Apr 12 Quartermaster General Montgomery C. Meigs approves burials at Vicksburg.

May 15 *"We must hurry. Many bodies have been washed from their resting places by the encroachment of the Mississippi River and have been floated to the ocean in their coffins or been buried in the sand beneath its waters."*
A planter at Milliken's Bend has leveled an entire burial plot to enlarge his cotton patch.
Another burial ground in Vicksburg has been leveled to build a racetrack.

Jun 20 A Warrenton site owned by A.B. Redding is being considered.

Jun 21 Provisions are being made for **20,000** burials.
$1.50 each is offered for assistance in finding a Union burial.

Jul 3 A.B. Redding is *"asking too much"* for the property.
Another site on the river north of Vicksburg is recommended.
The 40-acre tract is owned by Alney H. Jaynes.

Aug 21 5,000 extremely sad graves are estimated between Vicksburg and Lake Providence.

Aug 27 The 40 acres for the Vicksburg National Cemetery (VNC) will cost $9,000.

Oct 4 Bvt. Brig. Gen. Embury B. Osband, former commander of Grant's Provost Guard, dies and is buried in the levee at Carolina Landing, Miss., near Glen Allan.
He was a relocated cotton farmer.
It was Osband who arrested Mississippi Governor Clark and took control of state records in Jackson on May 22, 1864.

Oct 10 Capt. James W. Scully, appointed by President Andrew Johnson, is ordered to *"take possession of the land and prepare it for the burial of the dead."*

Oct 12 *"Bodies in the levee are daily being washed away."*

Oct 13 A contractor named Palmer is hired and provided coffins.

Oct 27 To reduce confusion, burial regions are defined.
Burials on the west bank of the Mississippi, from a point opposite Grand Gulf to the Arkansas Line, and on the east bank of the river from Rodney to the Arkansas Line, including both Rodney and Grand Gulf, will be removed to the National Cemetery at Vicksburg.

1866 (Cont.)

Oct 27 *Soldiers buried from the mouth of Red River to Rodney, and to a point opposite Grand Gulf, including Vidalia, La., will be reinterred in the National Cemetery to be established at Natchez.*

Nov 2 Scully reports that badly needed coffins have not arrived.

Nov 5 Scully: *"We have disinterred 1,000 but have no coffins!"*
The remains of 1,000 lie exposed to the elements and worse.

Nov 18 Louisiana resident E.V.M. Cramer complains about the careless desecration of remains during the removal process.

"I write to inform the public of the barbarous manner in which our dead are being treated by those engaged in removing their remains to the National Cemetery.

" They commenced digging up their remains on the levee and in the graveyard of the old Van Buren hospital about two weeks since.

"The coffins have rotted and the bones of the dead, many only partially decomposed, are thrown on the ground by the side of each grave. Upon these, the hogs and dogs are feasting.

"No battlefield ever presented a more hideous and sickening sight than the levee, for miles, presents now. It would have been far better to have let them rest where their comrades laid them than to remove them in so heartless a manner."

A Cold Harbor, Va., reburial party similar to that around Vicksburg.
An Alexander Gardner print from the Library of Congress.

1866 (Cont.)

Nov 21   Scully has hired 200 laborers for $40 a month and rations.
Scully purchases 1,500 coffins for $2.50 each.
He delays burials until a fence can be built to keep hogs away.

Nov 24   Scully demands reverence of his burial teams:
*"The work of reinterring the Union dead is, in reality, one
continued funeral ceremony. Everything that would be
out of place at a well-conducted Christian funeral would
also be out of place here."*

Dec 2   Scully refutes Cramer's point about *dogs and hogs.*
He says former Confederate soldiers and *Union officers
planting cotton* have done worse defilement of the graves.

Dec 10   Maj. Tredwell Moore inspects the Louisiana burial sites and
finds most of Cramer's allegations to be **true.**

200 burials on Pawpaw Island have been carried away by the
river through no cause but neglect.

Coffins are also reportedly opened by looting laborers with the
bodies are left to spoil.

G.M. Alexander states that remains and bodies are left to
animals and scavengers.

Dec 24   Capt. Scully disavows the witnesses against him personally.
Maj. Moore vindicates Scully.

1867

The Surrender Interview Site obelisk is moved to the Railroad
Depot after being vandalized for souvenirs.
An upright 42-pdr. cannon barrel replaces the obelisk.

May 25   Abandoning the site north of the city is considered, even
at a loss of the current *$65,000* investment.

Landowner Jaynes is criticized for *swindling* the Government.
He purchased the land two years earlier for $16.25 per acre
and sold the rugged land for the cemetery for $255 per acre,
the 2023 equivalent of $4,800 per acre.

Jun 1   The cemetery is under the oversight of Lt. Col. Luther H.
Peirce who supersedes Scully.

Early internments are washed out by a rain.
Terracing to solve the erosion problem has cost $40,000.

1867 (Cont.)

Jun 1 The internments are arranged to maximize terrace space.

100 weeping willow slips have been donated by President Johnson from his home in Greenville, Tennessee.
The parent trees came from Egypt in 1859.

Scully is working at multiple quartermaster positions from the Quartermaster Depot and delegating his duties to an unwell minister and a *rough, surly steamboat man.*
Inspector C.W. Folsom reports the system is not an optimum one and is leading to skyrocketing costs.
Folsom recommends most of Scully's foremen be discharged and that a commissioned officer be specifically assigned to the cemetery duties.

Folsom also recommends leaving the cemetery at its present location.

Jun 17 One foreman, Elias Schull, has been caught running a loan business among laborers whose pay was slow in coming.

Jun 29 Capt. Scully is relieved of duty, pending a court-martial that he requested
The charge is based on Scully allegedly taking kickbacks twice on coffins purchased from Julius Casparo in November 1866.
Scully was also charged with running a kickback scheme from a worker's sutler store he authorized to be set up in the VNC.

Jul 6 Brevet Col. Scully writes to Andrew Johnson:
"I demanded this court-martial to clear my name against Casparo who had to leave for forgery and swindling."

Jul 9 T.E. Halleck confesses to Johnson that he was the sole party working the system with Casparo.
He also reported that Scully had ordered Casparo to close the cemetery sutler store, leading to Casparo's charges.

Despite the evidence presented, Scully is found guilty of the *"first charge"* and is dismissed from service with a $5 fine.

Jul 25 Peirce reports many improvements in labor costs and time.

Aug 13 President Johnson overturns the court-martial and restores Scully to duty.

Oct 4 Maj. John G. Chandler, Quartermaster at Vicksburg, requests that a VNC *keeper* be appointed.

1868

Jan 29	Chandler reports 5,000 coffins have been requested for Lt. John Hynes, temporarily in charge pending the appointment of a permanent Superintendent, to meet the demands created by an ever-increasing number of reinterments.
Jan 31	Hynes has rented a barge and purchased a skiff to expedite the removal of remains along the river.
Apr 11	Hynes reports that open brick drains are needed at the foot of each terrace.
May 28	Julius Witkewski of Vicksburg is contracted for 500,000 bricks at $12 per 1,000 for Cemetery drains and culverts.
Aug 1	15,595 interments have cost $178,636, or $11 each, $230 each in 2023 dollars.

3,193 whites and 130 black are known.
6,589 white and 5,458 black are unknown.
83 of 133 officers are known.
Of 24 sailors, all but one are known.

White soldiers are placed in Sections A through H, and O.
The initial 543 black soldiers are interred in Section M.

The rumor that laborers are paid *by the skull* is debunked.
Laborers are paid a salary by the Quartermaster.

Aug 29	The first permanent VNC Superintendent is Alexander Henry.
Sep 9	Henry reports for duty.
Dec 31	The Cemetery *Superintendent's Lodge* is *ready for occupancy*.

The Surrender Interview Site obelisk is now on the Indian Mound at the Vicksburg National Cemetery.

1869

Jan 1	National landscape architect Frederick Olmsted advises the Quartermaster to hire James Gall to solve erosion woes.
Feb 26	Civil engineer James Gall is hired.
Apr 23	Quartermaster M.C. Meigs approves Gall's recommendations.
Jun 23	All names are classified on burial sheets according to native state, then forwarded to the respective state for correction. After corrections, the names are placed on an Honor Roll. Records of interment of the deceased are forwarded to the Adjutant General's Office in Washington.

1869 (Cont.)

Jul 11 National-level attention is being paid to VNC progress.
Horace Greeley, editor of the *New York Tribune*, writes to
Quartermaster Meigs, complaining of labor shortages at the
Cemetery that risk damage from the rainy season if work is
not soon completed.

1870

Jan 26 Vicksburg citizens have requested that a turnpike be built along
the river to the developing National Cemetery.
Meigs denies the request due to a lack of releasable labor.

Jun 22 A new Cemetery section is ready to receive 700 remains that
have lain *exposed in public view for over a year*.

Jul 14 Maj. Asher Eddy recommends moving the *deplorable*
Cemetery to a new site before the Mississippi River devours it.
He also suggests removing Henry as Superintendent.
These recommendations are ignored.

Aug 6 Wooden Cemetery headboards are decayed and need to be
replaced every four years.
The rotten headboards make registering graves difficult.
They also give a gloomy appearance and interfere with
maintenance.

Aug 9 Eddy is ordered to complete his assigned national cemeteries
before *"November next, before winter rains move in."*

The Vicksburg National Cemetery is prioritized.

Oct 12 Eddy recommends removing headboards and planting
trees between rows of headstones.

Dec 1 Meigs emphasizes the intent of the Cemetery Act.
*"Nothing less than a marker with name, rank, regiment, and
date will, in my opinion, satisfy the requirements of each
known grave.*
*"And to the unknown, we should at least give a specific
designation of the resting place of one who sacrificed his life
and the identity of whose remains has not even been
preserved by his comrades."*

1871

Jun 24 2d Lt. Isaac O. Shelby, Vicksburg Quartermaster, declares the
VNC construction *"completed, finished on a permanent and
substantial basis."*

1873

Mar 1   James Gall visits and comments on the VNC's *fine* appearance.

Mar 8   Secretary of War William W. Belknap has directed that two
              10-in. Columbiad guns lying near the steamboat landing
              and one 9-in. Dahlgren gun lying in the road halfway between
              Vicksburg and the Cemetery be removed to the Cemetery.
              The Cemetery already possesses seven 32-pdr. guns.

Mar 27   A separate VNC Superintendent's Office is recommended.

Jun 1   All 10 guns are lying near the Superintendents' Lodge awaiting
              disposition.

Dec 4   The Memphis and Vicksburg RR wants a riverside track near
              the VNC.

1874

May 8   The Superintendent is attempting to grow *eucalyptus* from
              seed.

Jun 15   Work is commenced on a brick VNC enclosure wall and gates
              by I.F. Baum and his partner, a Mr. Fischel.

Sep 29   Henry is recommended for dismissal due to drinking issues.
              John Trindle, Superintendent of the Natchez National
              Cemetery, is selected to replace Henry.

1875

Jun 30   Burials in the VNC total 16,588.
              Marble headstones mark all the known soldiers.
              Unknown markers for 13,000 are nearing completion.

Sep 1   VNC hours are between sunrise and sunset, by policy.
              Carriages must be kept to a walk.

Oct 21   The Superintendent's daughter, three-year-old Charlotte B.
              Trindle, dies.

1876

Apr 15   Trindle recalls James Gall to repair major landscape slippages.

Jul 1   Approximately 500 magnolia transplants, as well as a number
              of cedars, holly, and other deciduous and evergreen trees, are
              growing in the Cemetery greenhouse.
              The trees are neighborhood transplants.
              Plants for beautification are also grown in the greenhouse.
              The Cemetery horticulturalist is Charles H. Westphal.

Aug 15   Major repairs to the Superintendent's Lodge are completed.

1877

Sep 21   John Trindle requests a change of station due to health issues. He also has a painful stump from a leg lost to a war wound. His request is *delayed.*

1878

Jun 18   Congress appropriates $84,000 to attempt to keep the Mississippi River from changing course below Vicksburg. The soldiers buried in the Cemetery beside *their river* are used in an emotional ploy. The Mississippi River must be kept in its present alignment at Vicksburg so that the river continues *"to bring water and mementoes from every homestead of the poor fellows who lie there in eternal sleep where they fell in the service of their country."*

Jul 13   Trindle is asked if right-of-way has been obtained from citizens for the Cemetery Turnpike.

Aug 18   Vicksburg is experiencing a horrific yellow fever epidemic. The Trindles lose toddler, Eola M., to the disease.

Aug 22   The Cemetery is ordered closed due to epidemic impacts.

Aug 26   Trindle is authorized extended leave. The Superintendent's Lodge has been maligned for its bad ventilation.

Oct 11   The Trindles lose a son, William G., age four, to yellow fever.

Oct 28   Trindle reports himself well enough and attending to duty, despite the recent loss of two more children.

Dec 17   Right-of-way for the Cemetery Turnpike has been obtained. The contractor, J.J. Shipman, is onsite making preparations.

1879

Jan 13   Congress approves right-of-way for the VNC Turnpike and the Memphis and Vicksburg RR on the Cemetery tract.

1880

Apr 12   Former President Grant and Mayor W.O. Worrell visit the VNC. 3,000 people gather to welcome the former President. He does not visit the battlefield but places a flower on a grave.

Apr 13   The Vicksburg Herald reports, *"The reception of General Grant was free from partisan manipulation. Party lines and prejudices were blotted out in the heartiness of enthusiasm."*

1880 (Cont.)

Jun 23 The Cemetery flagpole is destroyed by lightening.
It will be replaced in a few weeks with a base from St. Louis.

1882

Mar 31 John Trindle is reassigned to the Chattanooga National
Cemetery, leaving three children in the VNC.

Apr 1 Henry Ward replaces John Trindle.

Nov 13 The VNC Turnpike and the new RR track are approved for
construction.

Nov 14 VNC gardener *"Waldie"* is installed as acting Superintendent.

Dec 24 George Haverfield is named VNC Superintendent.
Haverfield lost a lower leg at Fisher's Hill, Va., during the war.

1883

Apr 11 Several VNC outbuildings are being completed.

Nov 12 Former superintendent Henry Ward dies suddenly.

1886

Apr 6 Haverfield's VNC tour ends when he departs to be fitted with an
artificial leg in New York and does not return.

Jun 19 Thomas D. Godman replaces Haverfield.

1888

Jul 17 U.S. Rep. Thomas Catchings complains that the
Superintendent's Lodge is a *dilapidated eyesore.*

May 28 A fountain fed by Mint Springs Bayou has been constructed on
the cemetery's lower west level using a Columbiad gun.

1889

Jan 8 Cemetery workers are replacing the old brick greenhouse.

1890

Jul 21 Thomas Godman is relieved for issues related to his conduct.
Thomas France is named VNC Superintendent.

1891

Mar 9 Old-timers have *"never seen so much rain in such a short time."*

The Cemetery road is left in a dreadful state.

1893

Jan 14 Comrades of Brig. Gen. Embury Osband request authority to move his remains to the VNC from Carolina Landing on the Mississippi River 50 miles north of Vicksburg.

Jan 18 Osband, who arrested Gov. Clarke in 1863, is approved for reinterment in the VNC, its highest-ranking soldier.
He also commanded U.S.C.T. combat troops in the region after the fall of Vicksburg.

Jun 9 The VNC reports hosting *segregated* Decoration Day programs, blacks in the afternoon and whites in the early evening.

1901

May 1 President William McKinley steps from his train onto an improvised stage at the entrance to the Cemetery to address a crowd estimated at 15,000.
Two years earlier, he had signed the Act creating the Vicksburg National Military Park.
He is accompanied by his wife, Ida, Secretary of State John Jay, Postmaster Charles Smith, and Secretaries Ethan Hitchcock, James Wilson, and George B. Cortelyou.

1906

Aug 4 Vicksburg National Military Park (VNMP) Superintendent Capt. William T. Rigby requests permission to put bronze position markers in the Cemetery for the 25th and 31st Iowa.

1907

May 26 Judge Frederick Speed strongly but unsuccessfully seeks to halt destruction of the old greenhouse due to a lack of repair funds.

Oct 21 President Theodore Roosevelt visits the VNC and the VNMP.

1911

Dec 7 E.J. Bomar and S.J. Wilson complete an electric rail track and trolley service to the Cemetery.

1912

Jan 26 A northwest Cemetery section is opened for 125 new graves.

1914

Feb 13 John Trindle dies in Chattanooga and is buried in the VNC,.
Charlotte will join him and three of their children in 1935.

1924	
Jun 7	City water is approved on the VNC road.
Nov 15	VNC annual pay – Superintendent, $900; *Gardener, $1,080.*

1925	
Mar 31	The Columbiad fountain has been filled in with dirt.
May 20	VNC trees, shrubbery, and vegetation are being destroyed by the *Argentine Ant.*
Sep 17	VNC is given the resources to eradicate the Argentine Ant.
Oct 3	The Mississippi Power and Light Co. is licensed to deliver power to the VNC.

1927	
Dec 1	The VNC Superintendent's Lodge is badly damaged by fire. The records are the only property salvaged.

1928	
Apr 5	Construction begins on a new wooden Lodge under direction of Vicksburg architect Michael J. Donovan and builder R.B. Howard.
Aug 28	Superintendent Sullivan expresses delight at the new Lodge, the first electrically lighted building in the Cemetery.
Oct 6	The Cemetery Turnpike is paved by the Government.

1929	
Jul 9	The electric rail line to the Cemetery is officially terminated.

1930	
Dec 31	Average burials for the past five years: 29. Remaining spaces: 410.

1933	
Aug 11	The VNC, along with 10 other national cemeteries, is transferred from the War Department to the Department of the Interior.

Part VIII
Echoes of Anger
Concede to Reunification

*The smoke of war clears to
reveal challenges and opportunity
1866 to 1908*

Pax by William Couper, Minnesota State Memorial
(GJMC)

PART VIII
Echoes of Anger Concede to Reunification

January 1866

1   Historian Bradley R. Clampitt:
"The war and occupation transformed the daily lives of all Vicksburg residents."

8   Radical Republican Thaddeus Stevens offers to represent Jefferson Davis.

12   *The Chicago Tribune:*
"A Virginia trial would acquit Davis and say he had a perfect right to institute rebellion, that Virginia had a right to secede, and that the Government of the United States had no right to coerce the Southern states."

February 1866

1   Andrew Johnson asks Sherman to explain Special Field Order 15. The order distributed confiscated South Carolina lands to freedmen. Sherman: *"It was a wartime measure with no permanence."*

2   The U.S. Senate approves the Civil Rights Bill of 1866.

March 1866

6   44 remaining Army camels are put on the auction block.

10   **Frederick Douglass urges Johnson to spare Davis.**
Douglass states publicly that he holds no grudge against Confederates.

13   The U.S. House of Representatives approves the Civil Rights Bill.
"There are certain absolute rights which pertain to every citizen, which are inherent, and of which a State cannot constitutionally deprive him."

15   The Mississippi Constitutional Convention of 1866 nullifies the actions of the Confederate Secession Convention.

Washington Street in post-war Vicksburg.
From Harper's Weekly, June 1866.

March 1866 (Cont.)

22 The experiment of black occupation soldiers ends when Johnson orders them mustered out to appease white Southern voters.

27 Andrew Johnson vetoes the Civil Rights Bill of 1866.

April 1866

2 Johnson issues a Proclamation of Peace with Southern states.

Texas ratifies its new constitution.
Johnson does not yet issue a Peace Proclamation with Texas.

6 The U.S. Senate overturns Johnson's Civil Rights Bill veto.

Maj. B.F. Stephenson forms the Grand Army of the Republic (G.A.R). The organization will help struggling veterans transition nationally. He is a former surgeon of the 14th Illinois at Vicksburg.

9 The U.S. House overturns Johnson's Civil Rights Bill veto.

The Civil Rights Act declares all citizens born in the United States have certain full rights under the Constitution.

May 1866

5 The 52d Infantry, U.S.C.T., is mustered out at Vicksburg.

18 Calls are for Davis to be court-martialed to ensure his *execution*. There are concerns he will get off in a civil trial over secession.

24 The Natchez *Courier*:
"The jury is stacked if Davis is convicted. A large proportion of the public would reject such an outcome."

May 1866 (Cont.)

31 Horace Greeley to Salmon Chase:
"It would not be wise to maintain that 12 million Southern people may be governed by how 20 million people in other states see fit."

June 1866

5 Davis' lawyers demand that he be tried or released on bail.

July 1866

25 Congress creates the rank General of the Army for Grant.
Sherman is, at last, promoted to lieutenant general.
He had previously refused the rank to avoid outranking friend Grant.

August 1866

20 Johnson issues a Peace Proclamation with Texas.
Johnson: ***"The said insurrection is at an end."***
The War of Rebellion is officially concluded.

October 1866

Ben Montgomery asks former master Joe Davis to lease Davis Bend.
Davis offers him the land for $300,000 for a *"model black town."*
Montgomery is now *one of the richest former slaves in the nation.*

3 The New Orleans *Crescent:*
"Entrusting Davis' case to a jury risks opening the secession debate."

November 1866

1 Johnson has revoked Sherman's Special Field Order No. 15 that
distributed South Carolina lands to freedmen.
Maj. Gen. Oliver Howard, Freedman's Bureau head, objects in vain.

Jefferson Davis' constantly lighted cell and guards at Fort Monroe, Va.
Library of Congress image by Alfred R. Waud, 1865.

December 1866

31   Davis is still languishing at Fortress Monroe, Va., in an unheated bunker cell.
Some hope the sickly Davis will die to avoid a risky trial.

The black population of Vicksburg is 3,793.

January 1867

1   Joe Davis sells Davis Bend to former slave Ben Montgomery.

March 1867

2   Congress passes the Reconstruction Act.
The South is divided into military districts.
Vicksburg is in the 4th Military District commanded by E.O.C. Ord who commanded the XIII Corps under Grant at Vicksburg.

Illinois Secretary of State Sharon Tyndale works to successfully modify the state seal to downplay *state sovereignty*.
The words *State Sovereignty* are inverted and placed below National Unity.

Congress passes the *Tenure of Office Act*, preventing the President from removing certain office holders without U.S. Senate approval.

May 1867

13   Davis' lawyers tell prosecutors to bring their case.
The prosecution says it is not prepared to do so.
Davis is released on $100,000 bail, $3.2 million in 2023 dollars.

Davis' bail is paid by Horace Greeley, editor of the *New York Tribune*; business magnate Cornelius Vanderbilt; and Gerrit Smith, abolitionist, social reformer, and a member of the *Secret Six* that funded John Brown's raid.

Davis, *"thin, wasted, and careworn is emotionally exhausted by the strong men who came to offer support."*

Defense attorney Charles O'Connor:
"The business is finished. Mr. Davis will never be called on to appear for a trial."

14   A New Yorker:
"100,000 soldier graves cry out for revenge and he (Davis) is allowed to walk the streets on his own recognizance. Revenge deep and complete will be carried out on his damned soul."

18   The Philadelphia *Christian Recorder*:
"Refuse to try him and the secession issue is left open. Acquit him and the right of secession is acknowledged, to be repeated with impunity."

August 1867

12   Andrew Johnson flagrantly suspends Edwin Stanton, defying the
Tenure of Office Act while Congress is in recess.
He is attempting to replace Stanton with Grant.

September 1867

28   Former Davis slave Benjamin Montgomery is the newly appointed
Justice of the Peace for Davis Bend.
Maj. Gen. E.O.C. Ord, the commander of the 4th Military District of
Mississippi and Arkansas, made him the **first black to hold a
public office in Mississippi**.

November 1867

15   Sherman reminds the nation:
***"The entire nation is responsible for slavery and shared
in its profits."***

Johnson wants to add Sherman to his administration.

January 1868

13   Congress rescinds Johnson's suspension of Stanton.

February 1868

24   Andrew Johnson is ***impeached*** for the way he replaced Stanton.
The installation of Grant or Sherman as War Secretary draws fire.
Sherman testifies several *tortuous* days in support of Johnson.

April 1868

12   A *Vicksburg Herald* Letter to the Editor is signed *An Old River Man*.
It warns of disaster if river scouring at Delta Point is not checked.
The letter recommends sinking trees along the banks.

26   O'Connor, Davis' attorney, considers recommending to Davis that he
flee the court's jurisdiction.

May 1868

15   In Convention, both races adopt Mississippi's 1868 Constitution.

26   Johnson is acquitted by the U.S. Senate.
Stanton sees Johnson as the victor.

28   Radical Stanton resigns as Secretary of War.

June 1868

1   Maj. Gen. John Schofield becomes Johnson's Secretary of War.

August 1868

10   Columbia law professor Francis Lieber:
*"White Southerners and many northerners need to be convinced
to abandon their belief in state sovereignty."*

November 1868

3   U.S. Grant is elected President of the United States.

December 1868

15   Grant and Sherman discuss reorganization of the Army, giving
      Sherman new authorities once delegated to the Secretary of War.

25   ***The Christmas Amnesty***
      To avoid a Davis trial that might overturn the results of the war,
          Johnson, in one of his final acts, issues Proclamation 179.
      He grants full pardon for **all** Confederate Rebellion participants.

March 1869

4   Grant is inaugurated. ***"Let us have peace."***
      Sherman is General-in-Chief and full general.

13   Maj. Gen. John Rawlins is named Secretary of War.
      Ely Parker, Grant's wartime aide, is Commissioner of Indian Affairs.

26   Rawlins rescinds Grant's order giving Sherman more authority and
      strengthens the authority of the Secretary of War.

      Grant asks for Sherman to be patient on this issue, not wanting to
          "give more pain" to a dying Rawlins.
      Sherman's relationship with Grant cools.

May 1869

1   Lee visits Grant at the White House.
      Lee had invited Grant to visit him at Washington College.
      Grant had declined to avoid *imposing on Lee.*
      Lee accepted the invitation *on behalf of the South.*
      Inviting the South to the White House causes an uproar.
      Since the war, Lee has not allowed a word to be spoken ill of Grant
          in Lee's presence.

December 1869

1   The 1868 Mississippi Constitution is ratified by the people.

January 1870

1   *Key Vicksburg leaders start to fear the river will change course.*

      Sharecroppers, small farmers, tenant farmers, and plantation
          owners are growing **more cotton without slavery** than in 1860.

February 1870

3   Grant signs the 15th Amendment giving black males the vote.

23   Mississippi is readmitted into the Union.
      Republicans, led by Gov. James L. Alcorn, promise equality.

25   **Hiram Rhodes Revels is the first black U.S. Senator.**
Ironically, he fills Jefferson Davis' Mississippi seat.

March 1870

30   Grant signs the act to restore Texas to the Union.

May 1870

18   Anshe Chesed congregation is celebrating a new Cherry Street
synagogue, **Mississippi's first** *purpose-built* **synagogue.**

June 1870

30   Col. J.M. Macomb promotes surveys of eroding Delta Point.
Col. W. F. Raynolds: *"Apprehensions are only too well founded."*
83 percent of the city's cotton is moved on the river.
A $2.7-million stone project is recommended immediately.
Congress fails to fund the critical project.

September 1870

18   Joseph E. Davis dies at *Anchuca* mansion in Vicksburg.
Brother Jefferson visits and speaks briefly to an assembled crowd.
He is threatened with arrest if he *gives a speech.*

30   Ben Montgomery's Davis Bend long-staple cotton is awarded 1st place
at the prestigious St. Louis Agricultural and Mechanical Fair.

January 1871

31   Jefferson Davis has successfully sued Joe's heirs for *Brierfield.*

March 1871

3   The Southern Claims Commission is established to reimburse loyal
Southerners for losses in support of Union troops.

April 1871

20   Congress passes a law aimed at stopping the Ku Klux Klan.

May 1871

13   Alcorn Agricultural and Mechanical College is born from the former
campus of Oakland College at Lorman, Miss.
The $42,500 sale price is used to establish Chamberlain-Hunt
Academy in Port Gibson.
C.H.A. is named for Oakland's first president, anti-slavery Rev.
Jeremiah Chamberlain, who was assassinated on campus, and
"King David" Hunt, an area millionaire planter who helped fund
the creation of Oakland College and who ownd 1,000 slaves and 25
plantations before the war.
Two other benefactors of Oakland College were Smith Coffee Daniell
of *Windsor* Plantation and Dr. Rushworth Nutt of *Laurel Hill.*

May 1871 (Cont.)

13   **Alcorn A&M is the first black land-grant college established in the United States.**

November 1872

5   Grant defeats Horace Greeley for President.
Susan B. Anthony supports Grant over Victoria Woodhull, the first woman to run for President.
Woodhull's husband, James Harvey Blood, commanded the 6th U.S. Missouri under Grant at Vicksburg.

May 1872

22   The 19th anniversary of Grant's *bloodiest assault at Vicksburg*.
He signs amnesty for most office-seeking Confederate veterans.

August 1873

18   Capt. William Henry Harrison Benyaurd, Medal of Honor recipient, opens **the first U.S. Engineers office in Vicksburg**.

Benyaurd's task is to mark and clear war steamboat wrecks and repair war-damaged ports and other navigation resources.

November 1873

4   Peter Crosby, a former slave, is elected sheriff of Warren County.

With a net wealth of $230,000, former Davis slave Benjamin Montgomery is in the **top 7% of merchants in the South**. His wealth equates to about $8 million in 2023 dollars.

December 1873

7   Black sheriff Peter Crosby is removed on suspicious charges.
Scores of black citizens march toward Vicksburg to protest Crosby's removal.
The black citizens are ambushed at the Shirley House.
***Vicksburg's Massacre* claims the lives of up to 300 blacks.**

Anshe Chesed, Mississippi's second oldest Reform Jewish congregation, helps found the Union of American Hebrew Congregations.

June 1875

7   Deputy J. P. Gilmer wounds Sheriff Peter Crosby in the head.

October 1875

28   Peter Crosby fails in his re-election bid as Warren County sheriff.

November 1875

5   Grant is re-elected president, carrying 31 of 37 states.

April 1876

26 The Mississippi River cuts through DeSoto Point at Vicksburg. Vicksburg begins gradually losing its river and 50-foot harbor.

27 Grant learns of the river's course change on his birthday. 13 years earlier, he had just declared *his canal project dead* and was nearing Grand Gulf, Miss.

August 1876

1 Grant signs the Act of Statehood for Colorado, the only state created during his Administration.

October 1876

4 Brig. Gen. Sul Ross is the founding president of Texas A&M College.

February 1877

28 A bipartisan deal is made to elect Rutherford B. Hayes President. Democrats receive removal of Federal troops from the South to give electoral votes to Hayes. It is agreed that the white South will manage *"the Negro problem."* The *Jim Crow* era begins in the South.

July 1877

1 The Mississippi River diversion at Vicksburg has grown to 6,000 feet wide.

October 1877

19 It is revealed that Chief Justice Salmon Chase delayed the Jefferson Davis case because *"he feared the wrong outcome."* An innocent verdict could have overturned the war's outcome.

April 1878

26 The *Quarantine Act* aims to stop ship- and sailor-borne disease.

June 1878

18 Congress appropriates $84,000 to begin the project to maintain a navigation at the Vicksburg city front. Army Corps of Engineers DeSoto Point work will include: Phase 1: Stabilizing Delta Point to stop the cutting of the river. Phase 2: Building a bar dike to stop the harbor filling with mud. Phase 3: Using dredges to keep the harbor open. Phase 4: Diverting the Yazoo River into the city front.

July 1878

27 Two towboat crew members with yellow fever get off at Vicksburg. **The Vicksburg Yellow Fever Epidemic of 1878 begins.**

October 1878

10   Lt. Gen. Stephen Dill Lee is the founding president of Mississippi
Agricultural and Mechanical College.

June 1879

19   **President Rutherford B. Hayes restores John C. Pemberton
to full citizenship.**

August 1879

31   The river restoration project is paused due to yellow fever fears.

October 1879

27   James Eads, ironclad and river engineering genius, is appointed
to the Mississippi River Commission.
Cyrus Comstock, Vicksburg U.S. Siegemaster, is its first president.

November 1879

30   The work on the river restoration project has resumed.

December 1879

31   3,227 (25%) of Vicksburg's 13,000 have died of yellow fever.

August 1880

31   The river restoration project is suspended due to yellow fever fears.
There is concern that mobile workers might transmit the disease.

January 1881

21   **Mississippi's first telephone exchange opens in Vicksburg.**
The Louisiana Telephone Co. is at 102 ½ N. Washington Street.

December 1882

31   Vicksburg engineers have protected 4,800 feet of DeSoto Point.
Slow funding is pausing rail, river, and economic development.

October 1884

6   Vicksburg-financed passenger rail service is restored.
The Louisville, New Orleans, and Texas RR makes its first run.

24   Newspapers report the new First National Bank at Vicksburg.
It is located on the northwest corner of Crawford and Washington.

July 1885

25   The Vicksburg, Shreveport, and Pacific RR has recovered from
the war.

October 1885

27   Transfer boats begin moving trains across the river at Vicksburg.

The railroad transfer boat, *Pelican*, in front of Vicksburg bringing a train across. *(VFHP)*

January 1886

25 The Merchants Bank in Vicksburg opens at 1310 Washington St.

The glory days of steamboats are ending, replaced by railroad.
The vessels are evolving into towboats, pulling or pushing barges.

November 1886

30 Vicksburg celebrates a new waterworks plant.
Samuel R. Bullock and Company will supply water for 30 years.

December 1887

31 Isaiah Montgomery has realized his father Benjamin's dream by
buying 840 acres and establishing the **all-black town** of Mound
Bayou, Miss.
The modern town is heralded as a reflection of the *genius of the
African race.*

December 1889

1 Vicksburg's horse-drawn street cars have been converted to electric.

31 A 140-foot-tall steel tank on Castle Hill provides good water pressure.

February 1890

17 A guest's unattended cigar burns *Windsor* mansion to the ground.

December 1892

10 A diversion canal will move the Yazoo River to the city waterfront.
Congress has authorized and funded a plan to divert the Yazoo.
Rep. Thomas C. Catchings has led the appropriations battle.
A $1.2-million contract will use the Atlantic, Gulf, and Pacific Co.

March 1894

10 Vicksburg has a viable waterfront only at the highest river stages.

12 Vicksburg confectioner Joseph Biedenharn sells the world's first
bottled Coca-Cola from his Washington Street store.

December 1894

31 W.H. and Lucy Jefferson have opened a black funeral home.

December 1901

31 The steamer *Peter Sprague* has been completed in Dubuque, Iowa. **The Sprague is the world's largest steam-powered sternwheeler and a record-holder for pushing tows on the Mississippi River.**

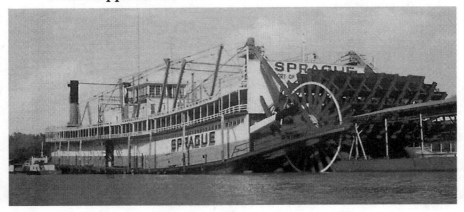

The *Big Mama of the Mississippi*, the Steamer *Sprague* at Vicksburg. *Image from a period postcard.*

March 1902

17 A streetcar breaks free and destroys a saloon, earning it the moniker *Carrie Nation* after a radical leader of the Temperance Movement.

December 1902

28 Only 19 city-front arrivals have been recorded since April 1876.

31 The Corps of Engineers area fleet is established adjacent to the National Cemetery Turnpike (North Washington Street).

January 1903

1 Vicksburg is the **world's leading producer** of long-staple cotton. It brings the highest prices on any domestic or world market.

Plantations can be paid off in three years growing this hybrid. The hybrid was developed by Mississippi's Delta planters.

28 A dike is removed to allow the Yazoo River to flow by Vicksburg. The contract dredge *California* has created the new channel. The diversion is 300 feet wide, averaging 25 feet deep.

January 1903 (Cont.)

28 The city executes an elaborate *Canal Day* dedication ceremony. Fireworks, a steamboat parade, and indoors programs are held. Mayor Murray Smith and the Corps' Capt. C.L. Potter preside.

April 1903

20 The city's Board holds its first meeting in the new City Hall. It replaces the 1848 structure on Monroe and Jackson streets.

About 30 area steamboats use Vicksburg as a base or terminus now.

Vicksburg, circa 1910, once again a prosperous river city. *(VFHP)*

June 1903

3 Mississippi dedicates its new capitol on Jefferson Davis' birthday. The state **pays $1,093,641 cash** for the construction with funds from a lawsuit with the Illinois Central Railroad.

July 1903

9 The *Vicksburg Post* prints a vigorous editorial against lynching.

December 1904

1 The $1.25-million project to divert the Yazoo River is paying off. Shipping rates are plummeting.

December 1905

31 Five automobiles are known to be operating in Vicksburg. The average citizen cannot afford a horse and buggy.

December 1908

22 The Yazoo and Mississippi Valley RR has a new depot in Vicksburg.

November 1910

18 Twelve passenger trains per day visit Vicksburg, many carrying
veterans of the Campaign of Vicksburg to the Vicksburg National
Military Park.

At peak, about two dozen trains will stop at Vicksburg's depot daily.

Vicksburg's Yazoo and Mississippi Valley RR Depot, circa 1910.
Image from a period postcard.

PART IX
Now, They Are But Echoes

*The giants of their age
pass into the Ages
1542 to 1956*

Image courtesy of the Oakland County, Michigan, Pioneer and Historical Society.

The last living *Echo* of the Vicksburg Campaign.

Private Joseph Clovese, 9th Louisiana and 63[d] U.S.C.T. Infantry, was the Vicksburg's Campaign's last living veteran and the last black dues-paying member of the Grand Army of the Republic Union veteran's organization. He very proudly attended the last gathering of Union veterans in 1949.

Private Clovese, who lived to be 107 years old, was born into slavery on a plantation in St. Bernard Parish, Louisiana, and escaped slavery in his teens to join the Union Army during the Campaign for Vicksburg. He served first as a drummer and later as an infantryman.

He was posted at Milliken's Bend, Louisiana, and participated in the legendary battle where freed slaves proved to the nation their value as fighting men.

He died July 13, 1951, in Dearborn, Michigan, beloved by the citizens of his adopted state. He had moved to Michigan several years before his death.

PART IX
Now, They Are But Echoes

1542
May 21   Explorer Hernando de Soto dies near present day Ferriday, La.

1687
Mar 19   French explorer René-Robert Cavelier, Sieur de La Salle, dies in present-day Navasota, Tex.

1775
Ethnographer Antoine Simon Le Page Du Pratz, who named the Mississippi River, dies in Paris, France.

1786
Nov 30   Bernardo de Galvez, colonial governor of Louisiana, dies in present day Mexico City, New Spain.

1799
Jul 18   Don Manuel Luis Gayoso de Lemos, governor of Spanish Louisiana, dies in New Orleans, La.

1807
Aug 10   Francisco Luis Hector, Baron de Carondelet, governor of Spanish Louisiana and West Florida, dies in Quito, Ecuador.

1815
Feb 24   Steamboat king Robert Fulton dies in New York City of *TB*.

1817
Dec 19   Samuel Gibson, founder of Port Gibson, Miss., dies.

1824
Jul 4   Samuel Emory Davis dies at Davis Bend, Miss. *Joseph assumes responsibility for his mother and Jefferson.*

1825
Jan 8 — Eli Whitney, Jr., dies in New Haven, Conn., of cancer.

1827
Jan 27 — Peter Bryan Bruin dies in Bruinsburg, Miss.

1835
Aug 22 — Ann Rutledge, the love of Lincoln's life, dies of typhus.
Sep 15 — Sarah Knox Taylor Davis dies of malaria in St. Francisville, La.

1837
Mar 30 — Dr. Rushworth Nutt dies at Laurel Hill Plantation, Miss.

1854
Jun 13 — Samuel Emory Davis dies of measles in D.C. at 23 months.

1862
Feb 20 — William Wallace *Willie* Lincoln dies of typhoid fever.
Apr 6 — C.S. Gen. Albert Sidney Johnston is killed at the Battle of Shiloh, Tenn.
Apr 25 — U.S. Maj. Gen. Charles F. Smith dies of a Shiloh injury in Savannah, Tenn.
Jun 21 — U.S. Col. Charles Ellet, U.S. Ram Fleet developer, dies of a Memphis leg wound in Memphis, Tenn.
Jun 26 — U.S. RAdm. Andrew Hull Foote dies in New York City of a foot wound received at Fort Donelson.
Aug 5 — U.S. Brig. Gen. Thomas Williams dies leading a charge at Baton Rouge, La.

1863
May 1 — C.S. Brig. Gen. Edward Dorr Tracy is killed, shot in the neck at Port Gibson, Miss.
May 7 — C.S. Maj. Gen. Earl Van Dorn is murdered at Spring Hill, Tenn.
Jun 17 — C.S. Brig Gen. Isham Garrott is killed by a sharpshooter at the Vicksburg Square Fort while trying to shoot one.
Jun 27 — C.S. Brig. Gen. Martin Green is killed by a sharpshooter at Green's Redan, Vicksburg, after scoffing at sharpshooters.
Jul 13 — C.S. Maj. Gen. John Stevens Bowen dies of dysentery near Raymond, Miss., nine days after working Vicksburg's surrender.
Aug 7 — U.S. Capt. Samuel DeGolyer dies of his May 25th Vicksburg wound in Hudson, Mich.

1863 (Cont.)

Aug 14	U.S. Brig. Gen. Thomas Welsh dies in Cincinnati of malaria contracted at Jackson, Miss.
Sep 21	U.S. Brig. Gen. Benjamin Hardin Helm, Lincoln's Confederate brother-in-law, is killed at Chickamauga, Ga.
Sep 23	C.S. Col. Leon Marks dies in Shreveport, La., from wounds received on June 28th while dining at the Stockade Redan.
Oct 3	William T. *Willie* Sherman, Jr., dies in Memphis, Tenn., of typhoid fever.
Nov 25	U.S. Col. Holden Putnam, 93rd Illinois, is killed at Missionary Ridge, Tenn., after surviving suicidal attacks at Vicksburg.

1864

Apr 3	Joseph Evan Davis, aged five, dies of an accidental fall in Richmond, Va.
May 1	U.S. Commodore William D. *Dirty Bill* Porter dies of heart disease in New York City.
Jul 22	U.S. Maj. Gen. James Birdseye McPherson is killed at Atlanta.
Jul 22	C.S. Maj. Gen. W.H.T. Walker is killed at the Battle of Atlanta.
Oct 7	C.S. Brig. Gen. John Gregg is killed leading a counterattack at Darbytown-New Market roads near Richmond, Va.
Oct 29	U.S. Brig. Gen. Thomas Ransom dies of dysentery in Rome, Ga.
Nov 30	Five key Vicksburg Confederate officers die at Franklin, Tenn. Brig. Gen. Hiram Granbury. Brig. Gen. States Rights Gist. Brig. Gen. John Adams. Col. William W. Witherspoon, 36th Mississippi.

1865

Apr 15	President Abraham Lincoln is assassinated in Ford's Theater in Washington, D.C.

1866

Jul 28	C.S. Maj. Gen. Martin Luther Smith dies in Savannah, Ga.
Sep 13	U.S. Brig. Gen. William Orme dies of TB in Bloomington, Ill.

1867

Feb 9	U.S. Maj. Gen. Jacob Lauman dies in Burlington, Iowa, from an old war wound.

1868

Jan 12	U.S. Maj. Gen. Frederick Steele dies after a buggy accident in San Mateo, Cal.

1868 (Cont.)	
Oct 16	U.S. Brig. Charles Matthies dies in Burlington, Iowa.

1869	
Sep 6	Grant's Secretary of War John Rawlins dies of TB in Washington, D. C. He was also Grant's Vicksburg chief of staff.
Dec 14	U.S. Col. Stephen Hicks dies in Illinois.

1870	
Jan 6	U.S. Maj. Gen. Joseph Mower dies in New Orleans.
Jul 12	U.S. RAdm. John Adolphus Bernard Dahlgren, ordnance developer, dies in Washington, D.C.
Aug 14	U.S. Admiral David Farragut dies of a heart attack while on vacation in Portsmouth, N.H.
Sep 18	Joseph Davis, Jefferson's mentor brother, dies at *Anchuca* in Vicksburg.

1872	
Jan 9	U.S. Maj. Gen. Henry Wager Halleck dies in Louisville, Ky., of liver disease.

1873	
Jan 26	Former *Vicksburg Daily Citizen* and *Vicksburg Herald* publisher James M. Swords dies in Vicksburg.
Jan 29	C.S. Maj. Gen. Franklin Kitchell Gardner dies in Lafayette, La.
Nov 27	Illinois war governor Richard Yates dies in St. Louis, Mo.

1874	
Jul 12	U.S. Col. William S. Hillyer, the last surviving member of Grant's original staff and Sherman's *czar of transportation*, dies in Washington, D.C.
Aug 28	U.S. Brig. Gen. Hugh Reid dies of *Bright's Disease* in Keokuk, Ill.

1875	
Jan 31	C.S. Artillery Col. Edward Higgins dies in San Francisco.
May 17	C.S. Maj. Gen. John Breckinridge dies of war-related issues in Lexington, Ky.
Jul 8	U.S. Maj. Gen. Francis Blair dies of lingering effects of a stroke in St. Louis, Mo.
Jul 31	President Andrew Johnson dies of a stroke in Elizabethton, Tenn.
Sep 10	C.S. Brig. Gen. John Vaughn dies of meningitis in Greenwood, Ga.

1876

Nov 8   U.S. Brig. Gen. Giles Alexander Smith dies in Bloomington, Ill.

1877

Feb 18   U.S. RAdm. Charles Henry Davis dies in Washington, D.C.

Nov 1   Indiana war governor Oliver Perry Throck Morton dies in Indianapolis, Ind.

Dec 24   U.S. ordnance developer Robert Parker Parrott dies in Cold Spring, N.Y.

1878

Feb 11   U. S. Navy Secretary Gideon Welles dies in Hartford, Conn.

Dec 2   U.S. Navy gunboat designer Samuel Moore Pook dies in Brooklyn, N.Y.

1879

Oct 27   C.S. Brig. Gen. John Whitfield dies at Hallettsville, Tex.

1880

Aug 19   C.S. War Secretary James Seddon dies in Goochland Co., Va.

Aug 29   C.S. Brig. Gen. Paul Octave Hebert dies in Bayou Goula, La.

1881

Jul 13   C.S. Lt. Gen. John C. Pemberton dies in Penllyn, Pa., of lung and prostate issues. His dying regret: ***"I would not have listened to Johnston."***

Jul 28   U.S. Col. James Richard Slack dies while visiting Chicago, Ill.

1882

Mar 27   U.S. Maj. Gen. Stephen Augustus Hurlbut dies in Lima, Peru.

May 5   U.S. RAdm. John Rodgers dies in Washington, D.C.

May 15   U.S. Maj. Gen. Cadwallader Washburn dies in Eureka Springs, Ark.

Jul 16   Mary Todd Lincoln dies in Springfield, Ill., of a stroke.

Jul 22   U.S. Maj. Gen. Michael Lawler dies in Shawneetown, Ill.

1883

Oct 29   Gustavus Vasa Fox, Union Assistant Navy Secretary, dies in New York City.

Nov 9   Capt. George Durell, Battery D, Pennsylvania Light Artillery, dies in Reading, Pa.

1884

May 6 C.S. Cabinet member Judah P. Benjamin dies alone in Paris, France, of heart-related issues.

1885

Feb 26 U.S. Brig. Gen. Charles R. Woods dies in Newark, Ohio.

Jul 23 U.S. Gen. Ulysses S. Grant dies in Gansevoort, N.Y., of throat cancer days after completing his *Personal Memoirs*.

1886

Dec 26 U.S. Maj. Gen. John A. Logan dies of old Fort Donelson war wounds in Washington, D.C.

Dec 30 C.S. Maj. Gen. William Wing Loring dies in New York City.

1887

Feb 19 U.S. Maj. Gen. Robert Potter dies in Newport, R.I.

Feb 25 Siege diarist Emma W. Harrison Balfour dies in Asheville, N.C.

Mar 8 Engineer genius and naval strategist James Buchanan Eads dies in Nassau, Bahamas.

Aug 26 Siege author Mary Ann Webster Loughborough dies in Little Rock, Ark. She wrote *My Cave Life in Vicksburg*.

Dec 14 U.S. Brig. Gen. T. Kilby Smith dies in New York City.

1888

Adeline Quincy Shirley of the *Shirley House* dies in Vicksburg.

Jan 2 U.S. Brig. Gen. Alexander Chambers dies in San Antonio, Tex.

May 1 C.S. Brig. Gen. Wirt Adams dies in Jackson, shot in the heart in a gunfight with a newspaper editor after a running feud.

Aug 15 C.S. Maj. Gen. Carter L. Stevenson dies in Caroline Co., Va.

1889

Apr 11 U.S. Col. Edward Hatch dies in Fort Robinson, Neb.

Oct 17 U.S. Maj. Gen. John Hartranft dies in Norristown, Pa.

Dec 6 President Jefferson Davis dies at 1134 First St., New Orleans, La., of pulmonary issues on his way to his home *Beauvoir* after visiting Vicksburg.

1891

Feb 13 U.S. Adm. David Dixon Porter dies in Washington, D.C., following an earlier heart attack.

Feb 14 U.S. Maj. Gen. William T. Sherman dies of pneumonia in New York City the day after Porter.

1891 (Cont.)

Mar 21   C.S. Lt. Gen. Joseph E. Johnston dies of pneumonia in Washington, D.C., after refusing to wear a hat in the rain as Sherman's pallbearer.

May 28   C.S. Brig. Gen. Winfield S. Featherston dies of paralysis in Holly Springs, Miss.

Sep 18   U.S. Maj. Gen. Isaac F. Quinby dies in Rochester, N.Y.

Oct 12   C.S. Col. Samuel Lockett dies in Bogota, Colombia, of illness and is buried there in an unmarked grave.

Nov 23   U.S. Maj. Gen. Alvin P. Hovey dies in Indianapolis., Ind.

1892

May 27   U.S. Brig. Gen. Ralph Buckland dies in Fremont, Ohio.

Oct 24   U.S. Brig. Gen. James M. Tuttle dies in Casa Grande, Ariz.

1893

Jan 11   U.S. Maj. Gen. Benjamin Franklin Butler dies in Washington, D.C.

Feb 20   C.S. Gen. Pierre Gustave Toutant-Beauregard dies in New Orleans, La.

Mar 28   C.S. General E. Kirby Smith dies in Sewanee, Tenn.

Jul 18   U.S. Col. William Milo Stone dies of pneumonia in Oklahoma City, Oklahoma Territory.

1894

Sep 1   U.S. Maj. Gen. Nathaniel Prentice Banks dies in Waltham, Mass.

Oct 18   Lt. Col. James Henry Burton dies a farmer in Winchester, Va.

Dec 2   U.S. Brig. Gen. Stephen Gano Burbridge dies in Brooklyn, N.Y., the infamous *Butcher of Kentucky unable to return home.*

Dec 17   U.S. Maj. Gen. Elias Dennis dies of pneumonia in Carlyle, Ill.

1895

Jan 9   U.S. Brig. Gen. Alfred W. Ellet dies in El Dorado, Kan.

Aug 16   C.S. Maj. Gen. Samuel Bell Maxey dies in Eureka Springs, Ark., of an intestinal ailment.

Aug 31   U.S. Brig. Gen. Ely Samuel Parker dies in poverty in Fairfield, Conn. The Seneca veteran served on Grant's staff from Vicksburg to Appomattox.

Sep 1   U.S. Col. Adam Gorgas, 13th Illinois, dies in Pine Grove, Pa.

1896

Jan 6   U.S. Maj. Gen. Mortimer Leggett dies in Cleveland, Ohio.

1896 (Cont.)	
Mar 8	U.S. RAdm. Henry Augustus Walke dies in Brooklyn, N.Y.
Sep 4	C.S. Brig. Gen. Francis Shoup dies in Columbia, Tenn.
1897	
Jan 20	U.S. Brig. Gen. Ely Parker is reinterred in Buffalo, N.Y., his Seneca tribal homelands.
Jan 22	U.S. Maj. Gen. John D. Stevenson dies in St. Louis, Mo.
Jan 29	U.S. Maj. Gen. John E. Smith dies in Chicago, Ill.
Jan 30	U.S. Maj. Gen. A. J. *Whiskey* Smith dies in St. Louis, Mo.
May 23	U.S. Col. Milton Montgomery, 25th Wis., dies in Omaha, Neb.
Jun 5	U.S. RAdm. Samuel Phillips Lee dies in Silver Spring, Md.
1898	
Jan 3	C.S. Brig. Gen. Lawrence *Sul* Ross dies in College Station, Tex., of cardiac issues.
Jan 21	U.S. Maj. Gen. Nathan Kimball dies in Ogden, Utah.
Feb 27	C.S. Brig. Gen. Thomas Dockery dies in New York City.
1899	
May 8	Medal of Honor recipient U.S. Maj. Gen. Manning Force dies in Cincinnati, Ohio.
Jun 16	C.S. Col. William Temple Winters dies in Fayette County, Ky.
Nov 21	C.S. Brig. Gen. Jeptha Harris dies in Lowndes County, Miss.
Dec 31	U.S. Brig. Gen. Edward Ferrero dies in New York City.
1900	
Jan 11	C.S. Maj. Gen. Dabney Herndon Maury dies in Peoria, Ill.
Aug 2	U.S. Col. John Loomis dies in Chicago, Ill.
Aug 12	U.S. Brig. Gen. Frederick Prime dies in Litchfield, Conn.
Sep 20	U.S. Maj. Gen. John McClernand dies in Springfield, Ill.
Dec 16	U.S. Maj. Gen. John Parke dies in Washington, D.C.
1901	
Jan 7	C.S. Brig. Gen. Louis Hebert dies in St. Martin Parish, La.
Jan 16	U.S. Sen. Hiram Revels Rhodes dies in Aberdeen, Miss.
May 17	U.S. Brig. Gen. Joseph Lightburn dies in Broad Run, W. Va.
Sep 14	President William McKinley dies of a Sept. 6 assassin's bullets in Buffalo, N.Y.

1902

Jan 8	U.S. Maj. Gen. F. Jay Herron dies a pauper in New York City.
Jan 14	U.S. Maj. Gen. Samuel Griffin dies in Keene, N.H.
Feb 8	U.S. Maj. Gen. William McMillen dies in Columbus, Ohio.
Sep 13	C.S. Maj. Gen. John Forney dies in Jacksonville, Ala.
Sep 23	U.S. Maj. John Wesley Powell dies in Haven Colony, Brooklin, Me., former director of the National Geodetic Survey.
Nov 13	C.S. Brig. Gen. Evander McNair dies in Hattiesburg, Miss.
Dec 14	Julia Dent Grant dies in Washington, D.C.

1903

Mar 30	C.S. Brig. Gen. William Jackson dies at Belle Meade near Nashville, Tenn.
Jul 28	C.S. Brig. Gen. Thomas N. Waul dies near Greenville, Tex.

1904

May 6	U.S. Brig. Gen. John Sanborn dies in St. Paul, Minn.
May 12	U.S. Brig. Gen. Andrew Hickenlooper dies in Cincinnati, Ohio.

1905

Jun 30	U.S. Maj. Gen. Hugh Ewing dies in Lancaster, Ohio.

1906

Feb 6	U.S. Brig. Gen. John Eaton, Jr., dies in Washington, D.C.
Mar 19	U.S. Maj. Gen. John Thayer dies in Lincoln, Neb.
May 15	U.S. Brig. Gen. John McArthur dies in Chicago, Ill.
Oct 16	Varina Howell Davis dies of pneumonia in New York City.

1907

Jun 22	U.S. Maj. William Le Baron Jenney dies in Los Angeles, Cal.
Jul 27	C.S. Brig. Gen. Edmund Winston Pettus dies in Hot Springs, N.C.

1908

May 28	C.S. Lt. Gen. Stephen D. Lee dies in Vicksburg after a Lawler Reunion address with Iowa soldiers and posing for his statue.
Aug 14	Martha *Pattie* Thompson Pemberton dies in New York City.
Aug 27	U.S. Lt. Col. William Vilas dies in Madison, Wis.
Dec 18	U.S. Brig. Gen. Green Raum dies in Chicago, Ill.

1910

Apr 20	C.S. Maj. Gen. Samuel French dies in Pensacola, Fla.

1910 (Cont.)

May 29 U.S. Brig. Gen. George F. McGinnis dies in Indianapolis, Ind.
U.S. Maj. Gen. Cyrus Comstock dies in New York City.

Dec 2 U.S. Maj. Gen. Eugene Asa Carr dies in Washington, D.C.

Dec 31 C.S. Brig Gen. John Creed Moore dies in San Marcos,
Coryell Co., Tex.

1911

Jan 1 U.S. Brig. Gen. John Curtin dies in Bellefonte, Pa.

Aug 31 U.S. Maj. Gen. Benjamin Henry Grierson dies in Omena, Mich.,
after suffering a debilitating stroke.

Dec 10 C.S. Lt. Col. James H. Jones dies in Woodville, Miss.

1912

Apr 12 U.S. Maj. Gen. Frederick D. Grant dies of cancer in Governor's
Island, N.Y.. His last public address was at the Wisconsin State
Memorial dedication at Vicksburg on May 22, 1911.

1915

Nov 15 Medal of Honor recipient U.S. Capt. Patrick White dies in
Menands, N. Y.

Dec 15 C.S. Brig. Gen. Francis Cockrell dies in Washington, D. C., as
Ordnance Director.

1916

Mar 4 U.S. Brig. Gen. Bernard Farrar dies in St. Louis, Mo.

1917

Jan 2 U.S. Maj. Gen. Peter Joseph Osterhaus dies in Duisburg,
Germany.

Aug 15 Medal of Honor recipient U.S. Sgt. Thomas J. Higgins dies in
Hannibal, Mo.

1921

Nov 7 U.S. Maj. Gen. Peter Hains dies at Walter Reed Hospital, the
only World War I soldier in uniform who fought in the
Civil War and the designer of the D.C. Tidal Basin.

1924

Feb 4 U.S. Cdr. Thomas O. Selfridge dies in Washington, D.C.

1930

Jan 27 Medal of Honor recipient Musician Orion P. Howe dies in
Springfield, Mo., the Medal's second youngest recipient at age
14 at the Stockade Redan.

1939

Apr 22   Priv. Louis Hornthal, Vicksburg's last veteran of the Civil War
             dies.

1951

Jul 13   Priv. Joseph Clovese, 9th Louisiana and 63[d] U.S.C.T., dies in
             Dearborn, Mich., the Vicksburg's Campaign's last living
             veteran and the last black member of the Grand Army of the
             Republic organization.
             He was a veteran of the Battle of Milliken's Bend.

1956

Aug 2   Albert Woolson, a Union soldier and the last living Civil War
             veteran, dies in Duluth, Minn.

Old Abe, mascot of the 8th Wisconsin atop his state memorial.
(GJMC)

The Rhode Island State Memorial, Frank Elwell's *"The Flag."*
(GJMC)

Part X
The Rumble of War
Melds into Memories

*Reunited enemies commit to
honor and perpetuate
1863-2025*

The 13th U.S. Infantry at the Stockade Redan, May 19, 1863.
A Library of Congress Prints and Photographs Division image.

The *Forlorn Hope's* Graveyard Road sprint at the Stockade Redan, May 22, 1863.
(MHL)

When Maj. Gen. William Sherman refused to send his XV Corps soldiers up the heinous heights at Vicksburg a second time, he called for 150 volunteers to prepare the Graveyard Road as an avenue of approach for Ohio regiments.

As they waited to attack into the *Beaten Zone*, they expected horrendous fire from all sides. They will not be shooting back immediately. They will be carrying logs, planks, and ladders so that following comrades will, at least, have some chance.

Part X
The Rumble of War Melds into Memories

1863

May 19   ***First at Vicksburg:***
After the 1st Battalion, 13th U.S. Infantry, suffered 43% casualties planting their flag first on the Vicksburg works at the Stockade Redan on May 19, 1863, William Sherman pro-claimed the unit's perfor-mance ***"unequalled in the Army."***

Sherman declared that their battalion colors could carry the words *"First at Vicks-burg."* The unit still uses that battle cry today in their crest at Fort Jackson, S.C.

May 22   The U.S. *Forlorn Hope* storming party at the Stockade Redan loses **72** of 150 in a failed suicidal assault. For their efforts, they will receive the most Medals of Honor given in one single-point action in U.S history, 78, on the Graveyard Road.

Oct 2   Under General Order 30, Maj. Gen. James McPherson creates a *"medal of honor"* for his XVII Corps soldiers who distinguish themselves in the field during the remainder of the war.

Dec 17   By a Joint Resolution of Congress, Grant is awarded a large commemorative gold medal for his Vicksburg Campaign victories.

The solid-gold medal weighs over a pound and is designed by Anthony C. Paquet, an assistant engraver at the U.S. Mint.

1864

Jul 4   A large crowd of Unionists, Union soldiers, and freedmen hold *"the largest 4ᵗʰ of July celebration in the state"* at Davis Bend, the home of Confederate president Jefferson Davis.

Union soldiers place an engraved commemorative obelisk at the site of the July 3, 1863, Grant-Pemberton Surrender Interview to replace a witness oak carried away as souvenirs.

Sep 26   8ᵗʰ Wisconsin veterans present their regimental mascot, the eagle *Old Abe,* to Gov. James L. Taylor who gives the young eagle a two-room aviary in the state capitol.

After leading his regiment into dozens of engagements and being wounded twice at Vicksburg, *Old Abe,* who was *"Wanted, Dead or Alive"* by the enemy, becomes a favorite national attraction.

State Historical Society of Wisconsin.

1865

Apr 25   A Lincoln monument is installed in the Ohio Statehouse, a portion of which commemorates the surrender of Vicksburg.

The Ohio Lincoln memorial's Vicksburg Surrender Interview.
From the Thomas Jones sculpture in the rotunda of the Ohio Statehouse.

May 16   Meyer Meyer is the first interment in the new Anshe Chesed Jewish Cemetery on the former 2ᵈ Texas Lunette.

1865 (Cont.)

Dec 31   Vicksburg, Pa., population, 136, honors Grant's victory.

© *2011 by Gerry Dincher. Modified from his image at*
creativecommons.org.

1866

Apr 6   The *Grand Army of the Republic* is formed in Decatur, Ill.,
by Dr. B.F. Stephenson, 14th Illinois surgeon at Vicksburg.
The G.A.R. provides political influence for veterans and aids
veterans with their difficult transition back into society.

May 5   The 52d U.S.C.T., newly mustered out, donates $700 ($13,000
in 2023$) for a new Lincoln sculpture in Washington, D.C.

May 15   The Vicksburg Confederate Cemetery Association is formed.
The 5,550 Confederate soldiers are largely unmarked.
This group predates national memorial activities by two years.

1867

Aug 20   One of the world's largest sequoia trees in California is named
the *General Grant*, to be followed by the *General Sherman*.

1868

Apr 29   Maj. Gen. John Logan is invited to speak to a Carbondale, Ill.,
crowd at an event honoring Civil War soldiers buried there.

May 5   Logan, as G.A.R. Commander-in-Chief, issues G.O. 11, calling
for a national day of commemoration to honor the Civil War
dead, not limited to Union dead.
He begins the national tradition of *Memorial Day.*

Dec 15   Sherman and Grant meet at Sherman's Peace Reunion of the
Armies of the Cumberland, Georgia, the Ohio, and the
Tennessee in Chicago.
An *unwell* Porter must regrettably decline the event.

1870

Jun 18   A team that will serve as the catalyst for the future Vicksburg National Military Park is formed.
Capt. William T. Rigby marries Sarah Evaline *Eva* Cattron, the sister-in-law of Capt. John F. Merry.
Merry's wife is Eva's sister, Emma.

1873

Mar 20   Rawlins County, Kansas, is named for Maj. Gen. John Rawlins. Grant, Sherman, Logan, and McPherson counties are created.

1876

May 22   The 8th Wisconsin mascot eagle *Old Abe* is touring with the American Centennial Exhibition.

Aug 1   Colorado is granted statehood under President Grant.
Counties are named for Maj. Gen. John A. Logan and Capt. James L. Routt (94th Illinois), the first Colorado governor.

1877

Feb 28   Maj. Gen. John S. Bowen's remains, moved from historic Bethesda Presbyterian Church in Edwards, now rest in Cedar Hill Cemetery *(today's Soldiers' Rest)* in Vicksburg.

1879

Nov 1   The Vicksburg National Cemetery entrance arch is complete.

The Vicksburg National Cemetery Arch, circa 1911.
From a period postcard by the Carroll Hotel.

1881

Jul 3 Davis' *The Rise and Fall of the Confederate Government* is published on the 17th anniversary of the Confederate defeats at Gettysburg and Vicksburg.

Nov 12 The Sons of Union Veterans of the Civil War is organized in Pittsburgh, Pa., for children of Union veterans.

1883

May 11 Rev. Henry A.M. Henderson, former commandant of the Confederate prisoner of war camp at Cahaba, Ala., is entrusted by former President Grant with the eulogy and funeral arrangements for his mother, Mrs. Hannah Simpson Grant.

Jul 25 The Women's Relief Corps is created in Denver, Colo., to aid the G.A.R. members in their struggle to return to peacetime.

1884

Jun 4 The Pomona, Cal., chapter of Vicksburg Post 61, G.A.R, is formed by U.S.C.T. veterans.

1885

Jul 18 Grant finishes his *Personal Memoirs* days before his death. *Davis refuses a Boston Globe reporter's effort to criticize Grant. "If it were in my powers, I would contribute to his peace of his mind and the comfort of his body."*

Grant's works will leave poor Julia an estimated $14 million (2023$).
Library of Congress image dated June 27, 1885.

1885 (Cont.)

Aug 15   The Century Company is publishing the wartime recollections
of Union and Confederate officers in its *Century* magazine.
The subscription series will serve as the basis for the invaluable
anthology *Battles & Leaders of the Civil War.*
The *Century series* represents the first major work to capture
and commercialize the soldiers' war memory.

Publications willing to pay for all manner of war recollections
are drawing veterans, who tended to keep *their war* to
themselves, out into the national mainstream.
The war is becoming a very public, profitable industry.

1887

Jun 11   **The first Campaign and Siege memorial** in the city of
Vicksburg *(below)* is dedicated by the Association of Louisiana
Veterans to its 9,000 Vicksburg soldiers of whom over half
died. Louisiana had 43 separate units engaged at Vicksburg.

(MHL)

1888

Dec 28   Jefferson Davis' last speech, to a group of young men in
Mississippi City, Miss., is being widely circulated.
*"The past is dead; let it bury its dead. Lay aside all rancor, all
bitter sectional feeling and take your places in the ranks of
those who will bring about a consummation devoutly to be
wished – a reunited country."*

1889

May 30   Post No. 7, the G.A.R. Post in Vicksburg, is now meeting.

Jun 10   The national United Confederate Veterans is organized.

Nov 2   North and South Dakota are granted statehood.
Counties are named for Maj. Gen. John A. Logan, Oliver
Perry Throck Morton, the war governor of Indiana,
Brig. Gen. Thomas Ransom, Col. Edwin McCook (31st Illinois),
Maj. Gen. James McPherson, and U.S. Grant.

Nov 8   Montana is granted statehood.
Powell County is named for John Wesley Powell, 2d Illinois
Light Artillery, and explorer of the Grand Canyon.

Nov 9   Jefferson Davis leaves Beauvoir for his final visit to Vicksburg.

Nov 11   Washington is granted statehood.
Grant County is named for U.S. Grant.

Dec 6   Davis' acute bronchitis claims his life in New Orleans at the
home of Judge Charles E. Fenner, 1134 First Street.

Dec 11   Davis' funeral *(below)*, the South's largest, is held in New
Orleans, La., where he is entombed in the Army of Northern
Virginia Tomb in Metairie Cemetery.

Library of Congress Prints and Photographs Division image.

1890

May 25   Col. Charles Conway Floweree of Vicksburg is president of the
national Blue-Gray Association.
U.C.V. Camp 32 and G.A.R. Post 7 host the Association's week-
long reunion in the *Spirit of Nationalism* in Vicksburg with
veterans from around the country.

1890 (Cont.)

May 25 Blue-Gray Association Reunion attendees are disturbed by conditions on the old battlefield and at the Vicksburg National Cemetery.

An appeal is made to former Lt. Gen. Stephen D. Lee who is willing to work with former Northern enemies and Southern comrades to encourage a Vicksburg national military park.

Aug 19 Congress authorizes the Chattanooga-Chickamauga National Military Park.

Aug 20 A black G.A.R. Post has been established in Vicksburg.

Aug 30 The Antietam National Battlefield Site is established.

1891

Iowa's *Governor's Greys*, a ceremonial militia unit led by Capt. John F. Merry, visits Vicksburg and interviews Southern veterans and citizens as to their views on the establishment of a national military park at Vicksburg.

Iowa exhibits a strong interest in preserving the battlefield. Iowa had the highest number of casualties at Vicksburg and the most Vicksburg soldiers per capita of any Union state.

Merry coaxes his brother-in-law, Capt. Will Rigby, to get involved. Merry will be busy with his railroad duties.

1893

(MHL)

April 26
The Confederate Memorial at Soldiers' Rest in Cedar Hill Cemetery is installed by the Vicksburg Confederate Cemetery Association.

Records of the Confederate burials are not known to exist in 1893.

The Confederate burial ground was a potter's field-type section directly behind the 46th Mississippi line on the north end of the battlefield.

1893 (Cont.)

May 27   Varina Davis is moving her husband's remains to Hollywood Cemetery in Richmond, Va., to great ceremony.

May 28   Jefferson Davis' Louisville & Nashville funeral train is being greeted by throngs of adoring veterans along its route.

Jun 30   After a chance meeting at a hotel in New York, Julia Grant and Varina Davis are developing a very close friendship.

1894

Feb 8   The Governor's Greys from Dubuque, Iowa, are at the New Pacific House Hotel on Washington Street in Vicksburg.

Feb 9   S.D. Lee seeks support from Southern states for the Park: *"Southern soldiers who fought so valiantly at Vicksburg deserve to be honored rather than shadowed by shame."*

Sep 2   Three members of the *Forlorn Hope storming party* are the first of 78 to receive the Medal of Honor for their valor on May 22, 1863, at the Stockade Redan.
These represent the most Medals of Honor ever awarded for one single action, more than the entire Battle of Gettysburg (64).

Sep 10   The United Daughters of the Confederacy is formed in Nashville, Tenn., to *"honor and perpetuate the memory and deeds of high principles of Confederate men and women."*

Dec 27   Congress authorizes the Shiloh National Military Park.

Dec 30   Local military park supporter, cave owner, and the battlefield's unofficial guide, Thomas E. Lewis, is hosting public visits to his Siege cave behind his home on east Grove Street.

1895

Feb 11   Congress authorizes the Gettysburg National Military Park.

Resentment is surfacing in Mississippi,
"We don't need a Yankee tribute park in Mississippi."

Feb 28   John Cashman, publisher of the *Vicksburg Evening Post*, petitions for a Vicksburg national military park.

Oct 22   Veterans led by Lee and Merry form the Vicksburg National Military Park Association (VNMPA) in the Piazza Hotel (New Pacific House Hotel).
Officers are elected representing both sides equally.

The VNMPA meeting is held in conjunction with the Western Waterways Convention. Many of the most powerful and influential politicians and business leaders in the Mississippi River Valley, mostly veterans from the North and South, are in attendance.

1895 (Cont.)

VICKSBURG NATIONAL PARK ASSOCIATION

President, Lt. Gen. Stephen D. Lee, Mississippi

Vice-President, Maj. Charles L. Davidson, Iowa

Secretary, Capt. William. T. Rigby, Iowa

Treasurer, Col. Charles C. Flowerree, Mississippi

Original Board of Directors

Gov. John M. Stone, Capt. W.W. Stone, and Capt. E.S. Butts, Mississippi; Gen. A.J. Weissert, Ex -Governor W.D. Hoard, and Gen. Lucius Fairchild, Wisconsin; Gen. George F. McGinnis, Gen. N. Walker, and RAdm. George Brown, Indiana.

Gen. A.J. Vaughan and Gen. W.H. Jackson, Tennessee; Col. Frederick D. Grant, New York; Gen. Robert McCollough, Missouri; Gen. R.A. Alger, Michigan; Gen. Thomas N. Waul, Texas; and Colonel J.K.P. Thompson, Iowa.

Gen. John B. Gordon, Georgia; Capt. J.G. Everest, Illinois; Gen. E. W. Pettus, Alabama; and Col. John P. Rhea, Minnesota.

1895 (Cont.)

Nov 18   The charter for the VNMPA is signed by Gov. John M. Stone, former colonel of the 2^d Mississippi Infantry.

Nov 20   100 VNMPA directors and members representing the Northwest depart Chicago by train for Vicksburg.

7:30 p.m. – Capt. Merry's VNMPA party arrives to a vast throng and military salutes.

An honor guard of resident blue and gray veterans and militia escort Gov. Stone and Gen. S.D. Lee.

Nov 22   10:00 a.m. – A meeting of the VNMPA incorporators is held in the parlors of the Carroll Hotel.

The Articles of Incorporation are read and adopted.

Wis. Gov. Lucius Fairchild recommends preserving the fortifications and interior lands not to exceed 4,000 acres.

A committee of Lee, Davidson, Rigby, Flowerree, and Capt. Edward Butts (21st Mississippi) is charged with preparing a Bill to establish the Vicksburg National Military Park (VNMP), presenting the Bill to Congress, and providing estimated land costs.

Local enthusiast Tom Lewis engages to help to get the Bill *"into the right hands."*

1895 (Cont.)

Nov 28 Fifty VNMPA shares sell for $250 ($9,000 in 2023 dollars).

Dec 31 Local owners have provided the needed park land options.
Their willingness to sell demonstrates a positive local park
sentiment.

1896

Jan 10 A VNMPA executive committee meeting is called by S.D. Lee.
Congressman Thomas C. Catchings has warned the proposal is
too costly to fund.

Rigby presents a proposal for just 1,200 acres at $35 per acre,
$1,260 per acre or $15 million total in 2023 dollars.
Startled VNMPA members approve the proposal anyway.

Jan 20 Catchings introduces H.R. 4339 to create the VNMP.
John A.T. Hull (R-Iowa) is chair of the Military Affairs
Committee.
Though favorably received in committee, the Bill does not pass.

Jan 31 H.R. 4339 is referred to the Committee on the Whole House on
the State of the Union.
The Czar of the House, Speaker Thomas Reed, refuses to allow
the Bill to reach the floor.
VNMPA members return home sorely disappointed.

Feb 15 Rigby is traveling New England to promote the VNMP.
He is meeting feverishly with state officials and G.A.R.
Departments.

Feb 19 Lee praises Rigby for his work for the proposed park.
*"You have certainly won your spurs by your work in the
interest of the Park, and I hope you, at least, will be
rewarded for it, if no one else is."*

Apr 9 Fred Grant is serving as New York City's police commissioner.
*"I am not at all surprised at Speaker Reed not desiring the
matter to come up in the last session of Congress, owing to
the financial condition of the country. However, the outlook
for the coming year is much better, and I presume his
objections will be less serious."*

Apr 23 Musician Orion P. Howe receives the Medal of Honor, the
second youngest in history, for a successful suicidal mission at
the Stockade Redan on May 19, though seriously wounded.

Apr 30 Lydia Barr Rigby, Capt. Rigby's mother, dies after a lengthy
illness.
Rigby has only paused his personal national VNMP lobbying
campaign to care for her.

1896 (Cont.)

Dec 5   The *U.S.S. Vicksburg*, PG-11, is launched from Bath Iron Works in Bath, Me.

Dec 14   David Henderson (R-Iowa) tells friend Will Rigby:
"I have been pushing the Speaker," but stressed, *"Much work is needed in that quarter."*
Henderson was John Merry's colonel in the 46th Iowa.

Dec 16   At a VNMPA board meeting in the Carroll Hotel, Lee, Rigby, and others are directed to D.C. to push for Catchings' Bill.
Fred Grant and members of the Society of the Army of the Tennessee join the Vicksburg party in visiting Speaker Reed.
Reed is not opposed to the park idea, just to the money needed.

1897

Feb 7   Stephen D. Lee laments:

Czar of the House Thomas Reed.
Library of Congress image.

"I feel all has been done that could be done for the Park Bill. The trouble is the empty treasury — and Mr. Reed has 8,000 arguments on his side.

"Although I think the Bill may pass in the next Congress, the options will all have expired and we can never renew them as favorably again.

"In the meantime, many an old veteran in both armies will have 'crossed over the river'."

Mar 4   William McKinley (R-Ohio) is inaugurated U.S. President.
He will be the *last President to be a Civil War veteran.*
He names VNMPA board member R.A. Alger as War Secretary.
Congress reconvenes to Rigby's petitions from legislatures in Illinois, Indiana, Michigan, Minnesota, Pennsylvania, and Wisconsin, *northern states only*, for the VNMP Bill.

Mar 10   The 54th Congress adjourns.
Speaker Reed ignores the pressure for the VNMP Bill.
H.R. 4339 dies.

Aug 27   The Mausoleum for Ulysses S. Grant is dedicated in New York.
One million view and over 55,000 march in freezing weather with 57 mile-per-hour winds.

The dedication of the U.S. Grant Mausoleum.
(NPS)

1897 (Cont.)

Oct 29   Lee tells Rigby that the failure of Congress to act on the Park
Bill means starting again – "how, when, with what money?"

Nov 26   *Iowan James K.P. Thompson (Musician, 21st Iowa):*
*"If there is a battlefield of the late war worthy of recognition
by the government, Vicksburg is that one. It was big with
results. Gettysburg was simply a display of remarkable
courage on both sides — no great results followed."*

Dec 9   Rep. Catchings introduces H.R. 4382 *"to establish a national
military park to commemorate the campaign, siege, **and
defense of Vicksburg**."*
"Defense of Vicksburg" indicates that the Confederate soldiers
will be honored equally.
The Park will capture the national mood of reconciliation among
the white sections of North and South.

1898

Jan 5   Lee to Rigby:
*"The speaker is the only obstacle. If his comrades in the G.A.R.
and other organizations cannot reach him, certainly I cannot."*

Jan 25   Rigby, in Indianapolis, Ind., to wife Eva.
*"I am assured, however, that the House Military Committee
will today vote to report the Bill favorably."*

Jan 29   Stuyvesant Fish, Illinois Central Railroad (ICRR) president,
gives Rigby $200 ($7,200 in 2023 dollars) to press on.

1898 (Cont.)

Jan 29 The ICRR will benefit from veterans traveling to Vicksburg. Stuyvesant Fish's father Hamilton was Grant's Secretary of State, the *pillar of his Administration.*

Rigby writes to Eva from Nicholasville, Ky.:
"I have succeeded with the Dept. of Kentucky and am going on to Chattanooga to get the Dept. of Tennessee in line. Passes are waiting everywhere from Fish and Merry."

Feb 14 Supporters in Massachusetts, Connecticut, and Rhode Island have sent letters to Rigby in advance of his visit to D.C. *Rigby's singular efforts rival a major political campaign.*

Feb 15 Rigby visits the G.A.R. Dept. Commander in Washington, D.C.

Feb 18 Rigby schedules visits with G.A.R. commanders in Indiana, Illinois, Iowa, and Wisconsin for the remainder of February.

Mar 1 The VNMP Bill is reported out of committee. Prospects for the VNMP are looking up.

Apr 1 Sgt. Thomas Higgins is awarded the Medal of Honor as the 99th Illinois flagbearer at the 2d Texas Lunette, May 22, 1863. *Defenders at the 2d Texas Lunette served as witnesses on his medal application when he could find none.*

Apr 21 Before the VNMP Bill vote, the Spanish-American War begins. Rigby's inertia pops like a balloon. Actions regarding the VNMP Bill are put on hold.

For the first time, Union and Confederates veterans are allowed to fight in the same army.

Apr 28 Rigby refuses to let the war steal the Association's momentum. He sends *Park Bill resolutions* to all G.A.R. Departments that have meetings scheduled in May.

Aug 13 Hostilities cease in the Spanish-American War.

Nov 8 Victory in the Spanish-American War sends Republicans and all VNMP supporters back to Congress.

Dec 11 The Treaty of Paris ends the Spanish-American War. Veterans' issues are of great interest to Congress. *The war has actually greatly enhanced the VNMP's status.*

Dec 28 The VNMPA meets in Vicksburg for a strategy session.

1899

Feb 4 Rigby and newly appointed VNMPA board member William O. Mitchell are in Washington D.C. Mitchell (13th Iowa) has replaced the late Capt. Edward Butts.

1899 (Cont.)

Feb 5   Even the tight-fisted Reed seems anxious to fund projects and programs of interest to veterans and drops his opposition to the VNMP measure.

Feb 6   Rep. Hull asks Speaker Reed to suspend the rules and pass the VNMP Bill.
As soon as H.R. 4382 is read by the Clerk, it is voted on and *passes unanimously.*

Feb 7   The *Vicksburg Evening Post* celebrates:
"No matter ever brought before the Congress has been more faithfully presented and worked for in the past three years than the Bill which passed the House yesterday under a suspension of the rules for the establishment of a National Military Park at Vicksburg."

VNMPA board member Mitchell, an Iowa state senator, joins in:
"It is conceded by everyone that Captain W.T. Rigby is entitled to practically all the credit for originating and carrying forward the enterprise. He has worked for it for nearly four years and it would be an outrage if someone else were appointed commissioner in his place."

Fred Grant, Stephen D. Lee, and a host of others are singing Rigby's praises.

Even Lt. Col. John P. Nicholson, powerful chairman of the Gettysburg Park Commission, is pleased to draft a letter of support.

Feb 9   Sen. Edmund Pettus of Alabama, a member of the Senate Committee on Military Affairs who had served under Lee's command with the 20th Alabama at Vicksburg, sends to the floor a companion Bill, S. 4382.

Feb 10   Mississippi U.S. Senator Hernando De Soto Money asks for *"unanimous consent"* to call up S. 4382.
After a reading, the measure passes.

Feb 20   The VNMP Bill goes to the desk of President William McKinley, an Ohio Civil War veteran, as were Grant, Sherman, and McPherson.

Feb 21   McKinley signs the Act creating the Vicksburg National Military Park.

Feb 24   Rigby is requested to appear before Secretary of War Russell Alger on March 1st at 10:00 a.m. regarding the VNMP.
Rigby is expecting an appointment to the National Park Commission from his fellow VNMPA board member.

1899 (Cont.)

Mar 1   The VNMP Commission is established of Lee and Rigby, as well
as James G. Everest who represents 36,000 Illinois troops.
The Commission members are all Vicksburg veterans.
The Commission's role is to establish the VNMP.
Lee, the Mississippian, is elected chairman.
Gen. John S. Kountz will be secretary and historian.
Charles Longley will serve as clerk.

Everest served with the 13th Illinois at Vicksburg.
Kountz was awarded a Medal of Honor with the 37th Ohio at
Missionary Ridge and was with Sherman at Vicksburg.
Longley was a sergeant with the Rigby's 24th Iowa at Vicksburg.
Rigby's youngest son is Charles Longley Rigby, b. 1874.

Only Rigby moves to Vicksburg where he manages the daily
business of the Commission as the *Resident Commissioner*.

Two Union veterans have elected their 1863 adversary at
Chickasaw Bayou, Champion Hill, and the battles for and
Siege of Vicksburg as their leader to advance the Park banner.

Mar 14   The Park Commission establishes an office at 100 N. Cherry St.

Mar 15   The VNMP Commission holds it first meeting.
The Park area surveyed is 1,248 acres valued at $52,670, about
$42.24 per acre ($1,520 per acre in 2023 dollars, $1.9 million).

Apr 28   Rigby, feverishly at work, declares,
"Enough land has been purchased to secure a park."

Sep 4   *The Czar*, Speaker Thomas Reed, resigns in protest of the
Spanish-American war.

Sep 10   As if by divine intervention, the new Speaker of the House is
Park friend David B. Henderson from *Dubuque, Iowa*.
Henderson will be the last Civil War veteran to serve as Speaker.
Henderson was wounded at Shiloh and later served as colonel
of Merry's 46th Iowa.

With Ohio veteran William McKinley as President, VNMP has
friends in the *highest of places*.
*Rigby's many seeds are about to produce a miraculous
harvest.*

1900

Mar 29   The Iowa legislature approves $150,000 for its state memorial.

Jun 18   Construction of Confederate Avenue is underway.
The route is easier than Union Avenue with its steep landscape.

1900 (Cont.)

Aug 18 The 10-inch Columbiad that sank the *U.S.S. Cincinnati* is buried on the Lum property on S. Washington Street.

Dec 20 An exhausted S.D. Lee asks that Rigby temporarily relieve him as VNMP Commission chair.

Dec 31 Alice Shirley Eaton has sold her parents' house and 60 acres to the VNMP.
Two conditions: The house must be the most prominent on the battlefield and her parents must be exhumed from Cedar Hill Cemetery and buried behind the home. Both are met.

1901

May 1 President William McKinley visits Vicksburg, four months before he is assassinated.

May 14 The Illinois Memorial Commission is established.

Sept 10 Stephen D. Lee turns to the press to stop VNMP budget cuts.

Sep 14 President William McKinley, signatory of the VNMP Act, dies of an assassin's bullets in Buffalo, N.Y.

Nov 20 An aged, unwell Lee reluctantly resigns as Commission chair.
Capt. Rigby is appointed to fill the post in the interim.
Capt. Lewis Guion, 26th Louisiana, Shoup's Brigade, is added to the Park Commission as its Confederate representative.

Nov 23 Members of the Illinois Memorial Commission meet in Chicago.

1902

Mar 2 S.D. Lee is president of the Mississippi Historical Society.

May 20 $3,000 is allowed for the restoration of the Shirley House, $105,000 in 2023 dollars.

Nov 14 The restored Shirley House is entrusted to the Park Commission.

1903

Jan 1 Period artillery tubes will be mounted on 112 iron field carriages made by the Chattanooga Car & Foundry Co.

500 battlefield description tablets will unite the Park.

Apr 15 Capt. Rigby officially becomes Park Commission chair, having performed those duties almost from the first.

May 15 Union Avenue, with its more severe terrain, is in development.
J.T. Crass will gravel the Park roads.
Union Avenue will feature 12 bridges.
Confederate Avenue will be bridged in three places.

1903 (Cont.)

Jul 28   Nine Melan arch bridges are being built by the William T. Young
Bridge Company.
An arch-truss steel bridge is being built on Confederate Avenue
by the Penn Bridge Company.

Oct 15   A massive memorial and plaza to Gen. William T. Sherman is
dedicated in Washington, D.C., still *untamed and unconquered.*

William Tecumseh Sherman's memorial, Sherman Plaza, recalls Vicksburg exploits.
From a period postcard.

1903 (Cont.)

Nov 14   The Massachusetts State Memorial, *The Volunteer, by* the
renowned *Theo Alice Ruggles Kitson* is dedicated, the first state
memorial erected on the VNMP.

Massachusetts governor John Lewis Bates also delivers *the first
state reconciliation message*:
*"A new era has dawned. We erect monuments not to mark the
division, but its disappearance.*
"We erect monuments in the **land that was once hostile
because it is now friendly**. *We erect them because* **old
things have passed away**."

*At the Park's first state memorial dedication, the VNMP's
first Commission president, Lt. Gen. Stephen D. Lee,
reciprocates the reconciliatory tone.*

1903 (Cont.)

Nov 14   *Lee:*
*"Our grand republic, willing to obliterate forever all vestiges of divisions and bitterness in our mighty civil strife, has established, on the noted battlefields of the war national military parks, giving equal honor to the Union and Confederate soldiers alike, and emphasizing the fact that the valor, patriotism and fortitude displayed and the hardships and sufferings endured, the blood spilt, and treasure spent on both sides is now **common property;** that **the glory of the Union soldier and the Confederate soldier is now the sacred heritage of the American people.**"*

Dec 15   The firm Jenney & Mundie is hired as architects for the Illinois State Memorial.
William Le Baron Jenney was Sherman's chief engineer.
As an architect, Jenney is known as the *Father of the Skyscraper*.

1904

Sir Henry Hudson Kitson submits a reduced bid on the Iowa State Memorial with more troop emphasis.

Stephen Dill Lee is elected Commander-in-Chief of the *United Confederate Veterans*.

Jan 27   The Wisconsin State Capitol is destroyed by fire.
The remains of 8th Wisconsin eagle mascot *Old Abe* are lost to history, with the exception of a few feathers.

Nov 30   The New Hampshire State Memorial, the VNMP's second memorial, has been erected adjacent to *Massachusetts* without a dedication ceremony.

Dec 31   State appropriations for monuments in the Vicksburg Park have been made as follows: Illinois, $250,000; Iowa, $150,000; Ohio, $56,000; Wisconsin, $30,000; Pennsylvania, $15,000; New York, $12,500; Massachusetts, $5,000; New Hampshire, $5,000. Aggregate, $523,500, about $18 million in 2023 dollars.

Urgent demands for educational facilities and public works of every kind delay most Southern memorial placements.

1905

Jan 1   Work commences on the Illinois State Memorial.
79 regimental and battery memorials and 80 regimental markers are also being created by Culver Construction Co. of Springfield, Ill.

1905 (Cont.)

Jan 1   Marble for the Illinois State Memorial is coming from Georgia. Bronze features are being crafted at the American Bronze Foundry Co. of Chicago.

Jan 9   The Shirley House becomes the first Park Museum.

May 22   The 39 Ohio State regimental monuments created in Clyde by the Hughes Granite and Marble Co. are dedicated.
Clyde, Ohio, is Maj. Gen. James McPherson's birthplace.

Ohio memorials to the 53ᵈ and 114ᵗʰ Ohio Regiments.
(GJMC)

1905 (Cont.)

May 25   A site for a proposed Ohio state memorial is being considered on Union Avenue near its juncture with Graveyard Road.

Dec 31   Iowa regimental temples, created by Edmund Prior of Postville, Iowa, have been installed.

1906

Jan 31   Legislation to build a Mississippi State Memorial, the largest Southern VNMP monument, **passes by one vote**.

Jan 1   Tom Lewis, cave owner and guide, is named Park Marshal.

Feb 28 $50,000 for markers and a Mississippi Memorial is authorized, $1.6 million in 2023 dollars.

1906 (Cont.)

Mar 27   The Pennsylvania State Memorial is dedicated.
Locally, it is known as the *Five Faces*.

Apr 15   The Illinois State Memorial is complete.

Apr 20   The New Hampshire State Memorial is accepted by the Federal
government.

Oct 16   Fred Grant arranges a military escort to accompany Varina Davis'
body from New York City to Richmond, Va.
Mrs. Davis had publicly stated in her newspaper column in 1901
that the *right side won the war*, ostracizing her as a true
Confederate lady who preferred life in the North.

Oct 26   The Illinois State Memorial is dedicated.
Illinois spent ¼ of its state budget on the memorial.

Nov 15   The Iowa State Memorial is dedicated.
Illinois and Iowa memorials are Rigby's *anchor* memorials.
With Iowa and Illinois, he is confident of adding other states.

The Illinois State Memorial, a temple to Peace and a temple of Fame.
(GJMC)

1907

A bridge to Maloney Circle is built for the proposed John
McClernand equestrian statue. *The statue location is later
changed and the bridge abandoned.*

Fred Grant, Vicksburg veteran and the General's son, visits the
Illinois State Memorial
He *requests* that *his* name be added on the bronze plaque next
to his dad as a wounded aide to the Commanding General.

1907 (Cont.)

May 24 The Minnesota State Memorial is dedicated.
Minnesota governor John Johnson reinforces the VNMP theme of sectional reconciliation:
"The things we fought over then no longer matter."

Nov 16 Oklahoma is granted statehood.
Counties are named for U.S. Grant, Maj. Gen. John A. Logan, and Col. Roger Mills, 10th Texas Cavalry.

Nov 23 The Virginia State Memorial, the first Confederate memorial, is dedicated to the Botetourt Artillery and to her native sons.

1908

Mar 28 Local favorite and original battlefield fixture and cave owner Thomas E. Lewis dies.
He was an early promoter of the preservation of the battlefield when few seemed interested.

May 25 Lee speaks to a reunion of Wisconsin and Iowa veterans and poses for his battlefield statue.
He is planning the next U.C.V. reunion on June 9.

May 28 Lt. Gen. Stephen Dill Lee dies in Vicksburg of a cerebral hemorrhage, beloved by blue and gray

Nov 11 The Rhode Island State Memorial, *The Flag*, is dedicated.

Dec 29 Indiana dedicates its unusual trapezoidal regimental markers.

1909

Jun 11 The Stephen D. Lee statue by renowned Sir Henry Hudson Kitson is dedicated.
Both sides have contributed to his memorial.
An Iowa soldier speaks of their former adversary:
"He was our friend. We want him to know the war is over."

Nov 13 The Mississippi State Memorial is dedicated, the largest Confederate memorial, despite Mississippi's earlier reluctance.

1911

May 22 The Wisconsin State Memorial is dedicated.
Maj. Gen. Fred Grant is featured speaker in his last public appearance.
Its bronze honors 9,800 Wisconsin soldiers and *Old Abe*.

1912

Jan 6 New Mexico is granted statehood.
Counties are named for U.S. Grant and Lt. Thomas Catron, Bledsoe's C.S. Missouri Battery and statehood leader.
These are the last counties named for Campaign veterans.

1914

Mar 31 The Maryland State Memorial has recently been dedicated.

1916

Nov 10 The Michigan State Memorial is dedicated.

1917

Jan 1 95% of today's VNMP monuments and markers are in place.

Edmond Quinn completes the John C. Pemberton statue.

Feb 25 *The Crisis*, a Civil War silent film featuring Vicksburg actors and scenes, has its general release.

Mar 26 Col. Willard D. Newhill arrives to supervise the October National Memorial Celebration and Peace Jubilee Reunion.

Oct 1 Col. George Hoskins and 1,250 soldiers of the 155th Infantry arrive for the Peace Jubilee.

Oct 6 Freeland Romans, 72d Illinois veteran, arrives for the Reunion. He is 10 days early, unable to wait any longer.
"The three months I spent in Vicksburg after its fall were the happiest days of my life."

Oct 16 The National Memorial Reunion and Peace Jubilee begins. It is attended by 8,000 blue and gray veterans. Its goal is to encourage young men to join the WWI effort.

Oct 17 Three memorials are dedicated during the Peace Jubilee: New York, U.S. Navy, and Missouri.

1919

The Florentine Brotherhood Foundry in Chicago completes the equestrian statue of U.S. Grant *(below)* by Frederick Hibbert.

(GJMC)

The Missouri State Memorial, *Here Brothers Fought,* honors both Armies. *(GJMC)*

1919 (Cont.)

Jul 10   Construction of the Louisiana State Memorial begins.

Jul 11   A Memorial Arch at the entrance into the Park is authorized using remaining Peace Jubilee Reunion funds.

1920

Oct 18   The Louisiana State Memorial is dedicated at a final cost of $43,500 ($1.5 million in 2023 dollars), including three off-site relief portraits.

Oct 20   The VNMP Memorial Arch is dedicated.
It is constructed of Stone Mountain, Ga., granite.

1921

Mar 24   Willis Meadows, 37th Alabama, makes national news when he coughs up the Vicksburg bullet in his head since 1863.
The guilty sharpshooter, Peter Knapp, 5th Iowa, and Meadows make *Ripley's Believe It or Not,* becoming pen pals until death.

1922

Nov 14   The West Virginia State Memorial is dedicated.

1923

Jun 26 VNMP historian Edwin Cole Bearss is born in Billings, Mont.

1924

Apr 17 James Everest, one of three original VNMP Commissioners, dies in Chicago, having represented 36,000 Illinois soldiers.

1925

May 18 The North Carolina State Memorial is dedicated.

1926

Jun 26 The Indiana State Memorial is dedicated.

Oct 22 Margie Riddle *(Bearss)* is born in Brandon, Miss.

1927

Jun 5 Alice Eugenia Shirley Eaton dies in Washington, D.C., and is buried with her husband in Arlington National Cemetery. Her former home is now the Shirley House Memorial.

Dec 24 U.S. Rep. Thomas Clendinen Catchings dies in Vicksburg. *He was the sponsor of the VNMP Congressional Bill.*

1929

May 10 Capt. William Titus Rigby dies while serving as Resident Park Commissioner, beloved by countless veterans and citizens across the country. His VNMP achievements and legacy are legendary. At each monument, marker, and tablet, the *Echoes* of Capt. Rigby and 107,000 soldiers can be heard where they fought, later came together to pinpoint their common spots in history, then celebrated their glory until they were no more.

1931

Mar 31 Jefferson Davis' home Brierfield south of Vicksburg has recently been destroyed by fire.

1932

Oct 29 Sculptress Theo Alice Ruggles Kitson dies in Boston, Mass. Having created 73 sculptures, she is the **Mother of the Vicksburg National Military Park**.

1933

Apr 13 Maj. Broadus Holt requests 150 men for VNMP Civilian Conservation Corps (CCC) camps.

Jun 30 150 of 200 CCC workers have arrived in Vicksburg.

Aug 10 VNMP is transferred from the War Department to the Interior Department along with other national military parks.

1933 (Cont.)

Dec 15   VNMP launches its *"tour stations"* for guides and visitors.
By noon, 900 visitors in 68 cars and 14 buses have toured.

1934

Apr 1   The last of four CCC camps (MP-4) is established along Union
Avenue south of Graveyard Road.

Apr 11   VNMP has a slide projector to illustrate presentations.

Apr 23   Vicksburg is being instructed in becoming *Military Park
Conscious* as efforts to publicly promote the Park continue.

1935

Nov 22   The South Carolina State Memorial is dedicated.

Dec 15   The Vicksburg National Military Park initiates a visitors' guide
program.
Below, the Warren-Hinds W.M.U. tours the battlefield in 1935.

(NPS)

1936

Apr 4   *Vicksburg's historian*, Gordon A. Cotton, is born in Yokena.

Nov 21   VNMP opens its first *Visitor Center*.

1937

May 22   Ulysses Grant III and John Pemberton III shake hands at the
Surrender Interview Site.

1938

Jul 3   The last great Blue-Gray Reunion is attended by 10,000 at
Gettysburg, 21 years after Vicksburg's last reunion, the Peace
Jubilee.

1939

Feb 17 The destroyer *U.S.S. Ellet, DD-398,* honors the family that includes founders of the Vicksburg Ram Fleet and Mississippi Marine Brigade.

1942

Aug 16 The 101st Airborne Division is created from the remnants of the 1921 Milwaukee, Wis., 101st Division of Organized Reserves.

The 101st carries forward the Reserves sleeve patch featuring the mascot of the 8th Wisconsin, the original *Screaming Eagle Old Abe*, with an added Airborne tab.

1943

Nov 6 A tornado practically destroys Bethel Church near the ruins of *Windsor* mansion at Bruinsburg.
Grant's soldiers on the Rodney Road shot the steeple bell while they were marching toward Port Gibson.

1944

Mar 28 The *U.S.S. Vicksburg, PG-11,* renamed the *Alexander Hamilton,* is put out of service.

1945

Apr 26 99-year-old Johnson Knight's death closes the Vicksburg G.A.R. Post 61 in Pomona, Cal.
Knight was the last of 436 Union Army veterans who attended meetings at the Vicksburg Post.

Oct 19 The *U.S.S. Hartford,* a Navy *relic,* is towed to the Norfolk Yard.

1947

Jul 4 Gen. Dwight Eisenhower's visit to Vicksburg is considered by some a break in Vicksburg's refusal to celebrate July 4th.
The festivities are called the *Carnival of the Confederacy.*

1948

Jun 3 The Old Court House Museum opens its doors after a lengthy campaign by Ms. Eva Whitaker Davis to save the icon.

1951

Jul 19 The Alabama State Memorial is dedicated.

1953

Apr 3 Davis heirs sell the plantation on Davis Island.

1954

Apr 17 The Florida State Memorial is dedicated.

Aug 2 The Arkansas State Memorial is dedicated.

1956

Aug 2 The Union veterans' fraternal and charitable organization, the Grand Army of the Republic, is dissolved.

The Alabama State Memorial, honoring the State and the heroic women at home. *(GJMC)*

1956

Nov 12 VNMP historian Ed Bearss pinpoints the *U.S.S. Cairo* wreck. The vessel was sunk on December 12, 1862.

Nov 20 The *U.S.S. Hartford*, beyond salvage, sinks in Norfolk, Va. The *Hartford* brought Farragut to Vicksburg in 1862.

1957

Dec 20 *Raintree County* with Montgomery Cliff and Elizabeth Taylor, which includes a key scene at the *Windsor* ruins, is released.

1959

Jun 12 John Ford's *Horse Soldiers* based on Grierson's Raid is released. The film features John Wayne and William Holden.

Oct 31 Divers have been descending on the *U.S.S. Cairo* wreck site. The divers bring items to the surface not seen in 97 years.

1960

Jun 30 The Kansas State Memorial is erected but will not be dedicated.

Sep 15 Raising *U.S.S. Cairo's* pilothouse heightens interest in raising her. She is the only *City Class* ironclad that remains of seven.

1961

Nov 4 The cornerstone of the Texas State Memorial *(below)* is dedicated, the largest Texas memorial outside of Texas.

Sealing the Breach stands on the Railroad Redoubt. *(GJMC)*

1962

May 31 The new Grand Gulf State Park museum has opened. Margie Bearss was contracted to develop the museum.

Oct 25 The Georgia State Memorial is dedicated.

Low water on the Big Black River has exposed the remains of the *Charm* and *Paul B. Jones*, Mark Twain's first boat as pilot.

1963

Jun 4 VNMP is authorized funds to reconfigure the park road and transfer lands to local government.

Jul 4 Vicksburg commemorates the centennial of its place in history. Again, the celebration is the *Carnival of the Confederacy*.

Oct 15 The Mississippi Agriculture and Industrial *(A&I)* Board is overseeing a fund-raising drive to raise the *U.S.S. Cairo*.

Raise the Cairo apparel is popular in the city.

1964

The lower quarter of the VNMP from Square Fort to the Mississippi River is quitclaimed to the City of Vicksburg and a thoroughfare *(Mission 66)* will be built through Vicksburg as a VNMP bypass.

Apr 30 The state legislature has appropriated $50,000 to continue the *U.S.S. Cairo* project.

The Warren County Board of Supervisors agrees to underwrite the salvage operation.

Aug 3 The great adventure to raise the *U.S.S. Cairo* begins.

Oct 17 Seven cables required to raise the *Cairo* are in position.

The face of the ironclad *U.S.S. Cairo* sees daylight after 102 years. *(NPS)*

1964 (Cont.)

Oct 18 The *U.S.S. Cairo* raising operation begins.

Four derricks, each lifting 1,000 tons, are pitted against her 512 tons.

The weight is too great and the *Cairo* is moved to a shoal.

Oct 29 An effort is made to put the *U.S.S. Cairo* on a sunken barge.

Two of the cables cut into her, ending hope of an intact lift.

Dec 12 A derrick raises the *Cairo's* last section onto a barge, 102 years to the day that she was sunk.

1965

Oct 1   The A&I Board barges the *U.S.S. Cairo* to the Gulf Coast. *Cairo* remnants are being hosted by Ingalls Shipbuilding in Pascagoula, Miss.

1972

Oct 12   Congress passes the *Cairo Restoration Act* to include exhibition. The VNMP is authorized to accept title to the ironclad.

1973

Harpers Ferry and Denver officials consider the best path forward for the *U.S.S. Cairo* restoration.

The former VNMP Administration Building and Museum on Confederate Avenue is demolished.

1974

Sep 30   A three-year design of the *U.S.S. Cairo Museum* is underway.

1976

Nov 30   Ingalls Shipbuilding needs the *Cairo* holding space vacated.

1977

Jan 15   Work to move the *U.S.S. Cairo* back to Vicksburg is underway. Lt. Col. Robert Calland, transportation expert, is in charge. Superintendent Dan Lee and maintenance crew are assisting.

Jun 19   The *Cairo* arrives in Vicksburg, pushed by the U.S. Army Corps of Engineers' *Motor Vessel Lipscomb*.

1978

Oct 17   President Jimmy Carter signs a Joint Resolution reinstating Jefferson Davis' citizenship.
"By posthumously restoring the full rights of citizenship to Jefferson Davis, the Congress officially **completes the long process of reconciliation that has reunited our people** *following the tragic conflict between the States."*

1980

The *U.S.S. Cairo Museum* opens.

1981

May 22   In 1863, local undertaker J.Q. Arnold kept meticulous burial records for C.S. soldiers at Vicksburg. The records were found in the early 1960s for 1,600 soldiers.

In 1981, the U.D.C. and Veterans' Administration acquired and had placed the corresponding massive number of stones at Vicksburg's Soldiers' Rest at Cedar Hill Cemetery.

1981 (Cont.)

At left, a color guard begins the dedication of the new C.S.A. tombstones at Soldiers' Rest on May 22, 1981. The author is at right.
(MHL)

Rodney, Miss., Catholic Church, Grand Gulf State Park, Miss.
(MHL)

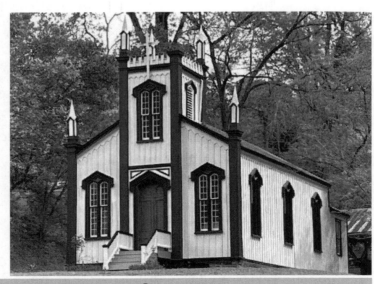

1983

Jan 1   The 1868 Rodney Catholic Church is the state's **outstanding example of carpenter gothic church architecture**.

1983 (Cont.)

In 1957, there were only seven communicants for the Rodney church. The Natchez-Jackson Diocese deeded the property to the Rodney Foundation which donated it to the State of Mississippi.

It is transferred to the Grand Gulf Military Monument Commission in 1983, a surviving *Echo* of the once prosperous town and people of Rodney.

1984

The restoration of the *U.S.S. Cairo* is complete.

25 craftsmen, engineers, and maintenance workers were engaged.

1990

Mar 28   Grant's DeSoto Point Canal is incorporated into the VNMP.

Sep 17   *The Occupation of Vicksburg* and *Reconstruction* are added to VNMP's interpretative mission.

1995

Jun 28   Illinois is adding gold leaf to the eagle *(below)* on its state memorial.

(GJMC)

1996

Jun 29   The Tennessee State Memorial is dedicated.
The cost is borne by the United Daughters of the Confederacy.

2001

Oct 1   The Kentucky State Memorial is dedicated.

2002

Oct 11   President George W. Bush authorizes the acquisition of John C. Pemberton's Headquarters on Crawford Street by the VNMP.

2004

Feb 14   The memorial to the *Soldiers of African Descent* is dedicated. The State of Mississippi and the City of Vicksburg are sponsors. Dr. Kim Sessums of Brookhaven, Miss., is the sculptor. The sculpture (*below*) stands on black Angola African granite.

(GJMC)

2006

Oct 7   Margie Riddle Bearss, author, historian, and great friend of Champion Hill and VNMP, passes away in Jackson, Miss.

2007

May 5   *Margie Riddle Bearss Day* is celebrated at Champion Hill.

2008

Jan 1   *The Friends of Vicksburg Campaign and Siege (FVCS)* organization is created.

Oct 14   The dedication of the Connecticut State Memorial completes the list of states represented by units at Vicksburg.

2010

May 8   The Kentucky Confederate Memorial is dedicated.

2011

Jan 1   VNMP is commemorated on a U.S. quarter dollar *(see below)*.

Jun 1   Key portions of the battlefield are being restored to their 1863 view by the FVCS, increasing the *wow factor* for visitors.

Apr 14   5th Iowa's Peter Jones Knapp's recently discovered ashes are buried in the Willamette National Cemetery near Portland, Oreg., to full military honors.

Knapp is the last veteran of Vicksburg to be buried and the cemetery's first Civil War burial.

He is remembered for shooting Willis Meadows in the eye.

He and Willis made national news when Willis coughed up the bullet 50 years later and became lifelong pen pals.

2013

May 23   Vicksburg's sesquicentennial is featured on a postage stamp.

2013 (Cont.)

May 25   The newly restored Iowa State Memorial is rededicated.

2017

Oct 17   The newly restored Missouri State Memorial is rededicated.

Dec 31   The Anshe Chesed congregation has deeded its synagogue and 2d Texas Lunette Jewish cemetery to the FVCS.

The Iowa State Memorial. The art, by Henry Hudson Kitson and Theo A.R. Kitson, honors the Union and Confederate soldiers in the Campaign. *(GJMC)*

2018

Apr 13   Bids are needed for a project to stabilize the north face of the Texas State Memorial due to failing loess soil.

2019

Jan 6   Vicksburg celebrates the Tercentennial of French Fort St. Pierre and the first French presence in the Gulf region.

May 3   A Champion Hill memorial is dedicated before a national crowd honoring Edwin C. Bearss, the nation's leading Civil War historian who, in earlier years, began the mission of preserving the Champion Hill Battlefield 25 miles east of Vicksburg.

2020

May 25   The History Channel features a three-part series on U.S. Grant.

Sep 20   National Park Service historian emeritus Edwin Cole Bearss dies in Richland, Miss., passionate about the past until his passing. He rests in Bethel Cemetery in Brandon, Miss.

2021

Mar 7   Vicksburg's beloved historian Gordon A. Cotton dies in the city.

Oct 30   Ed Bearss' life and legacy are memorialized in a posthumous portrait relief dedication in Bentonville, N.C.

2022

Aug 1   The FVCS refurbishes the Texas State Memorial at a cost of approximately $500,000.

2023

Jan 1   The 160th anniversary of the Vicksburg Campaign and Siege is commemorated. Vicksburg's bicentennial is being planned.

The Mississippi State Memorial, *"The Last Stand."*
The war claimed ¼ of Mississippi's war-age men and produced 10,000 orphans.
(GJMC)

Capt. William Titus Rigby, the *driving force behind* the Vicksburg National
Military Park.
(GJMC)

BIBLIOGRAPHY and RESOURCES

Ballard, Michael B., *Pemberton, The General Who Lost Vicksburg*, 1991.

Ballard, Michael B., *Vicksburg, The Campaign That Opened the Mississippi*, 2010.

Barry, John M., *Rising Tide*, 1998.

Bell, W. Scott, *The Camel Regiment, A History of the Bloody 43rd Mississippi Volunteer Infantry, C.S.A., 1862-1865*, 2018.

Betera, Martin N., *DeGolyer's Eighth Michigan Battery*, 2016.

Chatelain, Neil P., *Defending the Arteries of the Rebellion, Confederate Naval Operations in the Mississippi Valley, 1861-1865*, 2020.

Chernow, Ron, *Grant*, 2017.

Clampitt, Bradley C., *Occupied Vicksburg*, 2016.

Faust, Drew Gilpin, *This Suffering Republic, Death and the American Civil War*, 2008.

Flood, Charles Bracelen, *Grant and Sherman, The Friendship That Won The Civil War*, 2005.

Gibraltar Publishing Company, *In and About Vicksburg, An Illustrated Guide Book to the City of Vicksburg, Mississippi*, 1890.

Grabau, Warren, *Ninety-Eight Days, A Geographer's View of the Vicksburg Campaign*, 2000.

Groom, Winston, *Vicksburg 1863*, 2010.

Hermann, Janet Sharp, *Joseph E. Davis, Pioneer Patriarch*, 1990.

Hills, Parker, *Vicksburg National Military Park, the Art of Commemoration, Vicksburg Convention and Visitors Bureau*, 2011.

Johnson, Walter, *River of Darkness, Slavery and Empire in the Cotton Kingdom*, 2013.

Joiner, Gary D., *Mr. Lincoln's Brown Water Navy*, 2007.

Jones, John Pickett, *Black Jack: John A. Logan and Southern Illinois in the Civil War Era*, 1995.

Jones, Michael Dan, *The Vicksburg 28th Louisiana Infantry*, 2013

Klein, Maury, *Days of Defiance: Sumter, Secession, and the Coming of the Civil War*, 1997.

Marszalek, John F., *Sherman, A Soldier's Passion for Order*, 1993.

McPherson, James W., *Embattled Rebel: Jefferson Davis as Commander in Chief*, 2014.

Minnesota Historical Society, *Brother of Mine, Civil War Letters of Thomas and William Christie*, 2011.

Miller, Donald L., *Vicksburg, Grant's Campaign That Broke the Confederacy*, 2019.

Mills, Gary B., *Of Men and Rivers, the Story of the Vicksburg District*, 1978.

Mitcham, Samuel W., Jr., *Bust Hell Wide Open, the Life of Nathan Bedford Forrest*, 2019.

Mitcham, Samuel W., Jr., *Vicksburg: The Bloody Siege that Turned the Tide of the Civil War*, 2018.

Morris, Christopher Charles, *Becoming Southern: The Evolution of the Southern Way of Life, Warren County and Vicksburg, Mississippi, 1770-1860*, 1995.

Nicoletti, Cynthia, *Secession on Trial, the Treason Prosecution of Jefferson Davis*, 2017.

O'Connell, Robert L., *Fierce Patriot: The Tangled Lives of William Tecumseh Sherman*, 2015.

O'Neill, Cyril J., *Early Twentieth Century Vicksburg, 1900-1910*, 1976.

Smith, David W., ed., *Compelled to Appear in Print, the Vicksburg Manuscript of Gen. John C. Pemberton*, 2005.

Smith, Myron J., Jr, *The Fight for the Yazoo, 1862-1864*, 2012.

Smith, Timothy B., *Champion Hill: Decisive Battle for Vicksburg*, 2004.

Smith, Timothy B., *The Siege of Vicksburg: Climax of the Campaign to Open the Mississippi River, May 23-July 4, 1863*, 2021.

Smith, Timothy B., The Union Assaults at Vicksburg: Grant Attacks Pemberton, May 17–22, 1863, 2020.

Solonick, Justin S., *Engineering Victory, The Union Siege of Vicksburg*, 2015.

Taylor, William D., *A Fit Representation of Pandemonium, East Tennessee Confederate Soldiers in the Campaign for Vicksburg*, 2008.

Tucker, Phillip Thomas, *The Forgotten Stonewall of the West, Major General John Stevens Bowen*, 1997.

White, Ronald C., *American Ulysses, A Life of Ulysses S. Grant*, 2017.

Williams, Richard Brady, *Chicago's Battery Boys: The Chicago Mercantile Battery in the Civil War's Western Theater*, 2007.

Winschel, Terrence J., *Triumph & Defeat: The Vicksburg Campaign*, 1999.

Woods, Troy Woody, *Delta Plantations: The Beginning*, 2010.

MISCELLANY

A-Z Animals, *How the Mississippi River was Formed*, Accessed 1 Jan 2023. https://a-z-animals.com/blog/how-was-the-mississippi-river-formed/

Fleming, Walter L., *General W. T. Sherman as College President*, 1912. https://louisiana-anthology.org/texts/sherman/sherman--lsu.html Accessed 9 Jan 2023.

Johnson, Scott K., *Ancient Native American City May Have Been Done in by Mississippi Floods*, Ars Technica, 4 May 2015. Accessed 8 Jan 2023. https://arstechnica.com/science/2015/05/ancient-native-american-city -may-have-been-done-in-by-mississippi-floods/

Klinkenberg, Dan, *The 70-Million-Year-Old History of the Mississippi River*, Smithsonian Magazine, September 2020.

Mississippi Department of Archives and History, *Mississippi History Timeline*, accessed 1 Jan 2023. http://timeline.mdah.ms.gov/

Mississippi Humanities Council, *Mississippi Encyclopedia*, 2022. https://mississippiencyclopedia.org/

Missouri State Museum, *Museum Muse*, Vol. 5, No. 1, Winter/Spring 2014.

Wilson, Charles Reagan, *Mississippi Delta, Southern Spaces*, University of Mississippi, 4 Apr 2004.

Winschel, Terrence J., *Vicksburg Campaign Tour, Louisville Civil War Roundtable*, 24-26 Apr 2003. https://www.youtube.com/watch?v=V6PYZOIDgug

Van Arsdale, Roy B., and Cox, Randel T., *The Mississippi's Curious Origins*, Scientific American, 2007. Accessed 7 Jan 2023. https://www.scientificamerican.com/article/the-mississippis-curious/

Vicksburg National Military Park, *Linking Geology and History*, https://www.nps.gov/vick/learn/nature/geology-and-history.htm Accessed 22 Jan 2023.

Vicksburg National Military Park, *Vicksburg, Home to a World-Class Geologic Story*, Accessed 21 Jan 2023.
https://www.nps.gov/vick/learn/nature/geologicactivity.htm

Vicksburg National Military Park, *Administrative History, Vicksburg National Cemetery* by Richard Meyers, March 31, 1968, Accessed May 1, 2023, http://npshistory.com/publications/vick/adhi.pdf

City of Yazoo City, *The History of Yazoo City*.
http://www.cityofyazoocity.org/visit-yazoo-city/the-history-of-yazoo/
Accessed 20 Jan 2023.

The *U.S.S. Cairo* on display at VNMP preserves *Echoes* of Eades and Porter. *(GJMC)*